Silent Revolutions

D1638904

Gideon Haigh is the author of *Mystery Spinner*, which was Cricket Society Book of the Year, shortlisted for the William Hill Sports Book of the Year and acclaimed as 'a classic' by the *Sunday Times*; *The Big Ship*, a biography of Warwick Armstrong; *Many a Slip*, his diary of a club cricket season, and *Ashes 2005*. He also edited *Peter the Lord's Cat and Other Unexpected Obituaries from* Wisden, and his most recent book is *Downed Under: The Ashes in Australia 2006*-7. All are published by Aurum. He writes regularly for the *Guardian Wisden Cricketer* and cricinfo. He lives in Melbourne, Australia.

Silent
Revolutions
Writings on Cricket History

Gideon Haigh

First published in Great Britain
2007 by Aurum Press Ltd
7 Greenland Street, London NW1 0ND
www.aurumpress.co.uk

Published by arrangement with Black Inc., Australia

A catalogue record for this book is available from the British Library.

ISBN-10: 1 84513 226 2
ISBN-13: 978 1 84513 226 2

1 3 5 7 9 10 8 6 4 2
2007 2009 2011 2010 2008

Book design: Thomas Deverall
Typeset by J&M Typesetting
Printed in the UK by CPI Bookmarque, Croydon, CR0 4TD

CONTENTS

LIFE STORIES

MATTERS OF HISTORY

ODD MEN IN

INTRODUCTION

7584 and All That

Asked fifty years ago to estimate the audience for his autobiography, Arthur Mailey confidently predicted that it would sell 7584 copies. How, wondered his interlocutors, could he be so precise? Easy, answered Mailey: there were 7584 people in the English-speaking world who bought every cricket book published. He counted on them doing so again.

All I can say is: those were the days. Not that cricket books do not sell: they do, and in great numbers, at least when attached to a famous name or controversial saga. The trouble is that this begets a literature designed to be sold rather than read, where the book is essentially the receipt for a contribution to the player's testimonial fund. For those of us who also play the game but reached something of a plateau around the age of twelve, the pickings are somewhat slimmer.

If you've bought *Silent Revolutions* ... well, for one thing, thanks. It is a book with next to nothing going for it under prevailing market conditions, containing essays about cricketers who played more than five minutes ago, and events that have not been the subject of framed memorabilia available for sale on a 1800 number. This modern prohibition on the past is a powerful regime, subtly enforced. These days, no remark slips so trippingly off an athlete's tongue as 'that's ancient history'. The event concerned could be a decade ago, or a year, or a week – but, being past, it is perforce redundant and irrelevant. Arbitrary insertion of the bonehead phrase 'going forward' – as in 'what I want to do going forward' – is an increasingly popular expression of a related sentiment.

Nonetheless, when the historian Greg Dening wrote twenty-five years ago that 'there is nothing so momentary as a sporting achievement and nothing so lasting as the memory of it', he was more right than he knew. Steve Waugh might be the archetypal modern cricketer, but he must pose on the cover of his autobiography beneath the totemic Australian baggy green cap to achieve his full stature. His story might be compelling, but it would be diminished by lack of corroborative recollection. His record might be impressive, but it is meaningless without historical and statistical comparison. The past in sport, *pace* L.P. Hartley, is not another country. We live in it, even if its pervasiveness and familiarity sometimes render it invisible.

The title of this book appropriates a philosophy from Dr W.G. Grace, whose facility in making history did not render him oblivious to history's role in making him. 'In the thirty-five years over which my memory sweeps, cricket has undergone many changes,' he wrote in *Cricket Reminiscences and Personal Recollections* (1899). 'The game we play today is scarcely like the game of my boyhood. There have been silent revolutions transforming cricket in many directions, improving it in some ways and in others robbing it of some elements of its charm.' He was feeling in a reminiscent mood that season, his last in Test cricket. 'It's the ground, Charlie,' he told C.B. Fry. 'It's too far away.' But whatever the provocation, it was a perceptive obiter dictum. If cricket seldom convulses, it is strengthening, weakening, shifting, sliding, cross-referencing and cross-pollinating all the while – and not in spite of human effort, but because of it.

The work collected in *Silent Revolutions* is mainly from the last five years, and has appeared in a range of newspapers, magazines, books and websites. I've been fortunate in finding editors amenable to my historical meanderings, especially Sambit Bal, Stephen Fay, Peter Hanlon and Graem Sims. Thanks, likewise, to Morry Schwartz, Chris Feik and David Winter at Black Inc., who accepted this anthology with such alacrity, despite the distance to the glimmer of 7584. The book is dedicated to Trumper – not the loveliest of batsmen, but rather the best of cats, who has had a good view of much of the writing from the vantage point of my lap, and considerately kept her views to herself.

Gideon Haigh
Melbourne, 2006

ADVANCE AUSTRALIA

AUSTRALIAN CRICKET

A Brief History

C.L.R. James once drew a distinction between the idea of a cricketer from the West Indies and a West Indian cricketer. A similar
distinction can be made in this country. There is not so much
cricket in Australia as Australian cricket: a species of the game dis-
tinguishable from all others that expresses the nation's history, tradition and culture over two centuries.

Though cricket's origins significantly predate the British settlement of Australia, the prehistory of each contains curious echoes
of the other. As Dr John Campbell envisioned Terra Australis
Incognita in his *Navigantium atque Itinerantium Bibliotheca* in 1744,
so in that year was cricket framing its oldest surviving set of laws.
As Cook defined that continent's extent to the east in 1770, so were
cricketers agreeing to limit the extent of their bats to a width of 4.5
inches. The First Fleet embarked a week before the inaugural
match at Lord's; Matthew Flinders affixed 'Australia' to the land-
mass he had devoted his life to exploring in the same month that
Lord's opened at its present site.

No one should presume that cricket's rise in Australia was inevitable. The game has hardly prospered everywhere. It was well
established in North America by the end of the eighteenth century,
and had been played in Italy and France as well as India and South
Africa; there was a German instructional book before the first
English one. But there were propitious preconditions for cricket's
popularity here. It is appropriate that the first mention of cricket
in a contemporary publication, in the *Sydney Gazette and New South*

Wales Advertiser on 8 January 1804, is in the context of 'intense' and 'immoderate' weather: heat and light are indivisible from our cricket experience. Golden soil yielded our first grounds of significance, notably the space named Hyde Park by Governor Macquarie in October 1810; wealth for toil underwrote the pioneering Australian Cricket Club in Sydney (1826), the Hobart Town Cricket Club (1832) and the Melbourne Cricket Club (1838).

Above all, perhaps, a home girt by sea made us hanker for the culture left behind. Cricket was already, in James Love's catchcry, the 'glorious, manly British game', and to play it was an act of fealty and fidelity. As one old Etonian wrote to the *Australian* in July 1832: 'The game of Cricket is peculiarly English, and possesses a fascination to those who have been players in boyhood and youth, that no time eradicates ... Oh! For the days of youth once more, for these are the scenes which recall those long-forgotten memories of enjoyment, when cricket was my highest source of gratification.'

News took time to reach us in this era – the death of George IV on 26 June 1830 was not reported in Sydney until 1 November – and cricket in Australia developed in arrears of its English counterpart. Round-arm bowling was legalised in 1828, but did not take hold in Australia until the early 1840s; intercolonial matches commenced in 1851, but not for another five years was admission charged at such fixtures, something that had been in practice in England since the 1770s. The tours of H.H. Stephenson's and George Parr's English venturers in the early 1860s were thus more momentous than is commonly appreciated. They narrowed a gap in time as they bridged the span in space, and provided models to emulate as well as matches to entertain: it was after seeing George 'Tear 'em' Tarrant, for example, that Fred Spofforth decided he simply had to bowl fast. Charles Lawrence and Billy Caffyn, who remained behind from those trips, had an even more lasting impact, as Australia's first coaches of significance. The idea of an 'England' cricket team touring also gave impetus to the idea of an 'Australia' hosting, then touring in its own right: in retrospect, an even more remarkable initiative than cobbling together the

Combined New South Wales and Victorian XI that won what has become known, rather grandiosely, as the inaugural Test match.

There was a strong spirit of mercantile adventure to those early expeditions. When Dave Gregory's cohort met with unimagined success while visiting England in 1878, including a one-day rout of the MCC, they became both famous and rich. The eccentric epic poet Richard Horne became one of the first Australian intellectuals to complain about sport's disproportionate rewards: 'I learn that the cricketers have made each £1000 over there! Why, oh why did I not become an Australian cricketer … ? When years no longer smiled upon my balls and runs, I might have retired on my laurelled bat, and have published tragedies at my own expense.' Englishmen coming to Australia were lured by the prospect of easy pickings. 'If you bring a strong XI with the best new blood,' reads John Conway's unblushing invitation to Alfred Shaw's team of 1881–82, 'there is a cartload of money waiting for you.'

But Australians in England, who effectively formed companies, and collected gate monies and divided them at tour's end amongst themselves, could do even better, because of the shorter distances and numbers of potential opponents. Emboldened by early success, they drove a hard bargain for their services at home, as well: thus the strikes of 1884–85 and 1886–87. Not that the budding administrative class set a particularly pure example. 'There was never such a prominent case of folly,' wrote Lord Hawke when it turned out that both the Melbourne Cricket Club and the Sydney Cricket Ground Trust had invited English teams to Australia for 1887–88.

By the late 1880s, in fact, Australian cricket had squandered much of its early goodwill. Public interest was waning. The English had grown cynical about colonial motives. 'The Australians make their own terms, insist on them, not always very gracefully, and play too obviously for the money's sake,' complained one critic. 'They arrogate to themselves the rank of gentlemen.' Two events set the antipodean game back on its feet: an English nob called Lord Sheffield, who'd absorbed a big loss in bringing a touring team including W.G. Grace, left behind an endowment that the colonies – just – agreed to use to fund a shield for domestic cricket supremacy; then, a heady five-Test series in 1894–95 was won 3–2 by England under Drewy Stoddart's leadership, after they had taken the first match despite following-on. It was also the first series to take advantage of the new telegraphic cable. Taking an expensive gamble, London's *Pall Mall Gazette* published long cabled reports of the action within a day of its taking place; suddenly, commented *Wisden*, English cricket devotees were 'in closer touch with cricket in Australia than ever before'. They liked what they saw. Cricket's next two decades, Victorian stateliness steadily giving way to Edwardian brio, have been burnished as its Golden Age.

We owe this period much. Long before they were the nation's, green and gold became colours of the Australian cricket team. The Ashes tradition, dating from 1882, was rediscovered and made the motif of the Anglo–Australian rivalry. A distinctly nativist spirit was nurtured by successive captains – Harry Trott, Joe Darling, Monty Noble and Clem Hill – and expressed in the virtuoso talents of Hugh Trumble, Warwick Armstrong and Victor Trumper. In Trumper, one finds the prototype of 'Australian' batting: original, spontaneous, self-taught. 'You could talk to him and coach him,' wrote Noble. 'He would listen carefully, respect your advice and opinions, and, leaving you, would forget all you had told him, play as he wanted to play.' Few have been so idolised. 'Every member of the great crowd which darkens the Sydney mound knows "our Vic",' wrote Trumper's English opponent Albert Knight. 'If one hasn't been to school with him, he knows someone who has or he knows the champion's father, or touched the fringes of his garments somewhere. Trumper's batting moves them as neither victory nor defeat quite touch them.'

In the shape of cricket to come, however, just as important were the names, now less familiar, of Ben Wardill, Billy McElhone, Ernie Bean and John Creswell. Wardill – 'the Moltke of Australian cricket' as he was called by Pelham Warner, after Germany's military mastermind – was secretary of the Melbourne Cricket Club, which by the late nineteenth century had established itself as the peak body

6

for the organisation of Australia's international cricket adventures, running tours on the basis of an entente cordiale with the country's leading players. Popular, able and ambitious, he did not protest when the club was called 'Australia's Marylebone'. McElhone, Bean and Creswell, the best administrative brains at the associations of New South Wales, Victoria and South Australia respectively, had different ideas, fantasising about a representative, national cricket government controlling the game root and branch: tour revenues, selection, fixtures. Associations to that time had been starveling bodies, which saw nothing of the spoils of national teams abroad. Once their initiative gained impetus from Federation, it would indeed have been anomalous that a private club, however generous and public-spirited, maintained the level of authority in Australian cricket that Melbourne had gained. But the rise of the Australian Board of Control for International Cricket and Melbourne's steady eclipse, with the players' concomitant loss of influence, would resonate through almost every subsequent event. Although memories of the acrimony of this period faded with World War I, virtually no Australian cricketer of note has not found himself, at one time or other, on the wrong side of the board. The board, meanwhile, has enjoyed all the advantages, and been prone to all the susceptibilities, of a steady, slow-growth monopoly.

It was also in this period that Test cricket became truly an event – as it would, for long, remain. It is amazing to realise that in the 140 months from the end of the 'Big Six' dispute of 1912 – a final consolidation of the board's power – Australia hosted only five Tests. Anticipation was always acute; the smart of defeat lingered, and so did the afterglow of success. Visitors were often startled by the ardent nature of Australian allegiance. 'We in England do not always appreciate to the full the part which cricket plays in the national life of Australians,' wrote the great English all-rounder Frank Woolley. 'When Australia gets a really good player it does not merely just like or take a fancy to him, it literally idolizes him, almost worships him.' The rise of Donald Bradman after a fallow period in the late 1920s was thus unlike the kind of sporting celebrity enjoyed now; the foremost personality in the only game in town, he bore an unimaginable weight of expectation every time he batted, but again and again lived up to it. His effect was magnified, too, by another leap in communications. To the telegraphic cable was now harnessed the miracle of wireless. Australians could listen to Bradman's accumulations, in Australia and even England, described run by plenteous run.

They could hear the deeds of others, too. Bill Woodfull and Bill Ponsford scored runs in quantities little less copious than Bradman; Clarrie Grimmett and Bill O'Reilly were as formidable a slow-bowling axis as any in history. Bradman, however, was a symbol of aspiration as well as of excellence. Even when it seemed, albeit briefly, that he would renounce Test cricket in favour of a lucrative Lancashire League career during 1931, he had public opinion on his side. As one leader writer declaimed: 'A marvellous gift has been bestowed on him. It is sheer stupidity to imagine that it is his duty to remain in the land of his birth if his gift is more valuable elsewhere.' Fortunately for Australia, Bradman's sense of duty went untested, for sufficient monies were subscribed to make remaining worth his while. His influence did not, of course, go unchallenged. The strategy known as Bodyline evolved to defeat him when England toured in 1932–33, reducing his productivity to more mortal proportions: without Bodyline, in fact, there'd have been no duck of destiny awaiting Bradman at the Oval in 1948, curbing his average at 99.94. But no cricketer – and perhaps no athlete – has disappointed his countrymen's hopes so seldom.

Like many a brilliant individual before him, captaincy did not come naturally to Bradman at first: he was advantaged in leading Australia before World War II chiefly by his own presence in the team. Afterwards, somewhat older, in circumstances more to his taste, and with Lindsay Hassett as an able deputy, he was formidable. Australia enjoyed a period of supremacy with few parallels, winning twenty-six and losing only two of its first thirty-two post-war Tests. In Keith Miller they possessed an all-rounder of uncanny magnetism, in Ray Lindwall a fast bowler of unexampled artfulness, in Neil Harvey a batsman of dash and daring. Lord's remained cricket's meridian, but the maturation of South Africa, India, the West Indies and New Zealand involved Australia as much as England, sometimes to better effect. When Len Hutton's men toured the Caribbean in 1953–54, for example, the tour was disrupted by West Indian politics and English petulance: *The Times* nominated it as 'the second most controversial tour in history' after Bodyline. When Ian Johnson's team visited a year later, it was the most popular to make the journey.

*

Cricket had more challenges at home in the 1950s and 1960s. Australian tennis boomed; the Olympic Games loomed larger, especially once it annexed the Melbourne Cricket Ground for a glorious fortnight in 1956. With post-war embourgoisement came a search for newer, more fashionable recreations; where radio had blazed a trail, television now followed. Test cricket round the world became a noticeably grimmer game as bowlers' run-ups lengthened, over-rates declined and, in a perverse tribute to its prestige, captains felt they had more to lose by defeat than to gain by winning. The glorious exception to the period was the 1960–61 series between Richie Benaud's Australians and Frank Worrell's West Indians: a resounding win each between a unique tie and a gripping draw, ending with a narrow squeak for the hosts in the decider. The promise, however, could not be sustained beyond an entertaining subsequent Ashes series. Splendid talents were often on show: Alan Davidson, Graham McKenzie, Bob Simpson, Bill Lawry, Norm O'Neill. Yet it is hard today to conceive of games as futile as 1964's Old Trafford Test: Simpson with 311 on one side, Ken Barrington with 256 on the other, and eighteen wickets in five days. Such engagements seem more remote from us than Tests played at the turn of the twentieth century.

In the mid-1960s there then came a shock. Having never lost a series to a country other than England, Australia was beaten by the West Indies and South Africa in the span of two years. There was increasingly a sense of going to defend laurels rather than to add to them, with the result that they were steadily surrendered. In 1970 and 1971, Australia did not win a Test. England even regained the Ashes, having held them for only five of the preceding thirty-seven years.

The cycle turned in the nick of time. There was some luck. South Africa was scheduled to tour in 1971–72, and would likely have inflicted another heavy defeat; cancelled, as the world belatedly awoke to the iniquities of apartheid, the tour became identified with political rather than sporting ignominy. A rebuilt Australia – a 'team of goers', as selector Neil Harvey put it – went instead to England in 1972 and surprised itself by drawing 2–2. Its young captain, Ian Chappell, was an outspoken, sometimes provocative leader who irritated traditionalists, but as Chesterton said of Dickens: 'The critics blustered, the people wept and cheered.' With brother Greg and the West Australian pair of Dennis Lillee and Rod Marsh, he became the core of a rejuvenated unit. They played bold, brassy, sometimes belligerent cricket. Unlike the short-back-and-sides Australians of the 1960s, in this team a shaggy moustache and an insouciant air were de rigueur; they attracted sponsors, advertisers and agents to a game that had hitherto had few commercial entanglements. Historically conservative to the point of prudery, what was known from September 1973 as the Australian Cricket Board struggled to keep pace with the players' expectations, its attitude being famously summarised by its secretary: 'The players are not professional. They are invited to play, and if they don't like the conditions there are 500,000 other cricketers in Australia who would love to take their place.' But their monopoly was about to be broken.

For twenty years Australian Test matches and Sheffield Shield matches had been telecast, without advertisements and filmed from one end, by the Australian Broadcasting Commission. Cricket's renewed popularity, however, had made it a telegenic commodity for commercial broadcasters; by comparison with other forms of programming, in fact, it represented cheap local content.

Kerry Packer, proprietor of Channel Nine, was the first to do his sums. He liked sport, was fond of cricket, and was averse to cant, introducing himself to the Australian Cricket Board with the honeyed lines: 'Come on now, we're all whores … What's your price?'

The board was confident of not having to do business with such a man. But, while it owned cricket, it did not own its increasingly restive cricketers. Told of an independent circuit of international cricket matches, using the traditional five-day and increasingly popular one-day formats with vastly jazzed-up television coverage, players not just from Australia but from England, the West Indies, Pakistan and the banned South Africa fell over themselves to take the Packer shilling. Many signatures were obtained, piquantly, during the Centenary Test, which celebrated a hundred years of the established global game. Inevitably, the irresistible force of Packer's World Series Cricket against the immovable object of official cricket ramified loud and long.

This was, in a sense, a sequel to events at the board's foundation. In 1905, it had been the board constituting itself to rival the existing authority, the Melbourne Cricket Club and the players; now the board was the existing authority under siege from an interloper. The players, meanwhile, were fighting for the share of the exchequer they had lost at that time. The board mounted a successful holding action in WSC's first summer, 1977–78. The national team, rebuilt from young talent that Packer had not recruited, beat India narrowly under the leadership of Bob Simpson; WSC, meantime, struggled to find an audience, despite its galaxy of talent, grandeur of design and gaudiness of promotion. The 1978–79 season, however, found the roles reversed: while an inexperienced Test side was routed by England, WSC went from strength to strength. Packer's promotion was directed to making WSC look more like official cricket rather than less; his Australian team was more truly the representative of the people than its establishment equivalent, and the Chappells, Lillee and Marsh were a persuasive unit. Resistance crumbled: Packer obtained his exclusive broadcasting rights and more.

A new world beckoned. Commercial television's philosophy is Darwinian. It is interested only in sport's uppermost level: first-class cricket was thus deemed second-class product; tour matches were dismissed as costly anachronisms. Unlike other kinds of programming, sport depreciates fast, so there is a pressure to play more and more: that certainly was cricket's experience. But international cricket took away much from WSC as well, including the fruits of experiments with floodlit cricket, coloured clothing, helmets and drop-in pitches. Virtually every constituency in cricket was fundamentally affected. Cricketers, rewarded like star sportsmen for the first time, were wakened to their worth in the marketplace. Administrators, alerted to the value that the media imputed to their sport, came to recognise television rights as an important revenue source, and limited-overs cricket as a popular format. Audiences, wooed by mass marketing, embodied in the pop chant 'C'mon Aussie, C'mon' devised by the admen at Mojo, would in future come to participate in the urban spectacle as much as to admire the cricket. WSC's clearest on-field beneficiaries, meanwhile, were the West Indians, who in two years evolved from a group of gifted but inconsistent soloists into a tough and tight-knit ensemble; their pace-bowling ranks were as deep as broad. For the next fifteen years, they would be cricket's undisputed market leaders. Even when Australia rebounded from a mid-'80s slump by unexpectedly winning the fourth limited-overs World Cup in India, then wresting the Ashes from England two years later, the team led by Allan Border had to be content with being the best of the rest.

Australian cricket changed to reflect new realities. A professional game entailed professional administration. Having for most of its history been a relatively small secretariat, the Australian Cricket Board expanded considerably from the late 1980s. It employed for the first time a coach, the indestructible Bob Simpson, and a growing support entourage, including a psychologist and a media manager; it opened an incubator for embryonic talent, the Cricket Academy, in Adelaide; its executive and bureaucracy outgrew several premises as it took on a host of new functions, including, unhappily, investigation, when match-fixing loomed in the mid-1990s as a grave threat to cricket's integrity. The tendency to rely on innate talent and historic endowments was past; nature henceforward would enjoy a kick along. Seven of Mark Taylor's Australian team of 1995, which finally bearded the West Indies in their Caribbean den, were alumni of the academy, including Shane Warne, the most talented cricketer of his generation and perhaps the greatest bowler of all, and Glenn McGrath, our finest opening bowler since Lillee. Even Australia's selectors, under chairmen Lawrie Sawle and Trevor Hohns, had never been more conspicuous. Perceiving the divergence of Test and one-day cricket, they pressed successfully for specialists in each, and were vindicated when Australia maintained its Test edge and won both the 1999 and 2003 World Cups: not even the West Indies had maintained such an ascendancy. Australian cricket began the twenty-first century synonymous with the best. In the preceding 200 years, it had never been far from it, but there was now perhaps a new dimension: it expected to remain so.

200 Years of Australian Cricket: 1804–2004 (2004)

WARWICK ARMSTRONG
Mr Big

At his final playing dimensions of 140 kilograms and 200 centimetres, Warwick Armstrong was Australia's heftiest Test cricketer. It suited him. Everything about Armstrong was outsized, from his first-class record of 16,158 runs at 47 and 832 wickets at less than 20 to his impatience with authority and capacity for resistance.

Modern fans know him mostly by his voluminous shirt, like a clipper's main-topsail, which now drapes a tailor's dummy in the Australian Cricket Hall of Fame. But he has left many other traces: the highest Australian partnership for the sixth wicket (with Monty Noble), the second-highest for the seventh wicket (with Joe Darling), the third-highest for the ninth wicket (with Ted Windsor), a century and 5 wickets in an innings on four occasions, a hundred runs and 10 wickets in a match twice. Among the ten Australians with 10,000 first-class runs and 500 first-class wickets, Armstrong has the highest batting average and the second-lowest bowling average.

For his huge and heavy boots, also in the hall, authorities always thought Armstrong too big. A man of few, mainly terse words, he could be found at the bottom of disputes with the Victorian Cricket Association, and subsequently the Board of Control, on an almost annual basis for twenty years. Partly this was because Armstrong was a representative of the Melbourne Cricket Club, whose influence the VCA and board were intent on extirpating; mainly it was because Armstrong was a cricketer who played only on terms satisfactory to him, and who knew his value to the last shilling. As team-mate Arthur Mailey commented, Armstrong 'didn't have much time for arbitration unless he himself could act as the arbitrator'.

Most of Armstrong's career was before World War I, when he was a roundhead among cavaliers, a batsman of prodigious strength restrained by great patience, and a leg-spin bowler who made up for what he lacked in spin with immense accuracy and endurance. No Australian will better his 1902 runs at 50 and 122 wickets at 18.2 on a tour of England just over a century ago.

After the war he was more belligerent, taking only 205 minutes to score a match-winning 158 against England at the SCG: 'Even the great Victor Trumper in his heyday had shown us nothing better,' said the umpire Bob Crockett. But he was never other than an entirely uncompromising opponent. He made a timed-out appeal against an opening pair in a grade match. He was the first Australian to attempt a 'Mankad' run-out in a first-class match, more than thirty years before Mankad. Most famously, he remains the only man to bowl consecutive overs in a Test, having learned that his rival captain had declared illegally. Asked if his decision to bowl back-to-back overs had been deliberate, he simply 'smiled and looked away'.

In Armstrong's dealings with administrators, there was no ambiguity: everything, especially the coat-trailing, was deliberate. In 1902–03, he flouted the VCA by refusing to play under the state's captain, Jack Worrall, on account of Worrall's published remarks about a team-mate's bowling action. In 1903–04 and 1904–05, he enraged the VCA by playing as a professional because they had refused to pay his expenses as an amateur. In 1905–06, he was censured by the VCA for captaining the MCC in New Zealand rather than playing in the Sheffield Shield. In 1906–07, he censured the VCA for selecting him in a match for which he had notified them he was unavailable because of work commitments. In 1907–08, the VCA very nearly banned him permanently after another dispute over expenses, and he was ousted by his fellow players as Victorian captain. When the Board of Control then mooted its takeover of the finances of Australian tours to England, Armstrong was at the forefront of player objections. 'What are they going to do with the money?' he asked at a meeting of the players of Victoria and New South Wales in December 1908. 'The players are taking all the hard knocks and making all the money. We should have a little idea where the money is going.' He refused to sign his contract for the 1909 Ashes tour as a protest against the board voting themselves a cut, and only a job offer from the MCC kept him from accepting a lucrative coaching contract in New Zealand early the following year.

Victorian administrators would have been glad to see his broad back. In 1910–11, he wrangled with the VCA about his players' entitlement to complimentary tickets, then declined to represent an Australian XI because the fee was too small. In 1911–12, team-mate Jim Kyle revealed that the VCA was intent on engineering Armstrong's removal as Victorian captain. In 1912–13, Kyle having been excommunicated and others sidelined, Armstrong *was* replaced as Victoria's captain by a stooge at a gerrymandered player vote. In 1913–14, reappointed as a stand-in captain following that stooge's failure, he resigned at lunchtime on the first day when the VCA declined to make the appointment permanent. After all that, in 1914–15 he led Victoria to victory in the Sheffield Shield – perhaps simply to annoy his detractors.

Between times, Armstrong was at the heart of Australian cricket's seminal dispute, being one of the six refuseniks opposed to the board's organisation of the team to England in 1912. When the board stripped Australian players of their last remaining right – to choose their own manager – Armstrong maintained his allegiance to the players' choice: his Victorian team-mate and friend Frank Laver. With Clem Hill, Victor Trumper, Hanson Carter, Albert Cotter and Vernon Ransford, he forfeited selection. This disobedience was forgiven but not forgotten. When Armstrong became Australia's captain in November 1920 after the Great War, the board appointed him for only one Test, and only on the odd vote. If they imagined this would unsettle him, though, they were wrong.

In the next year, Armstrong scored 2282 runs at 56, bowled 5420 deliveries for 117 wickets at 15.5, and turned that one Test appointment into ten, for eight wins and two draws.

The VCA made one last bid to dispossess him, sacking him from the Victorian team in February 1921, ostensibly as a punishment for withdrawing with an injury from a Sheffield Shield game without informing the team manager; more generally for behaving like a state within a state in Australian cricket. But after 10,000 gathered outside the MCG to protest, Armstrong was recalled and Victoria's selectors narrowly averted a vote of no confidence. The climax of his career was a wildly successful Ashes tour, harnessing Australia's first great pace-bowling partnership: Jack Gregory and Ted McDonald.

For a generation, Armstrong was the personification of Australia: big, tough, taciturn, wanting everything, yielding nothing. After watching Armstrong in England in 1921, the dramatist Louis Esson wrote to the critic Vance Palmer that cricketers were representatives of Australia superior to its artists and politicians put together: 'England are really scared of Armstrong and the fast bowlers ... They are not pleasant players. A good English journalist described them as "hard-bitten", "grim" and "pitiless". We shouldn't be a soft, mushy, maudlin race. In politics we're a shingle short, a nation of grinning village idiots. The cricketers fill me with great enthusiasm. They can lose, for there is luck in cricket, but they'll never crack up like the English.' More than a century after Armstrong played his maiden Test, Australians would like to imagine that this still holds.

100 Not Out (2006)

AUSTRALIA 1920 V 2000

Two Teams, Two Worlds

Australia leaves on Monday for a tour of New Zealand, with a shot at a record that once appeared incontestable and unassailable. Victory in the First Test, at Auckland on 11–15 March, will equal the feat by Warwick Armstrong's 1920–21 Australian team of winning eight consecutive Tests; winning the Second Test, at Wellington a fortnight later, will consign another old landmark to oblivion.

In a sense, *Wisden* exists to capture the setting and surpassing of such milestones. Yet here is a case where it's worth proceeding a little further than the cold black type of its pages to demonstrate how statistics sometimes foster illusions of direct comparability. For the sides of Armstrong and Steve Waugh inhabit worlds so different that they could almost be participating in different sports.

Armstrong's eight victories were all at England's expense: an unprecedented and unrepeated 5–0 sweep of a home series, followed by wins in the first three Tests of a visit to England. In between, the teams even travelled to England together on the *Osterly*, where anecdotal evidence suggests that the Australians prevailed in all the deck games as well.

At home, the members of Armstrong's team also participated in a full suite of Sheffield Shield matches. In England, they had a ludicrously congested tour program of thirty-nine matches, further complicated by a lengthy coal strike in the British Midlands, which so scrambled train timetables that many early finishes were necessary. To top it all, they played six first-class matches on the way home via South Africa, including three Tests; by train and ship, in fact, the Australian tour covered more than 50,000 kilometres. Despite this, Armstrong's touring ensemble won twenty-seven matches, drew sixteen, and lost only a couple of games at the very end of the trip's English leg. Aggregating their Australian and English feats produces statistics that boggle the mind: Arthur Mailey bowled almost 8000 deliveries in bagging 215 first-class wickets, Warren Bardsley had sixty hits for 3000 first-class runs.

Steve Waugh's side traverses quite different terrain. Their victories, if they arise, will have been at the expense of four different countries: Zimbabwe, Pakistan, India and New Zealand. They will have been interlarded with nineteen one-day internationals – a form of the game undreamt of eighty years ago – but virtually no first-class cricket. Perhaps the greatest difference is the time it took Armstrong's ensemble to set its record and Waugh's to give it a nudge. The eight Test victories Australia achieved in 1920–21 were their first international competition for eight years and occurred over ten months. The seven Tests Australia won in 1999 followed hot on a tour of Sri Lanka and unfolded over ten weeks.

The only common ground between the two teams, one might reflect, is that they both played something called Test cricket. But even this obscures a multitude of dissimilarities, not least in terms of time. In 1920–21, Tests in Australia were timeless; Tests in England were three days in duration: it was twenty-five years before the standardised 30-hour format.

All this complexity and nuance is stripped from the bare tabulations that appear in *Wisden*, and currently festoon newspaper columns. Necessarily so, too. But the devil is in the detail. The feats of the teams led by Armstrong and Waugh are considerable. But they are about as comparable as Rachmaninov and the Red Hot Chili Peppers. As for imagining a contest between the teams, we can surmise only that Armstrong's team would be unbeatable at shuffleboard and quoits, and Waugh's the masters at PlayStation.

Wisden Online January 2000

BRADMAN IN ENGLAND

Genesis and Revelation

Australia's seventeenth and twentieth tours of England bracket Sir Donald Bradman's cricket career like the books of Genesis and Revelation. No Australian batsman has accomplished as much as he did in 1930, nor has any Australian captain paralleled his feats of 1948. On both occasions, he was perhaps fortunate. The English team of 1930, though it held the Ashes, was past its prime, with an average age pushing thirty-five. Eighteen years later, Australia's hosts were still enervated by World War II. Yet runs must still be made and matches won, and in both cases Bradman proved himself the acme of cricket efficiency.

The twenty-one-year-old Bradman's precocity was evident even before he walked down the gangway of the SS *Orford* on 23 April 1930. He had set a first-class record four months earlier with an unbeaten 452 against Queensland, and his average from fifty innings exceeded 90. But English geology and meteorology had confounded young Australians before.

In fact, Bradman assimilated English conditions like a talented linguist absorbing a new tongue. Chaperoned by his captain, Bill Woodfull, at Worcester, he hit twenty-eight fours in a total of 236: the highest score by an Australian in England at first blush. In twenty-four hours' batting over eleven innings before the end of May, he scored 1001 runs: the fifth man and first Australian to achieve this milestone. There followed a century on Test debut in England, albeit in a losing cause.

If Bradman sensed the growing swell of expectation every time he batted, however, he did not betray it. His first fifty in the Second Test at Lord's required three-quarters of an hour, to which he then added 101 between tea and stumps. Bradman described the eventual 254 as his finest innings, where 'practically without exception every ball went where it was intended to go.' When Australia passed 700, it was discovered that the Lord's scoreboard had not been designed to go past 699, and a small 7 had to be fetched to hang from a hook. *Wisden*, too, would need sturdier bindings by the time Bradman's business was finished.

Bradman left one record intact at Lord's – the standing Test-record score of 287 set by Englishman R.E. Foster in Sydney twenty-seven years earlier – but not for long. A dozen days later at Leeds, he shattered it in 315 minutes. His eventual 334 was composed of forty-six fours, six threes, twenty-six twos and eighty singles. What amazed as much as the volume of runs was the ease and comfort of their acquisition. The *Evening News* printed Bradman's grinning portrait beneath the legend: 'The smile that England can't knock off.' Watching from the committee room, English cricketing potentate Pelham Warner sighed: 'This is like throwing stones at Gibraltar.' Returning to the dressing room at the end of the first day on 309 not out, Bradman told Woodfull: 'That wasn't a bad bit of practice. I'll be able to have a go at them tomorrow.'

With the series in the balance in the Fifth Test at the Oval, Bradman played more soberly: his 232 spanned 435 minutes. But the prime objective was secured: four years after losing them at the same ground, Australia regained the Ashes. Even sixty-eight years later, Bradman's 1930 output makes one draw breath. The quantum is astounding: 974 runs in seven Test innings. The rate of accumulation is even more so: 40 an hour, 62 per 100 deliveries, and all without the aid of a single six.

Needless to say, it established Bradman as a wonder of the age. His magisterial progress was followed with unusual closeness in Australia: for the first time, the ABC was broadcasting regular score updates from cables overnight. In a winter of Australian economic discontent, nights around the radiogram became a source of consolation.

At the time, indeed, Bradman may have been easier to admire from a distance than up close. His absolute absorption in run-making came at a cost to relations with team-mates. Journalist Geoffrey Tebbutt mentioned in his tour book the acrimony when Bradman did not share with comrades a £1000 gratuity awarded by Australian soap magnate Arthur Whitelaw, and the general sense that he 'had been rather less than human in the way he took success'. Playwright Ben Travers likewise recalled playing golf on the rest day of the Lord's Test with Alan Kippax, who had seen out the last half hour of the previous day with Bradman: 'Bradman had by that time made a goodly proportion of his 254 and … had only thoughts of the morrow. Kippax confided to me his utter, bottled-up resentment of Bradman, who had taken care that he, Kippax, the newcomer, had the strike wherever possible.'

That Bradman was feted like a Caesar on his homecoming deepened grievances, especially when the feats of match-winning leg-spinner Clarrie Grimmett were largely overlooked. 'We could have played any team without Bradman,' averred Victor Richardson. 'But we could not have played the blind school without Clarrie Grimmett.' Bad blood between Bradman and his contemporaries would linger some years yet, and into his career as Australian captain from November 1936.

Much of that had changed, however, by 1948. Having been first among equals, Bradman was now unchallenged in his seniority. Fifteen colleagues had less than a hundred Tests between them. Left-hander Neil Harvey was young enough to be Bradman's son. As Bradman wrote: 'What a difference between the mental outlook of a captain who is 40 years of age and easily the senior member and that of one who is several years junior to some of the men playing under him. There are no longer any fears that they will query the wisdom of what you do. The result is a sense of freedom to give full rein to your own creative ability and personal judgement.'

The tour duly set benchmarks for Australian success. Eight of an omnicompetent side averaged more than 40; seven exceeded 50 wickets. Seventeen matches were won by an innings; none were lost; four of the five Tests were won in comfort. Bradman himself hit eleven hundreds in thirty-one innings, averaging 90.

Yet it is almost prosaic to confine commentary on 1948 to cricket, for rarely can a country have received an occupying army so gladly, even euphorically. The first Ashes tour for a war-torn decade was a cause for national rejoicing, and Bradman's presence warming to all. As English cricket writer R.C. Robertson-Glasgow put it: 'We want him to do well. We feel we have a share in him. He is more than Australian. He is a world batsman.'

The Australians arrived bearing gifts: 200 food parcels for presentation to the British Ministry of Food to ease the exigencies of continued rationing, in advance reciprocity of that which the Australians would consume on tour. It was a far-sighted gesture, for the team were feted at every turn. Bradman's address to the Cricket Writers' Club was broadcast live on the BBC. King George VI entertained the team for a day at Balmoral. The MCC presented Bradman with a 27-kilogram birthday cake. Readers of the *People* subscribed sufficient shillings to acquire for him an 11-kilogram solid silver replica of a priceless Roman antiquity, the Warwick Vase. Bradman would be knighted four months hence. 'To travel throughout England with Bradman is a unique experience,' reported Australian journalist Andy Flanagan. 'Cities, towns and hotels are beflagged, carpets set down, and dignitaries wait to extend an official welcome. He is the Prince of Cricketers.'

English players greeted Bradman in his first innings of the Fifth Test at the Oval on 14 August with a chorus of 'For He's a Jolly Good Fellow'. His average as he took guard was 101.3. Two deliveries from leg-spinner Eric Hollies later, it was 99.94. Australian radio listeners listening to English Test matches live for the first time heard the BBC's peerless commentator John Arlott describe the scene. 'Bradman bowled Hollies, nought,' he announced. 'And – what do you say under those circumstances? I wonder if you see a ball very clearly in your last Test in England on a ground where you've played some of the biggest cricket of your life, and where the opposing team have just stood around you and the crowd has clapped you all the way to the wicket. I wonder if you really see the ball at all.'

Age February 2001

THE LIFE OF BRADMAN
No Laughing Matter

'Don Bradman gone! It is unbelievable.' With these words did an obituarist at London's *Star* begin a tribute to Donald Bradman placed on file at that newspaper sixty-six years ago. Bradman had undergone surgery for a burst appendix in England at the conclusion of his second all-conquering tour of that country, and his condition was precarious enough to justify such a contingency.

Like so many notices filed at the time and in subsequent years, the *Star*'s tribute was, of course, never used. Yet, now that similar sentiments echo round the world to mark the passing of Sir Donald Bradman, they tell us something: he was a study not only in sporting greatness, but in the nature of fame. He was by common consent the outstanding cricketer – in relative statistical terms, perhaps the outstanding athlete – of the twentieth century. He was also probably more famous, and certainly famous for a greater proportion of his lifetime, than any other Australian.

This poses a problem when we contemplate aspects of his life. Are we dealing with the legend, or with the man? Of the former, we know much: no fewer than eighteen books about him have been published in the last twenty years. Of the latter, we know far less: for most of his life, in fact, Bradman successfully kept the world at a distance. Even in an age where public curiosity about the private doings of celebrity borders on the prurient, the detail in circulation concerning his domestic life was minimal. He maintained, perhaps, greater control over his image and reputation than any other noteworthy Australian. It took an Englishman,

Irving Rosenwater, to write the best Bradman biography of all, *Sir Donald Bradman* (1978), yet even it contains yawning holes in the story of the life, as distinct from the sporting deeds.

Why was this? The legend, frankly, is daunting. Bradman enjoys the status in Australia that other countries confer on those who lead revolutions, create immortal works of art or make great scientific breakthroughs. Superficially, this is odd: after all, he merely played cricket, a game many love and with an unusual grip on national consciousness, but a game nonetheless. Yet to regard his status as an indictment of the impoverishment of our national culture – as some have – would be mistaken. Lord Williams begins his *Bradman: An Australian Hero* (1996) with a citation from the Greek lyric poet Pindar: 'He achieved things that no mortal man had achieved before.' Appropriately, Pindar was extolling an athlete, Xenophon of Corinth, who won the short sprint and pentathlon on the same day at the Olympics of 484BC. When we contemplate Bradman, we draw on ancient regards. He raised an elemental act – that of hitting a ball with a bat – to a pinnacle of proficiency. Every aspect of his record is compelling, even his failure at the Oval in 1948, on the occasion of his final Test innings, to score the four runs necessary to round his batting average off at a neat 100: a *coup de theatre* that adds to his story that vital tincture of human fallibility.

Yet there is more to it, this infatuation with the works and relative incuriosity about their perpetrator. No one has written better about the feelings Bradman occasioned in his fellow Australians than the writer Philip Lindsay in his *Donald Bradman* (1951). It is a small book, but full of insight and sometimes deeply moving, for it describes not so much Bradman as one man's attachment to Bradman, and how it became an inspirational force in his life: 'For that tautening of my will, for the courage to take a risk, I must thank more than most things Don Bradman that day at Sydney; and I wonder how many hundreds, nay, perhaps thousands, of Philip Lindsays there are whose lives have been formed by someone who does not know of their existence.' This distance between himself and his hero, Lindsay confesses elsewhere, was of his own making and preservation: he never met Bradman, 'did not desire it, and do not desire it now'. He felt it 'safest to remain the spectator of a dream'. Perhaps this is the way we all wished it. 'Every man,' Lindsay reminds us, 'needs an ideal.'

*

On what, then, is the legend founded? The fifth child of a farming family working a small holding at Yeo Yeo, Bradman was born at the residence of a local midwife in Cootamundra on 27 August 1908. On the same day, in a three-room shack near Johnson City in south-western Texas, was born the thirty-sixth American president Lyndon Johnson. It is a neat coincidence. The United States has log-cabin-to-White-House stories; the optimum Australian route is log-cabin-to-Lord's.

The Bradmans moved to Bowral a little more than two years later, where Donald lived out what he described as 'normal boyhood days'. The chief cricket influences in his life were two maternal uncles, Richard and George Whatman, who instilled in him the value of practice and broadly oversaw his tuition. Yet it is essentially correct that he was self-taught, and self-directed. As Bradman described it, there were two particular drills, involving not a cricket ball but a golf ball: one involved hitting with a stump the rebounds from a tank stand; the other throwing over a distance of about ten metres at a rounded rail and fielding the results. 'I can understand,' Bradman wrote in his autobiography *Farewell to Cricket* (1950), 'how it must have developed the co-ordination of brain, eye and muscle which was to serve me so well in important matches later on.'

In *Don Bradman's Book* (1930), Bradman noted another characteristic that emerged early in his life: 'It is a trait in my make-up which it is quite impossible to explain, that I am an almost total stranger to that species of nervousness common to most people whenever involved in an unusual happening.' Such as batting. He scored his first century at the age of twelve and, not long afterwards, witnessed his first Test match at the SCG, in February 1921. Bradman dated his resolve to become a Test cricketer to this game: 'I shall never be satisfied until I play on this ground,' he told his father. The second Test he witnessed would be the first in which he played.

This youthful vow may make Bradman seem brasher than he was; he was probably surer of his purpose at this age than he was of himself. Even after the boy left Bowral to tackle Sydney grade cricket in October 1926, part of Bowral remained with the boy. He was a serious, somewhat self-conscious youth, feeling for some years afterwards the 'handicap that my education had been of a limited character and my experience of life comparatively negligible'. He did not drink, did not make friends easily, and ended up marrying a girl from his hometown. When he took up a bat, however, bowlers alone bore the burden of inferiority.

*

Bradman made a hundred in his maiden first-class innings in December 1927, and topped Australia's averages in his first Test series against England the following season, but the first sign he exhibited of talent beyond the ordinary was against Victoria at the SCG at the end of January 1929. He compiled an unbeaten 340 in eight hours and eight minutes: a painstaking innings, and the longest of his life. The unappeasable appetite for runs was evident; the allegro tempo of his scoring was still to come.

Calendar 1930 was then, in effect, the dawn of the Bradman era. It opened, on the same arena, with a world-record first-class score of 452 not out against Queensland, in not quite seven hours. It continued with a world-record Test score of 334 against England at Headingley, in six hours and twenty-three minutes. It concluded, in the totality of Australia's Ashes campaign, with the unsurpassed aggregates of 974 runs at an average of 139.14 in the five Tests, and 2960 runs at 98.66 from twenty-seven first-class matches *in toto*. His first-class aggregate for the year of 4368 runs also remains an Australian record.

These are merely a selection of Bradman's feats in that epoch-making twelve months; no recapitulation of his career can avoid a healthy proportion of statistics. In some respects, indeed, he was a harbinger of cricket's fetishistic fascination with numbers. Scores and averages had been part of cricket from its inception, but seldom regarded as definitive of merit, and in some circles were deplored as a crass measure of excellence. Just before Bradman's first tour, for instance, former Australian captain Monty Noble lectured in his celebrated *The Game's the Thing* (1929): 'Nowadays, far more notice is taken of batting averages than is good for the game. It is not how many runs a man makes but how he makes them that counts. Averages, like statistics, are sometimes capable of lying; merit cannot deceive.' By sheer productivity, Bradman brought numbers to the fore. He industrialised cricket, churning out runs like a factory, which required systems of inventory management. It is not insignificant, for example, that the last pre-Bradman edition of cricket's most famous record-keeping annual, *Wisden Cricketers' Almanack*, ran to 700 pages, and that the first post-Bradman edition ran to more than 1000.

Bradman's progress, however, transcended numbers. His scores, in scale, speed and style, represented a new paradigm; as the dean of English cricket writers, Neville Cardus, expressed it, he stood for 'the sum total, or synthesis, of all that has for years been developing in batsmanship, just as the *Queen Mary* is the sum total, or synthesis, of all that for years has been developing in the science of shipbuilding'. He had command of every stroke, plus a few of his own, and footwork of balletic precision. No aspect of cricket's multifarious arts eluded him. Once, batting in the first few overs of a county match, he pushed a ball to cover's left hand, usually a straightforward single. His partner cantered off, only to be arrested by Bradman's sharp rejoinder: 'No! He throws left-handed!' Bradman had watched the fieldsman warming up.

It was bold, it was brazen, and it was also Australian. Indeed, the solace Bradman offered his countrymen in a time of economic austerity – the chill wind of the Great Depression was then whistling round the world – has often been remarked on. In 1929, Australian exports totalled £139 million; in 1930, they totalled £99 million and Bradman. He excited everyone, from humble Philip Lindsay to great Henry Handel Richardson: visiting her in 1930, Vance Palmer found that the famous novelist could speak of nothing but Bradman.

What is sometimes overlooked in the legend is that the impact of the Great Depression was not lost on Bradman, either. Even at twenty-one, he handled fame as surely as he had acquired it. The English cricket writer Raymond Robertson-Glasgow recalled his first meeting with Bradman in a hotel at Folkestone in September 1930: 'I had rushed into it to dash off some postcard, and, as I addressed it, my eye caught a huge pile of letters; next to them – almost under them – sat Bradman. He had made his name in cricket … and now, quiet and calculating, he was, he told me, trying to capitalise his success.'

While the tour was in progress, Bradman frequently sequestered himself, either to answer his sackfuls of correspondence, or to make notes for a forthcoming autobiography, published in November 1930 as *Don Bradman's Book*. When he did go out, it was often to make public appearances or to discuss business: he lent his name to the 'Don Bradman' bat produced by the Yorkshire firm of William Sykes Ltd, for instance, and exhibited those bats with which he made the record first-class and Test scores in shop windows in Leeds and Manchester. Admirers singled him out for gifts and gratuities: the £1000 he received from the Fleming & Whitelaw soap tycoon, Arthur Whitelaw, exceeded his entire tour fee. He even made a gramophone record. Many of Bradman's more ardent admirers have lamented on his behalf that he was never able to enjoy the luxury of a 'normal life', that he was a prisoner of his prowess. Yet in 1930, renown was clearly anything but a burden.

There is little doubt that in rising up to meet his new fame, Bradman, however inadvertently, created a distance between himself and his fellows. This was particularly the case at tour's end when Bradman agreed, with the approval of the Australian Board of Control, to separate from the team on its arrival in Perth and travel home independently, making a series of public appearances beneath the banner of his employer, sporting-goods retailers Mick Simmons Ltd. 'I didn't like it,' Bradman later told his biographer Michael Page in *Bradman* (1983); did it occur to him how such a Caesar-like triumph might have irked his colleagues? It was the beginning of a relationship with cricketing contemporaries some-times more adhesive than cohesive. Some of the resultant friction undoubtedly sprang from jealousy. All the same, Bradman was so completely self-contained that he could appear oblivious to the mores and motivations of others. In *Farewell to Cricket*, for instance, he defended himself from the common complaint that he seldom socialised with team-mates off the field: 'There were those who thought I was unsociable because I did not think it my duty to breast the bar and engage in a beer-drinking contest.' It was a curious construction to put on the rituals of a post-match compan-ionship. At the close of Bradman's career, the eminent English broadcaster John Arlott found in him a certain pathos: 'I do not think cricket is under Bradman's skin but I believe it is under his skull – in close control. Therefore he has missed something of cricket that less gifted and less memorable men have gained. How, I wonder, would Don Bradman define happiness?'

*

Perhaps nowhere did Bradman's individualism emerge more strongly than in August 1931, when he entered into serious nego-tiations with the Lancashire League club Accrington, which offered him a contract worth an unprecedented £1000 a season. Acceptance would almost certainly have ended his Test career, yet he recalled being 'greatly tempted by it'. 'I don't think anyone could have blamed me if I had chosen to capitalise my cricket by accepting it,' he wrote in *My Cricketing Life* (1938). 'No one would criticise a singer for getting as much as he could for entertaining the public in his particular way.'

In the end, of course, he remained in Australia: local business interests quickly banded together to match Accrington's enticements. Yet Bradman's perception of himself as resembling a great singer, a solo entertainer, a box office drawcard, is intriguing. There is merit in it, too. By March 1932, after home series against West Indies and South Africa, he had scored 2695 Test runs at 107.8; opening batsmen who outstayed their welcome and delayed his entrance could expect heckling; bowlers who presumed to dismiss him were regarded as having spoiled the day's enjoyment.

It should not, perhaps, surprise us that, when an English team arrived in Australia six months later, it had plotted Bradman's downfall in great detail. For there can be no doubt that the fast leg-theory attack deployed by its captain, Douglas Jardine – colloquialised as 'Bodyline' when compacted into cablese – was aimed principally at curbing Bradman's productivity. There can be equally little doubt that it worked and that its after-effects lingered: having made a brave unbeaten 103 at his first brush with the tactics of the English fast bowlers Harold Larwood and Bill Voce in Melbourne, Bradman actually went twelve innings until he again reached three figures, at Headingley in July 1934 – a slump in his progress that stands out like the Wall Street Crash in a chart of the Dow Jones Average.

Bradman's response to the barrages of Larwood and Voce, with their retinue of close catchers on the leg side, was to draw away from the line of the ball and score in the depopulated off. It has been analysed in detail since; some have deplored it as funk, others have admired it as innovation. Chief among the former was Jack Fingleton, Australia's opening batsman from that series, who growled in his *Cricket Crisis* (1946) that 'even unorthodoxy blushed at some of Bradman's capers against bodyline'; Fingleton would become one of Bradman's most consistent critics, sometimes cogent, sometimes captious. Ablest of the latter was Johnnie Moyes, who argued in his *Bradman* (1948): 'Each batsman had a problem to solve. He had to solve it according to his own ability and conception of his powers of batsmanship'; Moyes being the only one of Bradman's biographers to know him well, his work is of immense value.

To recapitulate all the events of that tumultuous summer would take pages, at least: 'Bodyline' is cricket's Jarndyce case. Yet it would have been difficult for Bradman to dispute one aspect of Fingleton's analysis of 'Bodyline': that no cricketer exposed to the enfilade of Larwood and Voce that summer ever fully recovered their love for the game. If Bradman's cricket thereafter lost some of its initial gaiety – as was often contended – one suspects that 'Bodyline' can be considered the *causa rerum*. 'Test cricket is a serious business,' he opined on retiring, 'especially that between England and Australia.' As Robertson-Glasgow noted: 'There are humorously affectionate stories about most great cricketers ... but there are no funny stories about the Don. No one ever laughed about Bradman. He was no laughing matter.'

*

Throughout this turbulent period, Bradman continued to be plied with offers and commercial opportunities, and in February 1934 took one: to move to Adelaide with his wife, Jessie, to whom he had been married almost two years, and join the sharebroking house of Harry Hodgetts, a potentate on the South Australian Cricket Association. In no sense was it a token job, nor was Bradman of a sort to seek one. He became an avid student of the profession – one of the most fascinating digressions in *Farewell to Cricket* is a brief history of the joint-stock company – and later went into business under his own slate. It was not easy for Bradman to leave Sydney, and he arrived in Adelaide in what he described as 'very indifferent health', which could be diagnosed nonetheless as no more than a 'run-down condition'. Such mystery ailments were actually not an uncommon occurrence in Bradman's life, and Charles Williams conjectures, in *Bradman*, that they were in part psychosomatic, an internalising of the pressures under which he found himself; if so, his career is still more remarkable.

One illness very real indeed was the appendicitis which felled him at the completion of that year's tour of England. After an uncertain start to the tour, Bradman had again played a leading role in Australia's wresting of the Ashes, re-establishing his dominion with 304 at Headingley in the Fourth Test and 244 at the Oval in the Fifth Test; his condition became accordingly of, if not international, certainly imperial moment. During the health crisis, the Australian spinners Bill O'Reilly and Arthur Mailey dined at Canterbury with two leading Fleet Street journalists. As a hypothetical, Mailey wondered aloud how newspapers would react were Bradman to pass away on the same day as the Prince of Wales, next in line to the throne. The journalists winced and a lengthy discussion ensued, O'Reilly recalled, concluding with the judgement that front pages would simply have to be divided down the middle: 'Such was the fame of Bradman in England in 1934.'

The outpouring of public sympathy for Bradman and his wife – reading of her husband's grave illness from 12,000 miles away, and at one stage being told that he *had* died – was such that the aviator Sir Charles Kingsford-Smith offered to fly her to London. In the end, Jessie Bradman embarked on P&O's *Maloja*, cabling as she did so a tender reassurance: 'It's all right, Don. I'm coming.' She arrived only three days after her husband's release from hospital, and aided his convalescence by accompanying him on a gentle sight-seeing trip round England. As it was, more than two years would elapse before Bradman would again feel fit for Test cricket.

*

Bradman was next seen in Australian colours as captain, when England visited in 1936–37. As so often when a great individual is charged with leadership, some feared that the responsibility would compromise Bradman's form; they appeared vindicated when Australia were routed in the First and Second Tests. There were also rumours that, as the *Daily Telegraph* put it, there was 'an important section of the team that has not seen eye to eye with Bradman, either on or off the field'.

Rumours these remained, and it is difficult at this remove to disentangle fact from fancy. What is known is that four players – O'Reilly, Stan McCabe, Chuck Fleetwood-Smith and Leo O'Brien – were summoned to a hearing of the board, at which general charges of insubordination and indiscipline were read from a prepared statement by the chairman, Dr Allen Robertson, in an atmosphere O'Reilly described as 'mutual embarrassment'. Still more puzzlingly, when O'Reilly enquired whether he and his three comrades were the specific focus of these allegations, Robertson replied, 'No.'

Bradman disclaimed knowledge of the hearing, but by declining to accompany the players irked O'Reilly for many years after. 'I never really forgave him for it,' O'Reilly recalled not long before his death. 'I still haven't forgiven him now.' Historians have wondered since whether the episode manifested sectarian strains within the Australian XI – the four arraigned were Catholics of Irish descent, Bradman a freemason since the early 1930s – although this is more or less unprovable.

By the time of the hearing, in any case, Bradman's form had returned, like a force of nature: he completed the series with scores of 13, 270, 26, 212 and 169 in three emphatic Australian victories. When Australia next toured England, successfully defending the Ashes in 1938, he was still more effective, becoming the first batsman to average more than 100 in an English season. Still only twenty-nine, he had been cricket's foremost personality for almost a decade. 'It is strange, but I think true,' mused Jack Ingham of the *Star*, before the Fifth Test of that series, 'that all the time, day and night, somewhere in the world, somebody is talking about Bradman.'

*

That Fifth Test contained perhaps the most perverse tribute to the fashion in which Bradman had upped the ante of international cricket. As the hosts accumulated a Test-record score on a featureless pitch, Bradman took a turn with the ball and twisted an ankle. Only when it was clear that he would be unable to bat did England's captain Walter Hammond deign to declare at 7 for 903. As

Bradman was ferried from the Oval by team-mates, it seemed, too, that this would be England's last sight of him.

With the outbreak of war, Bradman enlisted in the RAAF, but after another bout of indeterminate ill-health, was invalided out a year later. 'I am quite certain,' he later concluded, 'that the over-exertion of my earlier cricketing days was exacting retribution in full measure.' There was, accordingly, considerable doubt whether his constitution, at the age of thirty-eight, would withstand Test cricket's rigours when Ashes competition resumed in 1946–47. 'Under no circumstances did I desire to make an attempt which would end in failure,' he recalled. 'On the other hand, cricket badly needed a good start in the post-war era, and I was anxious to assist in that direction if it lay within my compass.' Bradman elected to lead his country, beginning a dynasty continued by his deputy, Lindsay Hassett, in which Australia won twenty and lost only the last of its next twenty-five Tests: a period of dominance without parallel in our annals.

After the war, Bradman was not the batsman of yore: if the insatiability remained, the old alacrity was missing. He was probably, however, a superior captain, with a younger team who revered him unstintingly, and to whom he felt as a 'grandfather'. If there was a criticism of him, it was that, at times, he appeared simply too unyielding. On Australia's all-conquering tour of England in 1948, he demanded the utmost seriousness in even minor fixtures. The team's mercurial all-rounder Keith Miller recalled: 'Bradman would give a crooked little smile and say in his thin, piping voice, "I remember when England made 900 against us and kept us in the field for three days."' Yet Miller also remembered him as 'a shrewd captain' who 'looked after the welfare of his players'. And by pro-ceeding through this tour without defeat as captain, Bradman crowned his career royally.

The ultimate laurel, however, was a knighthood, bestowed in the New Year's Honours of 1949, which Bradman regarded as trib-uting 'the wonderful game of cricket and its importance in Empire relations'. To this game he continued to render yeoman service, remaining in the role of Australian selector – to which he had been appointed in November 1936 – until February 1971, with only two brief interruptions. He became the first former Test player to chair the Australian Board of Control in September 1960 – most conspicuously, in his role as the informal patron of the Frank Worrell Trophy – and served a second three-year term from September 1969. Even when Bradman closed his eponymous stockbroking firm in July 1954, after what he described as 'a serious warning' about his health necessitating 'complete rest', there was no slackening of his exertions as an administrator. Chris Harte's *History of the South Australian Cricket Association* estimates that Bradman attended 1713 meetings of the association in fifty years; very probably another record.

Bradman's retirement from active public life brought no end to the encomia or the honours and, if anything, increased the volumes of correspondence, to which he attended throughout his life with famous diligence. In his last interview, broadcast by the Nine Network on 29 May 1996, he told Ray Martin that he was receiving – and answering, spending four hours daily – 'more fan mail now than I ever did'. That interview was watched by 1.6 million people: Bradman was by now not only famous for being great, but famous for being famous; not merely the pride of cricket, but the embodiment of national virtue. As John Howard put it in the inaugural Bradman Oration on 17 August 2000, he was 'a man representing many of the values, much of the character of his countrymen'.

Such assertions fitted the legend rather better than the man. 'Stripped to the truth,' wrote Robertson-Glasgow in his famous essay in the *Wisden* of 1949, 'he was a solitary man with a solitary aim. It was what the man did rather than what he was that invited obedience.' There was a moment in Bradman's final interview when the unrelenting character lay momentarily exposed by probing regarding his valedictory Test innings: when, needing four to raise his Test average to 100, he was bowled second ball without scoring by leg-spinner Eric Hollies. With misplaced jocularity, perhaps expecting some sentimental appreciation of the event's exquisite romance, Ray Martin asked if Bradman 'laughed about it'. Matter-of-fact as ever, Bradman replied: 'No, I don't laugh much about it, because I'm very sorry that I made a duck, and I would have been glad if I had made those four runs so I could finish with an average of a hundred.' Bradman's business was achievement; the romance was our work.

Bulletin February 2001

ARTHUR MORRIS

Gentil, Parfit Knight

On the table next to Arthur Morris is a new biography written of him, by Sydney's Jack McHarg. Very flattering to be judged worthy of such a publication, Morris reasons, but it does have disadvantages. 'Good thing about getting older is that you forget all the ridiculous ways you got out,' he says, puffing quietly on a Davidoff. 'But now I read that I had a few failures, too. The chairman of the board I'm on at Trust Company, he always introduces me as "The man who never scored a duck." And I say, "Perfectly right, too." Truth's out now.'

So it is. But the truth is that the ridiculous ways that Morris found to get out in forty-six Tests were vastly overshadowed by the handsome ways that he stayed in to acquire 3500 runs. 'He plunders bowlers tastefully and changes rubbish to cultured art,' Neville Cardus rhapsodised. 'I never tire of watching him.' Morris's batting, moreover, was true to the man: civilised, courteous, unaffected. From his veranda, he returns the salutes of Cessnock passers-by, and acknowledges the car horns that sound in greeting. 'Lovely town, really,' he says. 'Everyone so friendly.' To the little girl on her mother's hand walking past: 'Give us a wave, Kelly Jo.'

There's a streak of self-mockery, too. The den is trophy-lined, but he first reaches to show you a coffee mug, a favourite gift from his former opening partner Ken Archer. It shows the pair coming out to bat, with the caption, 'Who's the Old Bloke next to KA?' Friendly? Morris supposes he is, but then you should have met Arthur Mailey: 'You'd say to Arthur, "Arthur, isn't there anyone you dislike?" He'd say, "Well, some people do disappoint me."'

Only occasionally – when a car backfires, or he hears voices raised – is Morris's composure slightly disrupted. 'I suppose that when I hear voices raised, even today I remember my parents. God alone knows how they ever got together; they were such different people. The old man, being a schoolteacher, he lived a pretty monastic life: didn't drink, didn't smoke, didn't go out with sheilas. My mother liked a party. Smoked a hundred cigarettes a day from the age of fifteen till she died at ninety-one. They'd have a big argument and off we'd go.'

Cricket was a happy refuge from his parents' estrangement. Morris joined St George at fourteen as a left-arm spinner, where the club captain was Bill O'Reilly, whom he watched in a dramatic SCG Test when Allen's Englishmen overthrew Bradman's Australians just before Christmas in 1936. Morris recalls, 'I always enjoyed watching until Bill bowled. It seemed that all the beautiful strokes stopped when he came on, and I couldn't understand what he was doing to make the batsmen prod and miss. It was only as I got older I learned what a great bowler he was. That Test was the first time I realised that first-class cricketers swore, actually. I was down there on the third man boundary, as naive as they come, and Maurie Sievers came running down towards the fence but the ball just beat him. And he goes, "Fuck it!" I'd heard the word before but, with a very proper upbringing, I was quite shocked.'

As a sixteen-year-old first-grade cricketer firmly under O'Reilly's spell, Morris slipped snugly into the nook of number one and never looked back. At seventeen, he was a state second XI opener in a team led by Ken Gulliver and including Colin McCool and Ron Saggers, tackling a Victorian second XI incorporating Ian Johnson and Keith Miller. At eighteen, Morris was opening the batting for his state and scoring an unprecedented brace of centuries against Queensland. 'Bloody terrified, I was,' Morris says. 'It turned out all right.'

It was December 1940, however, and white uniforms were being swapped for khaki. Private Morris of the AIF spent his war at Finschhafen and Lae in Papua New Guinea, fortunate that his movement-control unit came no closer to the Japanese than sporadic bombings, but unfortunate in that cricket was virtually out of the question. For the next six years, he played only once with his St George compadre Ray Lindwall, and then in a softball game against the US Army. Their roles, for once, were reversed: Morris pitched, while Lindwall prowled the deep field in front of the tree line. 'This big negro came in and hit it so hard that it was headed for the jungle and we would never have found it,' Morris recalls. 'And Ray flew up in the air and took this great bloody catch. If he hadn't taken it, that would probably have meant the end of the game.'

A belated demob returned twenty-three-year-old Morris to Sydney just in time for the first post-war Ashes series against Wally Hammond's Englishmen, reuniting him with a character first spied from the far side of an SCG fence almost a decade before: the mercurial, massively gifted right-hander Sid Barnes. 'I can still remember Siddy the first time I played him. He played a long innings while O'Reilly went through Petersham, and this whipper-snapper rolls up to Bill in the showers and says, "Well bowled, Tiger. That was some of the best bowling I've faced." I'd've walked up to Bill and said something like, "Excuse me, Mr O'Reilly, may I have a word?" But Siddy's going: "Yes, Tiger, you bowled very well out there." Bill just about swallowed the soap.'

Barnes proved an inventive, unselfish and agile ally. 'More than anybody, Sid lost his best years to the war,' Morris says. 'He was such a great player before it; afterwards he was more calculating, didn't take any risks and stayed on the back foot, got himself in a bit of a hole. But you've never seen a stronger player through point.' The pair succeeded almost at once. Having failed in his first couple of Tests, Morris greeted 1947 with consecutive innings of 155, 122 and 124 not out. 'Is that right?' he asks. 'All I can say about that first century is that there was a big bloody sigh of relief at the end.' Then, characteristically, there's the tribute to a rival: 'I tell you who bowled marvellously at me, did me all the time, did all of us: that was [wrist-spinner Doug] Wright. He'd jump and he'd go over the stumps; he was too quick. But because of his run and his jerky action he'd bowl a couple each over you could get at.'

The Morris–Barnes alliance was ratified and validated when the pair went to England as part of Donald Bradman's unchallengeable 1948 side, rooming and opening together for four months and averaging 87 and 82 respectively. Both scored hundreds in their maiden Lord's Tests – Barnes having staked £8 on himself to do so, at 15–1 – as Australia won by the small matter of 409 runs. The tour's pinnacle was Morris's triple-century partnership with Bradman at Leeds, underwriting a successful Australian last-day chase of 404. Now that was fun, Morris assures you. There's almost a mischievous glint in his eye. 'All the press'd said, "Thank God, this is the day we've been waiting for, where we finally beat these Australians." And suddenly you get that perverse feeling that you want to stop them and, before you know it, you can take on the world. They weren't bowling at all badly but, when you're batting well, you make your own rubbish, and we just kept going. [England captain Norman] Yardley, he had to go for a win so the field was always in, and I hit twenty fours in my first hundred.'

At lunch Morris decided that the bowler he most needed to neutralise was Denis Compton, who had beaten Bradman several times and had him dropped at slip. 'Denis was a pretty handy left-arm bowler, but he wasn't regular,' Morris says. 'So I thought that whenever he pitched up, I'd get stuck into him and loft.' In a famous photograph of them resuming after the adjournment, the Don is imparting some advice, but Morris appears preoccupied, tight-lipped, staring ahead, perhaps finally resolving on his forthcoming contest with Compton's chinaman. 'He was bowling like a batsman,' Morris recalls. 'Trying to do too much: if I started coming down, he'd throw it up further. So I'd keep coming.' Compton's first two post-lunch overs yielded Morris seven boundaries, a pivotal period that restored Australian momentum. Morris made 182, his stand with Bradman yielding 301. 'Bradman earned the better part of his knighthood on that day,' wrote Denzil Batchelor. 'And Morris was surely unfortunate to have missed … an OBE.'

Morris rounded out the tour at the Oval with 196 in what was known to be Bradman's last Test and – thanks to the disintegration of his relations with the Australian Board of Control – also proved Barnes's swansong. Their last stand was 122, dwarfing England's all-out 52, and though Morris had fruitful alliances with the likes of Jack Moroney, Ken Archer and Colin McDonald, he never attained quite the same simpatico as he had with Barnes. Morris recalls, 'When Siddy went I lost a lot of support, because he'd always get ones. Jack was a good player but, well, you had to get a two before Jack'd come one, because he didn't back up. Then I ended up with Ken Archer, who was a beautiful batsman to watch but played very firmly: mid-off, mid-on, bang, all the time. You'd look up at the scoreboard after twenty minutes or so, and you'd had six hits or something. Ken says – and I deny it completely, of course – that I came up to him after twenty minutes of one Test match and said, "Ken, I don't want all the strike, but can you at least give me 50 per cent?" I'm sure I could never have said such a thing, but he swears that I did.'

Morris also came to know a constant English thorn: Alec Bedser. Bedser dismissed Morris eighteen times in Tests; Morris scored eight of his twelve Test centuries against Bedser. Their subsequent correspondences and communications – for they became lifelong friends, in faith with the spirit of their rivalry – still freely refer to both. Some days, it was Morris's nerve and judgement that prevailed. In one Test at Old Trafford, Morris was paired at the top of the order with stand-in opener Ian Johnson. Johnson watched from the non-striker's end as Bedser bowled a wicked first over, moving the ball one way then the other at the very last instant. Morris met every ball in the middle of the bat, then conferred with Johnson in mid-pitch. 'It's doing a bit,' he confided, deadpan. 'We better stick around.' For the next hour, Morris took every ball from England's master of medium pace, absorbing him like a punching bag. Other days, of course, it didn't go according to plan. Bedser achieved an incontestable edge by eclipsing Morris six times in eight innings worth 60 runs, while touring with Freddie Brown's Englishmen in 1950–51, the nadir an anti-climactic duck in the SCG Test. 'Bloody ridiculous, really, on this beautiful wicket,' Morris says. 'Alec bowls a long hop, at quarter-power, just to get his arm over; I walk inside to touch it to leg, and it goes, "Flick." And there it is, before all these people, bowled for a blob. I started to laugh halfway back, because I came in to just dead silence.'

The tide turned in Adelaide. On the morning of the Fourth Test, Morris came down to breakfast to find he'd been allocated a seat at table thirteen. He paused superstitiously, then sat down anyway; what would be, would be. For the next day and a half, Morris was occupied in making 206: 'watchful, phlegmatic with hardly a hint of mortal error', commented E.W. Swanton. Finally, with the last man at the crease, he donated his wicket to finger-spinner Roy Tattersall; a photograph of the dismissal shows Morris smiling cheerfully as if released from the cares of solemnity.

Among contemporaries, there was always the feeling about Morris that he could summon resources as he wished. Ken Archer recalls a meeting one morning before a Shield match at the Gabba, where his friend advised: 'Not feeling too well, dear boy. Don't think I'll want to bat too long today.' But when a couple of wickets fell early, the New South Welshman flashed Archer a long-suffering look, and proceeded to blast 253 out of 400, the last 50 in seventeen minutes.

Yet Morris seldom gorged himself at the crease. Batting was a pathway to pleasure, not a road to records, and dismissal merely postponed enjoyment rather than thwarted ambition. He was phil-osophical even when run out for 99 by partner Neil Harvey at the MCG in the Fifth Test against South Africa, in February 1953. 'Last ball of the over I was at the bowler's end, so I was really thinking about getting my hundred next over,' says Morris. 'Tayfield was on to Neil, and he hit it to cover and took off. It was his call, so I had to go, and I probably hesitated because I wasn't expecting it.

And that was the difference ... between being run out by four yards rather than six!'

Perhaps the yen for big scores had faded by that stage. When Morris was back in England as Lindsay Hassett's vice-captain a few months later, he passed 50 a dozen times but only transited once to a century. But how could anyone describe this as a disappointing tour? Why, Morris met his future wife, Valerie Hudson, a willowy showgirl appearing with Bud Flanagan and Teddy Knox's 'Crazy Gang' show *Ring Out the Bells* at the Victoria Palace. When she took an assisted passage a year later, they married at the Sydney Registry Office. Morris hadn't thought of himself as the marrying kind. 'Would you have been, with the example of my parents?' he asks. 'Ian Craig says that the first time we met, when I was driving him and Richie Benaud after a game, I really ripped into them: "Whatever you do, don't get married. It'll be the end of you." Because, me, I'd seen it all before, hadn't I?' But there he was, married. Funny how things turn out.

It was destined, though, to be a tragically brief union. They'd been together only five months when Morris joined Australia's first tour of the West Indies in March 1955. He opened the trip with 157, then scored 111 in the First Test at Port-of-Spain, batting with all the brio of his early years and completing a notable record collection. Ray Robinson's chapter on Morris in *On Top Down Under* is called 'Saying Hello with Hundreds': an allusion to Morris's uncanny facility for immediate acclimatisation, for he scored centuries on his first appearances in Australia, England, South Africa and the West Indies. But when Morris returned from the West Indies, he learned that Valerie had been diagnosed as suffering breast cancer – she had refrained from informing her absent husband – and would live less than eighteen months. Morris's playing days were over at thirty-three.

'I had to retire,' he says. 'I knew we wouldn't have long together, five years at the outside. The one thing I wanted for her was to take her to England a last time, which wasn't easy because we had no money, but I was a very lucky man.' One of Valerie's former impresarios, Windmill Theatre proprietor Vivian van Damm, sent a cheque for £1000 to the 'best showgirl I ever had', and an envelope arrived from Lindsay Hassett containing another £500. 'He'd written this ridiculous letter,' says Morris. 'Lindsay says, "I'm building a house and I don't know where the money's going. You just pay me when you can."' Morris paid his way in England by writing cricket for the *Daily Express* during Australia's 1956 Ashes tour, at the conclusion of which Valerie died.

Arthur Morris remarried, to Judith, in 1967. Behind his neat front garden and the brass plate at the front door for 'A. Morris', he lives for his competition tennis and intermittent bus trips to Sydney. One other thing: like his father, he's always voted Liberal. He was even approached during 1949 to run for a safe seat, but refrained: the disdain of Labor voters on the Hill would've been too much to bear. Sir Robert Menzies was a friend and familiar during and after Morris's cricket career, although, as if to ward off any suggestion of political partisanship, the player refers warmly to Arthur Calwell and 'Doc' Evatt, the deputy prime minister. Evatt took Morris after his first-class debut to Stan McCabe's sport store in George Street and told him to choose a bat. Morris adds that he also found Paul Keating 'quite charming' at a charity breakfast before a Prime Minister's XI game. 'Actually, I was sitting next to Sir James Balderstone,' he recalls. 'And I said to him, "Do y'know? I'd love to have seen Keating and Menzies at it in Parliament together. They'd score off each other beautifully." Keating goes over the top, but he's a first-rate politician. And Menzies, of course, was just about the finest debater you could wish to see. It would have been better than the bloody Tivoli, it would! Front pages every day!'

Ah, yes, but you can't compare champions of different eras, can you?

Test Team of the Century (2000)

MILLER'S 185

Brakes Off

'The day you walk through an applauding Long Room at Lord's,'
Keith Miller once wrote, 'it seems as if you have had a hallmark
stamped on your career.' He knew the feeling better than anyone
– and never was the applause more heartfelt than when he represented Dominions against England in August 1945.

An RAAF Pilot Officer who'd had an arduous war in Beau-
fighters and Mosquitos, Miller had once walked away from a crash
landing with the nonchalant line, 'Nearly stumps drawn that time,
gents.' His cricket had the same air of carelessness in the face of
danger. An unheralded presence in the five Victory Tests, he had
headed the batting with 443 runs at 63.29, and collected 10 cheap
wickets; by the time he came to play in this glorious match, he was
already a force to be reckoned with.

Dominions was composed of servicemen from Australia, New
Zealand and South Africa, led by the mighty West Indian Learie
Constantine; the Englishmen featured nine past or future Test
players, led by Walter Hammond (who made twin centuries). But
Miller as *Wisden* said, 'outshone them all'. His first 61, scored in the
last seventy-five minutes of the second day, included one six onto
the top tier of the pavilion. It was then the morning of the third
day which Pelham Warner reckoned was the greatest exhibition of
hitting he saw in sixty years as a player and potentate. In ninety
minutes of mostly orthodox but inexpressibly powerful batting,
Miller added 124, with six further sixes: one carried to Block Q
on the right of the pavilion; another landed on the roof of the

broadcasting box, then atop the home team's dressing room. 'The hit came up over mid-on, rising all the time as it came,' recalled the commentator Arthur Gilligan. 'On hitting the pavilion it fell into a hole that had been made in the roof of the commentary box by shrapnel, and the ball had to be poked out by a stick.' So violent was the attack that some elderly members, so the story goes, abandoned their favourite positions and adjourned to the bar, where it was safer – although this may be fond Australian imagining.

The bowlers were, strange as it may sound today, chiefly two outstanding English leg-spinners: Eric Hollies, Bradman's conqueror in his final Test innings three years later, and Doug Wright, who claimed 10 for 195 in the match and would take more than 100 Test wickets. Keeping faith with the event, they kept trying to get Miller out, even as Miller strove to entertain: his partnership with Constantine was worth 117 in forty-five exuberant minutes. The old sage C.B. Fry equated the Australian with the greatest of his forebears: 'Apart from his technical excellence, Keith Miller has something of the dash and generous abandon that were part of Victor Trumper's charms.'

Like the most skilful pilot Miller guided Dominions to a 45-run win, in a game of 1241 runs, with minutes to spare. But the result was secondary to the spirit of the contest – something that would be true of Miller's whole career. If ever an innings was in tune with its times – relieved, reviving, heady, hopeful – this was. After years stale with austerity and discipline, it was a breath of extravagance and irreverence. 'From the moment he takes guard,' wrote R.C. Robertson-Glasgow after watching Miller that summer, 'he plays each ball just that much below its supposed merits that scratches a bowler's pride ... It is dignity with the brakes off.'

Inside Edge: The Greatest – Top 50 Innings by Australian
Batsmen (2004)

THE DEATH OF MILLER
Nugget

The office of Australia's longest-serving prime minister, Sir Robert
Menzies, was famously decorated by two framed images. One was
a painting by the artist Tom Roberts, capturing the austere, sun-
blasted beauty of a bush landscape; the other was a photograph of
Keith Miller putting the finishing touch on a square cut at the
Sydney Cricket Ground in 1950.

Any symbolism was unconscious. Yet here, in their time, were
the first and last words on Menzies' country: the elemental and
primal antiquity of the land, and the breezy and expansive youth-
fulness of its people. For no athlete since World War II has fitted as
exactly as Miller the bill of 'Australian in excelsis' – to borrow Sir
Neville Cardus's famous phrase.

An Australian might hope to have been born a Bradman, but
there was only really room for one Don in the firmament. Miller
not only did everything a cricketer would want to do, but the way
they would want to do it, wrapped in an infectious personality that
radiated carefree ease one moment, and virile hostility the next.

He batted with classical technique and utter abandon. He could
touch speeds of bowling reserved for few, so that rivals were loath
to rouse him. 'The worst mistake a batsman could make,' recalled
Sir Leonard Hutton, 'was to hit him for four.' Lounging deceptively at slip, Miller stood out even when unoccupied. He was a
game of cricket in himself. When the boy Ian Chappell was taken
to his first Test, his father Martin offered one piece of advice.
'Miller,' he said. 'Just watch Miller.'

Miller could even, when the circumstances dictated it, ooze boredom. Though Australians distrust exhibitionism, they esteem the natural, the open, the spontaneous. And Miller was more than simply an entertainer: he had that uncanny knack of commanding attention without apparently ever seeking it.

In Australia, Miller is also an historical embodiment. Just as Bradman is often seen as the sporting solace of the Great Depression, Miller is associated immediately with World War II, the warrior who beat his sword into a bat rather than a ploughshare. A sense of destiny infests his name: Keith Ross Miller was christened as a tribute to the aviators Keith and Ross Smith, who, in the week of Miller's birth, landed in Melbourne after a pioneering trip from England. And it would be in reversing their journey at the outbreak of war as a pilot officer in the Royal Australian Air Force that Miller underwent what was almost certainly his defining life experience.

In his book *Cricket Crossfire*, Miller allots his war years ten pages. They read, at first, light-heartedly. Then you notice, dropped in laconically, phrases like 'who later in the war was killed', 'he crashed ... and was killed,' and 'six or seven of my pals had been killed.' If his cricket had an air of nonchalance, then, there is little wondering why.

His first big cricket ensued, in fact, in the so-called Victory Tests of the English summer of 1945, where he capped off leading the batting averages with a famous innings of 185 for Dominions against England. Lord's became a venue that he cherished as much as it cherished him: he made a fine Test hundred there in 1953, and reaped 10 wickets three years later.

No appreciation of Miller, though, should be burdened with too many facts. It just wasn't him. Just about every Australian can tell you Bradman's batting average; only a real aficionado can be exact about Miller's figures. He stood out by other, pre-statistical criteria. In an era when cricketers did not routinely resemble athletes, he assuredly did. In an age when cricketers were not famed for their photogenia, the camera loved him, almost to distraction. Cricket, too, was simply the game he played during the day. He did not care to think about it too deeply in hindsight. A journalist once accosted him, wanting to know how he'd just taken 7 for 12 in a Sheffield Shield match against South Australia. 'There's three reasons,' Miller replied. 'First, I bowled bloody well. Second, I, er ... second ...' There was a long pause. 'You can forget about the other two reasons.'

And make no mistake: Miller had 'it'. Presence, charisma, an aura – call it what you will. It was said that men wanted to be like him, women simply to be with him. He was thankful in later life that the media had, in his own time, been a relatively tactful institution. Over lunch in Sydney one day, a mutual friend opined that Miller would have been worth millions to the modern game, and would have been paid accordingly. Keith looked askance. 'You know,' he said, 'Bill O'Reilly said to me, just before he died: "Keith, we were lucky to play cricket when we did." He didn't have to say anything else. I knew exactly what he meant.'

I have one particularly vivid recollection of that meeting, for I did something I seldom do, and asked Keith for his autograph – to sign a copy, as it happens, of that same photograph that had hung in Menzies' office. The mutual friend laughed, not without reason, that a park-cricket plodder like myself should feel an affinity with such an image. Only after returning home did I peep at Keith's dedication. It reads: 'Good shot this. Try it sometime.' Perhaps it explains something about Miller's personality that just contemplating him makes me feel I ought to.

Guardian October 2004

QUEENSLAND

Good PR

Let's be honest. The history of an Australian state cricket association? Surely it should come with matchsticks for the eyelids. This one looks more than usually like an exercise in corporate vanity: not only is it a heavy object loaded with big colour pics on glossy stock, but the publisher's imprint on the spine is 'PR'; short for Playright, one supposes, but suggestive of something to be given away rather than read. You can hear them at the Gabba now, can't you? 'Yes, this is our association history. Handsome, eh? Haven't read it myself, though it's certainly got lots of words in it ...'

Not so fast. As it happens, cricket bibliophiles have done rather well out of Australian state associations over the years. Phil Derriman's New South Wales history, *True to the Blue* (1985), is a super book. Robert Coleman's Victorian equivalent, *Seasons in the Sun* (1993), and Anthony Farmer's *The WACA: An Australian Cricket Success Story* (1998) are at least very good. Chris Harte's *The History of the South Australian Cricket Association* (1990), despite some stylistic eccentricities and the look of having been bound together as it emerged from his typewriter, is also a useful reference; having bought my copy at the Adelaide Oval for $5, where it was on next-stop-the-dumpster display, I've no complaints. So put aside your prejudices. Would you rather be reading *Punter: The Making of a*

Review of *Green Hills to the Gabba: The Story of Queensland Cricket* by Ian Diehm (Playright Publishing, 2000)

Champion? Be warned that *Green Hills to the Gabba* doesn't do the lay reader many favours. It's not written with any great flair or fluency; at times, it's a downright slog. But concealed in its bulk, and sometimes almost lost in their deadpan delivery, are recollections and ruminations of surprising colour and candour.

Queensland cricket administration in this century has been dominated by autocrats, most notably Jack Hutcheon and Norm McMahon. They enjoyed triumphs: Hutcheon ushered Queensland into the Sheffield Shield and secured Brisbane its first Test; on McMahon's watch arrived such luminaries as Wes Hall, Greg Chappell and Jeff Thomson. Yet their management model was essentially feudal. Players and spectators were annoying distractions. Des Hansen recalls that team-mates in the 1930s refrained from outfield dives because the QCA wouldn't pay laundry expenses. Jack McLaughlin remembers that, when Wally Walmsley arrived as coach in the 1940s, his family had to live in a tent; Mrs Walmsley suffered a nervous breakdown. Ron Archer recollects the knee injury that ended his career: 'The expense of getting my knee better at six pounds a week was too much ... I didn't ask the QCA for help because I knew I wouldn't get it.'

Some stories are comical: former Brisbane lord mayor Clem Jones relives the day when, appalled by the quality of the food served to members, he pushed a putrid banana into Hutcheon's face. Others aren't: McMahon, a taxation official, appears to have used his day job for political intimidation. When he fell out with Ray Lindwall, the great fast bowler's florist was submitted to a seven-year tax audit. When Greg Chappell ran for the QCA executive, McMahon glowered: 'I hope you've got your tax affairs in order.' Says Chappell: 'That was the start of a ten-year battle with the tax man that ended in a draw.'

It's not all parsimony and perfidy, of course. Some inspirational characters emerge, such as stalwart Ernie Toovey. Threatened with the loss of his ulcer-ridden leg when a POW under the Japanese, he told doctors: 'You can't take my leg off because I've got to play cricket for Queensland.' There are also some charming vignettes.

The widow of Charlie Andrews, a talented Queensland import of the late 1920s, offers a succinct account of why she and her husband wed that could be straight from Jane Austen: 'I used to go to a dance at the Palais every Saturday night and I danced with Don Bradman, Stan McCabe and Charlie. He took me home and I married him.' Again, that's not something you'll get in *Punter*.

Wisden Cricket Monthly September 2000

NEW SOUTH WALES

A Team of the Century

VICTOR TRUMPER
ARTHUR MORRIS
SIR DONALD BRADMAN
DOUG WALTERS
ALLAN BORDER
MONTY NOBLE (C)
RICHIE BENAUD
BERT OLDFIELD
ALAN DAVIDSON
RAY LINDWALL
BILL O'REILLY

TWELFTH MAN: STEVE WAUGH
COACH: BOB SIMPSON

Federation in Australia, in 1901, changed the constitutional basis of the Australian colonies, but not their cultures. Though New South Wales is to all intents just one among six states, its people have always regarded themselves as *primus inter pares*, reflected in the car number plates, which still boast of theirs being 'The Premier State'. Where cricket is concerned, with a record of winning forty-two Sheffield Shields over ninety-two seasons, they have felt especially secure.

Choosing a New South Wales team from across the ages is, accordingly, to squeeze a quart into a pint pot: the dozen representatives seem paltry when standing in for the whole of history. At times on the cricket field over the last 150 years, New South Wales has been virtually synonymous with Australia. Immediately after World War I, for instance, it was providing as many as eight members of the home Test XI, and in 1921, ten of the fifteen who toured England. It was regarded as a lamentable development when, thirty years ago, Australia walked onto a Test ground for the first time without a son of New South Wales.

With such a constellation of talent to choose from, omissions from this XII will strike some readers more forcefully than the inclusions. No place can be found here for heroes of yore such as Fred Spofforth, Charlie Turner, Warren Bardsley, Jack Gregory and Alan Kippax, or modern masters such as Mark Taylor, Mark Waugh, Michael Slater and the underrated Geoff Lawson. The elevation of Doug Walters will surprise some. His four unsuccessful tours of England impair appreciation of him: it happens that his record in all other climes was 4612 runs at 56.24, accumulated with the haste that turns games, including three Test centuries scored in a session. That said, were this team to be scheduled English fixtures, I'd consider either princely Stan McCabe or gubernatorial Charlie Macartney.

My selections are on a state-of-origin basis. This excludes Keith Miller and Neil Harvey, Victorians to whom New South Welshmen sometimes impertinently lay claim, on the basis of their having moved north for reasons of employment. But it includes Sir Donald Bradman, who played as many Sheffield Shield matches and scored more centuries for South Australia, and Allan Border, now as Queensland as XXXX – and rightly so, for it was their upbringings, in Bowral and Mosman respectively, that were the making of them. I've also required of each player a minimum of twenty interstate matches. That precludes the consideration of Glenn McGrath and Brett Lee, but so be it: both are cricketers from New South Wales rather than of it. Such an exercise as this causes one to reflect on how conditioned we have become to thinking in terms only of national and individual identities. As with all it touches, globalisation has weakened our senses of local and regional affiliation in cricket. More's the pity.

Whatever Elysian field this team took, a great game could be anticipated. Quality reportage would be guaranteed. You could count on Australia's best cricket writers, in Jack Fingleton and Ray Robinson, and its best broadcasters, in Alan McGilvray and Johnnie Moyes, for descriptions of play worthy of the participants. New South Wales has been unproductive only of good umpires – a paucity, of course, not confined to that state.

Wisden Asia August 2002

KERRY PACKER

TV Eye

Kerry Packer was an exception to the old adage that the first generation acquires, the second consolidates, the third squanders. His grandfather Robert Clyde Packer was a journalist turned proprietor; his father, Sir Frank, a proprietor turned mogul; Kerry was a mogul turned symbol, his hulking figure, heavy jaw and harsh manner making him the most recognisable businessman of his generation. At his death, Australia's richest man controlled a fortune worth US$5 billion; he had also just been deemed by Cricket Australia second only to Bradman in his influence on Australian cricket: a bouquet unthinkable when the main work towards it was done almost thirty years ago.

Very little about Packer's life, however, was predictable. Packer had a luckless childhood stricken by polio, a horrid education retarded by dyslexia, and a painful upbringing in which he was mocked and monstered by the tyrannical Sir Frank. He succeeded his father only because brother Clyde fled the family fold in 1972, after one dispute too many. But Kerry was very much his father's son. 'He [Kerry] was more politically opportunistic than Sir Frank and, although intensely loyal, more capable of unsentimental profiteering,' believes Dr Bridget Griffen-Foley of Macquarie University, whose *The House of Packer* (1999) charts the family's rise. 'But although brutalised by his father, the pair also had much in common; the late Clyde Packer, by contrast, was more like his namesake and the family patriarch, Robert Clyde Packer.'

Packer's early work was in his father's magazine stable, where he oversaw the relaunching of the hardy perennial *Australian Women's Weekly*, and the inauguration of the successful *Cleo*. But he had not long succeeded to the top job on his father's death in May 1974 than he began reinvigorating Consolidated Press's underperforming television arm, the Nine Network, with a heady cocktail of sport, soaps and current affairs. All were solutions to the challenge of providing local content for new rules laid down by the Australian Broadcasting Tribunal, but the greatest of these was sport, of which Packer was obsessively fond, especially golf, rugby, horseracing and, later, polo.

Cricket, however, was the white whale to his Ahab. He was endlessly frustrated in his pursuit by the cosiness of relations between the Australian Cricket Board and the Australian Broadcasting Commission, and let it show in perhaps his most famous remark – 'We're all whores ... What's your price?' – to ACB chairman Bob Parish and treasurer Ray Steele, in July 1976. When the authorities proved strangely immune to his charms, he was receptive to the proposition by John Cornell and Austin Robertson of an independent, international, professional cricket attraction. Cornell and Robertson brought the players – sixty of them by the time recruiting was done – to which Packer added money, marketing and an implacable determination to have his way.

It is worth pointing out that Packer didn't make cricket popular. He coveted it because it *was* popular, and perceived it as underpriced because you could buy the services of the players cheaply, relative to their market value. What he improved was cricket's ability to exploit its popularity through commercial means. This he did in a variety of fashions, jazzing up television coverage, promoting the players as personalities, pitching the game as a product to the public that could be consumed over five days or one, by day or night, in white and coloured clothing. When that did not work at once, he tweaked the popular patriotic nerve with a slogan centred on a pop song. Initially reluctant, the public turned to support World Series Cricket in overwhelming numbers, the turning point being a game between the WSC Australians and the WSC

West Indies at the SCG in November 1978 attended by more than 50,000 people. Within six months, the ACB had sued for peace, not only granting Nine the exclusive broadcasting rights for Australian cricket but also handing over marketing responsibilities to Packer's PBL Marketing.

The Packer Risorgimento in cricket became a model for the reinvention of a sport: Gary Kasparov once said that what chess needed was 'its own Kerry Packer'. By the same token, it was hardly an act of selflessness, for Nine obtained hours of popular and profitable summer programming at hugely advantageous terms. 'The deal with PBL was hardly a goldmine for cricket,' revealed former ACB CEO Graham Halbish in his autobiography *Run Out* (2003). 'The Board still had all its obligations to look after the game but it had to share considerable revenue with PBL Marketing ... When the agreement with PBL ended in 1989, after what many believed to be a fruitful and lucrative decade, the ACB's net assets had increased to $2.5 million. That hardly was megabucks.' So while, on the whole, it has been decided that Australian cricket did well out of Packer, it's arguable he that did far better out of Australian cricket.

Packer would forever be identified with cricket, partly because sport is the measure of so much in Australia, partly because he was never again so public: he privatised the Consolidated Press empire in 1983, buying out minorities for a song at the end of a recession. Yet while he enjoyed cricket, he loved television most of all, boasting of watching it for four hours a day. In *The Rise and Rise of Kerry Packer* (1993), his biographer Paul Barry painted a vivid, somewhat melancholy portrait of Citizen Packer in his Bellevue Hill Xanadu: 'He never read because he was dyslexic, rarely went out because he didn't drink, and had time on his hands because he was a lonely man with few friends. Instead of books his library at home had videotapes So each evening he would sit at home and watch television.'

That made his eventual decision to part with the Nine Network in April 1987 all the more startling, although the deal showed just how much his father's son Kerry was. Offered an unrefusable price by Rupert Murdoch in 1972, Sir Frank had set aside sentiment and sold his best loved media property, Sydney's *Daily Telegraph*. Fifteen years later, Kerry knew that the $1050 million offered by Australian entrepreneur Alan Bond for Nine was vastly in excess of the network's value, and sold with a parting mot: 'You only get one Alan Bond in your life and I've had mine.' In fact, Bond's management proved so ruinous that Packer was able to buy the network back for a fraction of its value within three years.

Packer was also his father's son in his attitude to life. Sir Frank, wracked by ill health, lived every moment at though it was his last; Kerry brazened out his many intimations of mortality. In October 1990, he actually died, being without pulse or respiration for six minutes after having a heart attack following a game of polo. He came back defiantly: 'The good news is there's no Devil,' he said. 'The bad news is there's no heaven.' He developed into the highest of rollers, and his gambling exploits became legend; he won and lost corporate fortunes in positions he took in the foreign-exchange market; he set a punishing regime of travel for business and pleasure.

Packer got another lease on life in 2001 when his pilot donated him a kidney, although his battles with illness lent his features an eerie plasticity. His face, which had once had a craggy grandeur, began to look like one of Dr Moreau's less successful experiments. Yet, even then, he hardly slowed down. He lived just a few months longer than did his father, dying at his home in Sydney's Bellevue Hill ten days after his sixty-eighth birthday, and shortly after flying back from Argentina to take over high-stakes negotiations by the Nine Network for Australian Rules football broadcasting rights.

Packer was an object of such fascination in his lifetime that even his death seems like another event to be analysed; it's tempting simply to echo Metternich's famous remark on the death of Talleyrand: 'I wonder what he meant by that.' Now the mantle of running the house of Packer falls on his son James, it is also tempting to prophesy decline. Yet one shouldn't be overhasty. In

1977, after all, you'd have obtained good odds on Packer's death eventually being marked by a minute's silence at the MCG, as there was on the morning of 27 December – the sort of odds that might even have appealed to the man himself. And Kerry Packer provides the best evidence that the next generation is always an unknown quantity.

Cricinfo December 2005

PACKER'S LEGACY

A Game Half-bought

> Probably the most imaginative piece of sporting promotion
> ever devised. A staggering coup ... Australians will be treated
> to what is expected to be some of the most magnificent cricket
> ever seen ... the move is expected to provide the greatest boost
> Australian cricket has ever experienced.
>
> —'The Great Cricket Story', *Bulletin*, May 1977

When Kerry Packer published the first details of his World Series
Cricket in his news-magazine the *Bulletin* almost thirty years ago,
his minions seemed to have hit a piercing high C on the hyperbole
register. Oddly enough, the hype has stood up well: World Series
Cricket was 'most imaginative', very much a 'staggering coup',
would produce some cricket worthy of the description 'magnificent', and proved enough of a 'boost' to cricket to justify a minute's
silence at the MCG on the news of Packer's death: thirty years ago,
the rights to broadcast Australian cricket were worth an annual
$70,000; today, the figure is $45 million.

Yet this is also misleading. One of the tricks history plays on us
is making events appear to be manifest destiny when they are
actually coalitions of circumstance and character. In his evocative
history of the first century of Australian settlement, *A Land Half
Won* (1980), Geoffrey Blainey devotes a fascinating section to the
movement for secession of north Queensland, even producing a
speculative chronology for the unborn colony. 'There can be no
discussion of a powerful event without realising that it is like a

63

traffic junction where a society is capable suddenly of changing direction,' he points out. 'In writing history we concentrate more on what did happen, but many of the crucial events are those which almost happened.' The secessionist movement of Kerry Packer's World Series Cricket *did* happen. But what if it had not?

For it very nearly didn't. The origins of WSC lie in two parallel ambitions. One was Packer's desire to obtain exclusive Test-match broadcast rights, as a means of winning cheap and popular summer content for his Nine Network; the other was the abiding sense of grievance among Australian Test cricketers in the 1970s about their paltry emoluments, and the search for a solution by the successful television comedians Paul Hogan and John Cornell when they learned of it through their friend and wannabe player-manager Austin Robertson. Both stories contain a common enemy: the Australian Cricket Board, which had slammed the door on Packer, and dealt grudgingly with the players' complaints. But Packer was unaware of the players' restlessness, while neither the players nor their allies knew that Packer had tried without success to prise open a handshake deal between the ACB and the Australian Broadcasting Commission in June 1976.

The narratives might never have intersected had Packer not headhunted Hogan and Cornell from the rival Seven Network three months later, and even then might have led nowhere had the individuals been differently disposed: after all, it seems as incongruous as Morcombe and Wise encouraging Lord Grade to patronise a World Rugby Sevens competition. As it was, when Cornell discussed some sort of independent Australian cricket circuit, Packer instinctively upped the ante: 'Why not do the thing properly? Let's get the world's best cricketers to play Australia's best.'

In his famous High Court judgement which swept away the International Cricket Council ban on World Series Cricket's signatories in November 1977, Justice Christopher Slade contended: 'The very size of profits made from cricket matches involving star players must for some years have carried the risk that a private promotor would appear on the scene and seek to make money by promoting cricket matches involving world-class cricketers.' But had Packer not been that 'private promotor', it is unlikely anyone would have come up with a scheme as grand as WSC. The likelier course would have been a continuation of smaller-scale private promotions – such as Jack Neary's World Double Wicket Competition in Australia and the Cavaliers in England – tolerated by the authorities for as long as they represented no perceived threat; the alternative of going head-to-head against a hundred-year-old brand-name, Test cricket, was open to Packer only because the content it generated could be integrated into his television schedules.

The players? Without Packer's irruption, they would probably have continued hustling for commercial opportunities individually. As Greg Chappell noted at the time, 'Players were becoming so heavily committed to their personal promotional pursuits that it wasn't uncommon to see half the team race off on the eve of a Test to engage in this type of activity.' At the time of Packer's entrance, too, Australian cricket was obtaining unprecedented sums through the sponsorship of the tobacco conglomerate Amatil, which, because of the impending ban on cigarette advertising, was building its Benson & Hedges brand into a big name in sports sponsorship. Belated increases in Test fees might have alleviated some discontents.

Nonetheless, Australian cricketers' grudge against their administrators derived from conditions as much as pay. Flashpoint had very nearly been reached in South Africa in March 1970, when Bill Lawry's team, exasperated and exhausted by five months on the road, had privately boycotted a Fifth Test agreed to by the ACB over their heads. It would not have been surprising had they been susceptible to inducements offered by agents for interests other than Packer.

South Africa, in fact, coincidentally destined to be exiled from international cricket soon after that Fifth-Test-that-never-was but still warmly connected to the game in Australia, was the likeliest source of such enticements. During the summers of 1974–75 and 1975–76, the three Chappell brothers, Dennis Lillee, Max Walker,

Ashley Mallett, Terry Jenner, Gary Gilmour, Martin Kent, Alan Hurst, Dav Whatmore, Johnny Gleeson and Malcolm Francke had all visited the country, some more than once, as part of multiple tours by the Derrick Robins XI and the International Wanderers; the latter were even managed by Richie Benaud.

Future visits were made problematic by the Soweto uprising in June 1976, and the UN declaration against apartheid in sport and the Commonwealth's signing of the Gleneagles agreement the following year. But the window-dressing merger of the South African Cricket Association and the 'non-racial' South African Cricket Board of Control, in October 1977, kept alive the illusion that the game there was 'normalising' of its own accord, and it is probable that overtures from Johannesburg would have been as enticing to peeved Australian Test cricketers in the late '70s as they were to Graham Gooch's jaded Englishmen a few years later. As it was, leading South Africans were among Packer's eagerest enlistees: Eddie Barlow reputedly snatched the pen and signed his contract without reading it. But it is just possible that the schism in the game caused by Packer prevented a deeper schism in the game over South Africa.

If we are to contemplate life had secession never happened, it might also be worth considering cricket had secession continued. By early 1979, what had begun as a domestic dispute had become an international incident. Packer had five dozen players on his books from six countries, including some from the next generation. WSC had toured New Zealand, was about to tour the West Indies, and would have been welcome in South Africa. The united administrative front had crumbled: only England's Test and County Cricket Board refused to tarry with Packer, and even it was concerned about disruption of the forthcoming World Cup.

There was the potential, at the time, for Packer to mobilise a cricket circuit coeval with Test cricket along the lines of Lamar Hunt's World Championship Tennis; or to become a cricket impresario as his pal Mark McCormack, at IMG, was to golf and tennis. While he had not invented one-day cricket, he essentially controlled the patents on its night, coloured and tri-cornered variants. Some of his men were tiring of the routine. Even Joel Garner and Imran Khan, of whom it made stars, later admitted to an abiding hankering for Test cricket. 'Beyond a certain point,' commented Imran, 'it is difficult to bowl to brilliant batsmen or face a battery of fast bowlers day after day simply in order to prove one's individual worth.' But Packer had also begun investing in young players such as the promising left-hander Graeme Wood, whom he'd signed on a five-year contract, while the South Africans would have played forever. 'To this day,' wrote Mike Procter, 'I don't know why it [WSC] disbanded so suddenly and why Kerry Packer packed it in.' To Clive Rice, it 'was as if someone had taken away my right arm'.

As it was, one of Packer's chief business gifts was not losing sight of the main game: he had gone into WSC to obtain broadcasting rights from the ACB; he decided he would settle for these, with the bonus that he would control Australian cricket's promotion and profitability through PBL Marketing. And while he had set up WSC in the spirit of competition with the official game, he was also a believer in monopoly, which he restored when he effectively gave the ACB back its players in April 1979. He rested content with an imaginative, staggering, magnificent boost – and a healthy piece of the action for himself.

Wisden Cricketer February 2006

BOB PARISH

One of the Old School

The death in Melbourne of Bob Parish, on 11 May, four days after his eighty-ninth birthday, did not mark the end of an era, for the era of Australian cricket administration which he personified is long ended. But he was, in a sense, the last of his kind. Until a few years ago, Parish was still coming in to the Australian Cricket Board a day or two a week, mainly to deal with historical enquiries. In their smart, shiny new premises, he seemed almost like a museum exhibit, whose case should have borne the taxonomic description 'Cricket Administrator, Australia, circa 1960s'.

Parish's longevity in cricket governance is hard, these days, to credit. A good-enough medium-pace bowler to take 197 district first-XI wickets at 26 in the 1940s, he was on the committee of his club, Prahran, for more than sixty years. He became the club's delegate to the Victorian Cricket Association in 1950 and gave the VCA forty-two years of service, including twenty-nine as chairman – and 'gave' is the right word, for his work was entirely honorary.

Parish also had two spells as chairman of the ACB, from 1966 to 1969 and from 1975 to 1980, in thirty-three years as a Victorian representative. He managed the Australian team on tours of the West Indies in 1965 and England in 1968, although he is best remembered as the board's dignified but beleaguered boss when Kerry Packer's World Series Cricket challenged the ACB's seventy-year monopoly on the international game in Australia.

Parish was not without a capacity for innovation. He had negotiated the sponsorship for the first domestic one-day competition with Vehicle & General Insurance; he had guided the first years of the board's long-term relationship with Benson & Hedges and been a prime mover in the triumphant Centenary Test. But he was easily appalled by the effrontery of Packer when first they met in June 1976 to discuss Channel Nine acquiring exclusive Test-match broadcasting rights. Though words uttered to an honorary cricket administrator have been better chosen than Packer's, Parish under-estimated the implacability of the media mogul. To be fair, he was not the only one.

In some respects, Parish epitomised what Packer's new attrac-tion was a reaction against. Parish was a born patrician, who fol-lowed his father into a successful family timber business after schooling at Melbourne Grammar, and was awarded the OBE in 1975 and the CMG in 1981. Courteous and tactful but rather pon-derous in speech, he had nothing in common with the players of the era, resentful of their poor rewards, who called him 'Bob the Snob'. Once World Series Cricket blended its riches and razzama-tazz with some old-fashioned nationalism, the ACB was always destined to be a loser in the confrontation.

The irony is that the champion of the underpaid players should have been Australia's richest man, and the defender of the estab-lishment one who devoted every Saturday for years to manning the scoreboard and serving the drinks at Prahran's Toorak Park home ground. But they were strange topsy-turvy days, and long, long ago.

Wisden Cricketer June 2005

AUSTRALIA'S RISE

Four Non-stars

The summer of 1985 has a golden glow in English memory: a time rich in juicy half-volleys, when every English father interested in cricket wanted his daughter to marry David Gower. For the very same reasons, it looms in the Australian cricket memory as an annus horribilis: the country was represented by Allan Border and ten A.N. Others who believed in the myth of Botham little less fervently than Botham, and treated Richard Ellison like he was Richard Hadlee. The only season more likely to be the subject of an unnerving flashback is the sequel in Australia, eighteen months later, when England's inability to bat, bowl or field to Martin Johnson's satisfaction did not prevent their retaining the Ashes with discombobulating ease.

To explain how Australia got good in the '90s, it is necessary to revisit this period, in which it went so bad. The obvious inflexion point is the five days in February 1984 when it seemed like Australia came to a standstill to bid farewell to first Greg Chappell, then Dennis Lillee, then Rod Marsh during a Sydney Test against Pakistan. Australian cricket's malaise, however, was more general. In truth, although it is thanks to an Australian, Kerry Packer, that professional international cricket came to pass, it took time here for professionalism to mean other than being paid more money for what one had previously done for damn-all. And while it is usually the stars who take the credit for the Australian resurgence, one should not underestimate the impact of four individuals not so obviously telegenic: the aforesaid Marsh, and Bob Simpson, Lawrie Sawle and Errol Alcott.

In Montreal in 1976, an Australian team failed, for the first time in memory, to win a gold medal in an Olympic Games. From the jolt of realisation that the country could no longer rely for athletes on sun, sea and natural ability emerged the Australian Institute of Sport, an incubator for raw athletic talent as advanced as any in the world. From the experience of consecutive Ashes defeats a decade later emerged a similar commitment to make Australian cricket happen rather than trust that it always would, using the Australian Institute of Sport's Del Monte training facilities at Henley Beach, in Adelaide. Though its first head coach was Jack Potter, the cricket academy came to be identified with his successor, Marsh, whose views on cricket were too trenchant for Channel Nine but who became a gruff paterfamilias to a generation of Australian cricket youths. The academy's honour boards eventually teemed with more than 120 first-class players and thirty internationals, including Ricky Ponting, Shane Warne, Glenn McGrath, Adam Gilchrist, Justin Langer, Damien Martyn, Brett Lee and Jason Gillespie.

The old Aussie dictum that the coach is for arriving in was further violated by the first ever appointment of a full-time coach for the national team. The country had, in Border, a Horatius; what it needed was a Cincinnatus, a former great summoned from retirement to restore order. The leathery, ornery Bob Simpson believed that Australian cricket, despite its professional pretensions, was too individualistic, too undisciplined: 'There were still talented players around, but it was obvious that many of them did not have the work ethic it would take to put Australian cricket back on its feet.' Simpson worked cricketers hard, which suited Border, a dedicated cricketer but loath to enforce his authority. His speciality was fielding, which he felt coaches generally overlooked. Dynamic fielding was the cornerstone of Australia's surprise victory in the 1987 World Cup. They executed thirteen run-outs in seven games, ending games as dusty as Bedouins from throwing themselves around to cut off boundaries.

When Simpson took over as coach, Sheffield Shield cricket featured no fewer than forty-four players with some taste of international cricket. 'A joke,' said Simpson, not known for cracking them. 'There has never been a period in history when Australia had forty-four players good enough to play for their country.' One who agreed was Simpson's former opening partner for Western Australia, Lawrie Sawle, who, in one of his first acts as Australia's chairman of selectors, earmarked a core group of sixteen to which discussions were generally confined, and additions to and deletions from were made only after lengthy deliberation. Sawle believed in forthright discussion, but also to commitment to the common weal. No selection, it is said, ever went to a vote. If a dissenting minority formed, it would always yield. Belief in continuity has been a hallmark of the chairmanship itself. Sawle served a decade in the role, as has his successor Trevor Hohns.

For continuity in the Australian set-up, however, nobody out-does its ageless physiotherapist Errol Alcott. He joined, coinciden-tally, in the same month that Chappell, Lillee and Marsh left; he turns fifty in December, though you'd scarcely guess it. While some of his treatment regimes are famous, such as keeping Dean Jones from evaporating completely in the second tied-Test, at Madras, and rebuilding Steve Waugh's calf in time for his inclu-sion in the Oval Test four years ago, Alcott's contribution to the team has been more in what has not happened rather than what has. English injury management has traditionally been on the lines first advocated for Humpty Dumpty. Alcott has, in the mean-time, been turning notorious hypochondriacs into fearless stoics with a mixture of planning, plain speaking and placebos. Brought up on folklore accumulated from previous teams, Australians have generally dreaded touring the Sub-continent. Alcott helped change that with a stock of practical medical wisdom from a doctor father and fastidious attention to detail: he was known for pulling a thermometer out at meals to test whether they had been sufficiently heated up.

After the disasters of 1985 and 1986–87, the basis of a new Australian hegemony was laid during the Ashes of 1989, with Simpson as coach, Sawle as manager and Alcott as physiotherapist all lightening Border's load. The academy, meanwhile, was bearing its first graduates, including Michaels Bevan and Slater. For Australia, the bad old days were about to become the stuff of history; for England, the stuff of nostalgia.

Guardian: Ashes Special July 2005

THE TRIANGULAR SERIES
Twenty-five Not Out

The best inventions catch on so quickly that they soon seem to have been around forever. So it is with the tri-cornered one-day series, which this year marks its twenty-fifth consecutive Australian season.

In the summer of 1977–78, Australia played no one-day international games at all; the idea that half of the summer of 2003–04 would be devoted to biffing and bashing under lights, in coloured clothes, would have seemed unthinkable. By 1980–81, when Australia won the second World Series Cup in immensely exciting fashion and consolidated the event in the cricket calendar, almost the reverse seemed true: so accustomed had we become to change by this point that the odds on us doing the same thing with the same format over the same distance twenty-three years later would have seemed long indeed. Yet here we are, approaching 400 games and about a million Mexican waves, with most of the features we started with: white ball, black sightscreens, field-restriction circles and, of course, Channel Nine.

The concept's durability is especially remarkable when its origins in Kerry Packer's World Series Cricket are considered. WSC was originally envisaged as a contest between an Australian team and an all-star World XI; it only became a three-way competition because Packer's agents were so successful in recruiting West Indians that they ended up constituting a separate side. From this happenstance came Packer's requirement for the season of 1979–80 that Australia square up against two visitors, West Indies and England, in Test and one-day matches: the sizeable acorn that matured into today's towering oak, under whose shade two-thirds of Australia's one-day internationals have been played. The continuity is reflected even in the nomenclature. In an era of commercial promiscuity, the tournament has undergone only one – forced – changed of sponsor, Benson & Hedges giving way to Carlton & United Breweries when the boom was finally lowered on tobacco cash in sport, in 1996.

For all of its being an indigenous idea, the home side took time to assimilate the rigours and rhythms of the one-day game. It won four of the first ten cups – not bad, but hardly dominant in a three-horse race – and the impression was of a team that tried as hard to beat one-day cricket as its opponents. Gospels of containment sat ill with local mores. It was with distaste that Dennis Lillee wrote after the inaugural tournament: 'I know it sounds un-Australian, and I almost find the idea offensive, but in limited-over cricket we must learn to think negatively.' Of Australia's performance in that series, *Wisden* noted: 'Greg Chappell made it clear he disliked this defensive form of cricket. He attempted to win his matches without resorting to negative bowling or spreading his fielders round the boundary.' In a sense, the notorious underarm conclusion to the third World Series Cup final of February 1981 was as much a reflection of Chappell's contempt for one-day cricket as of the shortcomings of his sportsmanship, a sort of *reductio ad absurdum* of its principles. That contempt showed again when, in a decision costly for Australia, Chappell opted out of the 1983 World Cup: something that now seems unthinkable.

The irony is that the turning point in Australia's one-day fortunes came when it realised that some cricket fundamentals lay beneath the hitting and giggling: fitness, fielding, full-length bowling and running between wickets. And when coach Bob Simpson instilled these in Allan Border's young team, it not only became formidable in the limited game but in the unlimited one as well. Australia's one-day tournaments have borne witness to its two-pronged advance: the home side has won eleven of the last fourteen trophies, while building its Test hegemony.

Not everyone, of course, finds satisfaction in cricket's truncated variant. The World Series Cup–C&U–VB Series has – like all one-day cricket – been beset by a single intractable problem. Its greatest strength and weakness is the same: that it takes place in a day. Being able to offer an innings from each team and a result within eight hours is a great virtue; yet few limited-overs matches leave an impression that last beyond them. Recollection becomes fragmentary, jumbled. There was that game with Bevo, wasn't there? And Gilly hitting those sixes, remember that? Hey, what about Viv? Whenever that was ...

The accent of the recall is usually telling. This has been a batsman's tournament: the white ball has never been a bowler's joy here. Richards was indeed the tournament's first centurion, and his dismissive 153 not out from 140 balls (sixteen fours, one six) at Melbourne in December 1979 looms as large on paper as it does in the imagination: Lillee, Thomson, Hogg, Bright and Chappell were the bowlers who could not restrict him. Batting has seldom been made to look easier than when David Gower whisked 158 from 118 deliveries against New Zealand at Brisbane in January 1983, with eighteen fours and four sixes, although Adam Gilchrist made nearly as merry in his 154 from 129 balls against Sri Lanka at Melbourne in February 1999, and Mark Waugh in his 173 from 148 balls against the West Indies two years later.

Mayhem, of course, has been expected of such names. Perhaps even more memorable have been the unlikely. The history of the cups is strewn with cameos of big hitting, from Rod Marsh's 24 and out in a Lance Cairns over at Adelaide Oval, in November 1980, to Cairns' own 50 from 21 deliveries, with six sixes, at Melbourne just over two years later – both, coincidentally, in losing causes. And to its hasty percussion, the one-day beat has found some unexpected toe-tappers. Openers as obstinate as Geoff Boycott and Geoff Marsh and as improvised as Junior Murray and Romesh Kaluwitharana have prospered. Bruce Laird took an unbeaten 117 off a West Indian attack of Roberts, Holding, Marshall, Garner and Croft with sparkling cuts and hooks he seldom hazarded in Test matches.

Dean Jones and Javed Miandad curbed their instincts and became masters of placement between fielders and helter-skelter between wickets, broadening our understanding of the essence of one-day batting. Few more fascinating innings have been played than Javed's undefeated 59 against the West Indies at Perth in December 1992, which contained no fewer than forty-five singles: not so much cricket as cat-and-mouse.

For bowlers and fielders, rewards have been scarcer. The 10-over restriction has probably cut off many great spells in their prime, while even great bowlers have at various times been humiliated, such as Bob Willis, struck for 22 by David Hookes in the last over at Brisbane in January 1983, and Bruce Reid, struck for 18 in the last over by Allan Lamb at Sydney four years later. To attack, captains have tended to need all circumstances in their favour, or bowlers some other stimulation – such as, in Curtly Ambrose's case, being asked by Dean Jones in the first final of January 1993 to remove his white sweatbands.

This is odd: perhaps the case of conventional wisdom eclipsing common sense. It is remarkable how often early losses have not brought about the coup de grace but the laissez-faire, fielding captains succumbing to the temptation to squeeze in a few cheap overs. This was seldom better seen than in January 2002 when, reduced to 6–82 in pursuit of 8–245, Australia were allowed by New Zealand to regroup and eventually win: Michael Bevan's 102 not out off 95 balls, abetted by Shane Warne, Brett Lee and Andy Bichel, was a marvel of management and manipulation; only his own 78 not out, including a last-ball four, to beat the West Indies at Sydney on New Year's Day, 1996 ranks with it for stealthily-accumulating drama.

Bevan himself incarnates a different aspect of one-day cricket. That there was a particular subset of one-day cricket skills was acknowledged long before the idea that this might entail an entirely new team. Specialists were created, both successful (Simon O'Donnell, Simon Davis) and unsuccessful (Glenn Trimble, Glenn Bishop). But not until 1997–98 did Australia come into line with what had become an international custom of selecting discrete Test and one-day XIs. Even then, there were plenty of pitfalls along the way: Australia won the C&U Series that season after winning six and losing five, compared to South Africa's eight wins and three defeats. They then made their task more difficult in 2001–02 with a practice of player rotation that ended up corkscrewing into the ground.

It is true, nonetheless, that players of older orthodoxies and taboos have been known to struggle under one-day pressures here: recall Sunil Gavaskar's 92 not out in 50 overs in a total of 4–192, when his team was actually chasing 292, in January 1986. One-day cricket can be majestic; it can also be ugly, brutal, scrappy, incompetent. There are thrills, but there are also many spills. The twenty-five one-day cups have seen batsmen out handled-the-ball (Mohinder Amarnath), shoulder-charging an opponent trying to run him out (Roshan Mahanama), sent back to the dressing room because they've tried to bat too early (J.J. Martin), stumped off a wide (Mark Waugh), and run-out in consecutive matches by their brother (Steve Waugh). Fielding sides have dropped as many as eleven catches (Australia v Sri Lanka at Perth, December 1989); keepers have dropped their hats on the ball, costing their team 5 runs (West Indian Ridley Jacobs against Zimbabwe in Sydney, three years ago). Even ground staff have caught the bug, like those at the WACA Ground fourteen years ago who caused a game to be stopped after two minutes, when it was realised that the fielding circles had not been marked.

When the third team in the competition is weak, moreover, there seems an irreducible proportion of cricket either dull or inept. Zimbabwe has been a game participant in three of the last ten tournaments, losing one astonishing match against Australia at Perth in February 2001 by a single run in a combined total of 603, but has never seriously looked like a finalist. Those arcane rules in which one-day cricket seems to abound have had their effect, too: sometimes excitingly, as when Allan Border nudged Pakistan out of the finals in January 1982 with slogging that bunked up Australia's run-rate as rain closed in; sometimes cynically, as when Stephen Fleming nudged Australia out of the finals in Perth, twenty years later, by deliberately conceding a bonus point. (Funny old world, eh? When results are orchestrated secretly, it is called match-fixing; when contrived publicly, it is called professionalism.)

Uglier and stupider still, in recent years, has been spectator behaviour. Fixtures have seemed to have less to do with cricket, and more to do with crowds making their own 'entertainment': Australia's meeting with Pakistan at Sydney in January 1997 infamously was interrupted six times by intruders, one of them crash-tackling the stumps. This led to some soul-searching in Sydney, and security was tightened, albeit with mixed success: there was only one intruder in December 1997 when South Africa was the visitor, but this was a barbecued chicken thrown at Pat Symcox. It was a shock for Australians, but no one else, to learn fourteen months ago that the International Cricket Council regarded the MCG as one of the world's worst three venues for interruptions in play, trespassing and unruly behaviour; season 2001–02 had seen thirty arrests and 500 ejections. England supporters have an excuse for inebriation: their performances would drive anyone to drink. It seems strange that Australian fans need alcohol when their team has played cricket of such intoxicating panache in recent years.

None of these problems, of course, is endemic to Australia; nor, now, is the tri-cornered one-day tournament. The round robin and finals series between three or four teams for a cup of some name or description spread round the world from Australia via Sharjah, where the first, the Rothmans Trophy, was held in March 1985. England finally admitted the idea to its season with 2000's Natwest Series, bravely conceding that a structure successful for twenty-one years might have something to recommend it.

The challenge might now be said to be that of ensuring that the invention doesn't trample everything in its path. Much of the urgency and enterprise we appreciate in Test batting now is a result of the insinuation of attitudes from the limited-overs arena. But

Test bowling now seems increasingly pervaded by one-day ideas of economy and rigidity – check out the way modern slip-fielders applaud a maiden in which 4 balls have passed unmolested to the keeper – and that is not so welcome a development. The principles of Test and one-day bowling are far more different than those of Test and one-day batting: you actually spend a lot of time in one-day cricket trying to prevent the ball behaving as you'd like it to in a Test match, like swinging and turning. If Test cricket is becoming a batsmen's game, as it seems to bc, it may be because it is becoming more like one-day cricket, which always has been.

Inside Edge: Twenty-five Years of One-Day Wizards (2004)

KIT AND KABOODLE

BATS

Release the Bats

To launch its inaugural edition last October, *Inside Cricket* magazine devoted fifteen pages to deciding its 'Bat of the Year', based on the votes of a dozen judges after handling twenty-five popular bats: a formalisation of the average cricketer's sports-store ritual, in which a stroke must be mimed with as many bats on the rack as time permits. It would be a mistake to place too much weight on such exercises. After all, as my cobber and colleague John Harms sagely points out, the Holden Camira was once a *Wheels* magazine 'Car of the Year'. Bats, of course, vary within their brands, and according to their hands: it has consistently amazed me how mine develop sweet spots immediately I lend them to team-mates.

There was a competition of sorts here, however, and that was between the names, a genre as evolved as the titles of Robert Ludlum novels, if even less explicable to the uninitiated. The judges settled on Ricky Ponting's preferred brand, which rejoices in the name Kookaburra Kahuna Captain, although they must have been arrested by the rival rhythms of the Fearnley Bat Wing Test, the Gray-Nicolls Phoenix Hayden 380 and the BAS Vampire Test Selection.

They must have had questions, too. Do proceeds from sales of the Puma Tribute go to the Worldwide Fund for Nature? Are royalties paid to the estate of Alistair MacLean on each Newbery Navarone (shortly to be matched, no doubt, by the Newbery Ice Station Zebra and Newbery Where Eagles Dare)? And which young marketing genius at MRF settled on calling his company's product the

Bonzer, as distinct from Ripper, Pearler and Absolute Bloody Ball-Tearer?

The tradition of naming bats, however, like much in cricket, has an unsuspected antiquity. Originally, markings on bats established ownership. The oldest bat in existence, owned by the Surrey County Cricket Club, is marked on its back 'JC1729', in honour of its owner James Chitty and the season. The 262-year-old bat owned by James Osmond Miles that survives from the first match of the great club Hambledon is initialled 'J.O.'

The first bat to sport a brand name per se seems to have been the King Willow, manufactured by Duke & Son of Penshurst in Kent from 1848. To promote it, moreover, the family firm did something unique, sponsoring a song in its honour, 'Willow the King', the sheet music for which one could obtain free by post. The words, by E.E. Bowen, feature the refrain: 'So ho! So ho! May the courtiers sing! / Honour and life to the Willow King.' The bats, one can only imagine, were superior.

That year, too, was born W.G. Grace who, among his many feats, would be perhaps the first cricketer of consequence to confer his fame on a bat: the L.J. Nicolls Automatic, whose cane handle was cut in interlocking halves, patented in 1888. Scoring more than 2000 runs with it, Grace kindly dubbed it 'my record bat' – something the maker eagerly picked up in advertising copy. It's arguable, mind you, that the batmaker has enjoyed a fame as enduring as the batsman. Nicolls' eponymous firm merged with H.J. Gray & Sons of Cambridge in 1940 to create the most famous compound name in cricketware.

The 1880s was a particularly vibrant period in experimentation with bats, and endorsements were useful for establishing names in the marketplace. Ponting's support for the Kahuna Captain seems unadventurous compared with the endorsement that an earlier Australian skipper, Percy McDonnell, offered in *Wisden* to Browning's Patent Triangular Bat – a bat, triangular in cross-section with three faces, that never caught on, but a specimen of which survives in the Lord's Museum.

Yet it's open to us to ask exactly what branding adds to bats, apart from a fair whack to the retail price because of the cost of the contracts of Ponting and his contemporaries. And it's high time, surely, that someone improved on the endorsement template: 'I use Slazenger. They are great. Signed A. Famous Cricketer.' (Perhaps Hermann Goering's most famous line might be profitably redeployed in a bat advertisement: 'When I hear the word "culture", I reach for my Gunn & Moore.')

What would be revealed if bats were stripped of their thick layer of stickers? There may have been a hint in the 'lab test' carried out for *Inside Cricket*, as part of its 'Bat of the Year' special, by two cricket-crazy boffins from the chemistry school at the University of Sydney, who ascertained the innate static power of each bat based on its rebound qualities. Here the Newbery Navarone came up trumps: another reason to expect the release next season of the Newbery HMS Ulysses. Like good scientists, Scott Kable and Tim Schmidt included a control in their experiment: a rather handsome plank of wood that emerged with an honourable mid-table position when assessed on its power-to-weight ratio. And given that most bats feel like planks of wood in my hands, it may be that an actual plank of wood is what I need to feel like I'm using a bat. 2005 shapes as the year of the Haigh P.O.W. Nought (Not Out).

Age January 2005

R.M. CROCKETT & SONS
Australian Made

In a recent club game, a teenage opponent emerged for his innings with a bat that looked like it should have been behind glass at the MCG. A team-mate sniffed a sledge in the making: 'That bat looks like yer granddad gave it t' ya.' The boy replied, 'He did.' It was a beauty, too: light, sweetly sprung, dark from many loving applications of oil. Closer inspection revealed a faded inscription: Crockett National Choice. A Crockett, by golly! The ball usually leaves the bat at speed when I'm bowling. This day I didn't mind so much.

Readers with a span of memory longer than a decade or two will recognise the name immediately. At one time the perky slogan 'It Just Isn't Cricket Without Crockett' had more foundation than most advertisements. And it was an enterprise with a particular significance to Australian cricket: not since it faded has Australian leather felt the touch of Australian bat willow, at least in the first-class arena.

A hundred years ago, this was a source of vexation in our cricket community. 'Why should Australia flog an English-made cricket ball with an English-made bat?' asked the *Bulletin* in one of its nationalist fulminations, deploring that the cricket equipment in a country famous for its teams and traditions was manufactured in and imported from England. Then came R.M. Crockett & Sons Pty Ltd.

The name would be revered in cricket annals anyway. Bob Crockett is perhaps the best umpire Australia has had, and certainly the most respected: by the end of his thirty-five-year career, he was routinely called the 'Chief Justice of Cricket'. His roots were in Daylesford, in country Victoria: a Crockett Street lies at the entrance to the town's secondary college. His father, a Scottish ship's captain, established the family there when he forsook the sea in favour of fortune-hunting, founding a farm with his Liverpudlian wife when gold proved elusive.

Born 140 years ago, Bob came to Melbourne in his teens to qualify as an assayer, but instead joined the Melbourne Cricket Club in 1887 as a ground bowler; in those days the club provided professional ground bowlers for the services of members as fitness clubs today provide dumbbells and rowing machines. He umpired his maiden first-class game in 1891, and his maiden Test a decade later, his involvement in batmaking allegedly springing from the latter.

The story goes that, during a break in play amid the heat of a Melbourne Test in January 1902, Crockett fell into conversation with England's seigneurial skipper, Archie MacLaren. MacLaren expressed surprise that Australia did not cultivate its own bat willow; Crockett suggested that MacLaren forward some cuttings and, amazing to say, six arrived six months later, acquired from Kew Gardens in London. Only one had survived the equatorial heat: 'a dying bud as large as a crumb', according to one account. But, nursed by Crockett's younger brother John, a horticulturalist, it begat 5000 further trees on Shepherds Flat, Daylesford.

Nothing changed overnight: trees take even longer than cricket. But World War I then brought opportunity. Inventories of English equipment in Australia were almost exhausted. Having bestowed hundreds of bats and balls on military camps and struggling clubs, for instance, the Melbourne Cricket Club was, by January 1919, 'desperately short'. It was a shortage of which Crockett had both intimate knowledge, being pavilion keeper at the club in addition to his umpiring duties, and a means of remedy. A number of players, including Crockett's friends Warwick Armstrong and Edgar Mayne, asked if they might obtain bats fashioned from wood grown at the plantation. To Mayne fell the honour of the first

Sheffield Shield hundred with a bat of indigenous *Salix alba v. caerula*, in December 1919 against South Australia (less promisingly, it broke during the next game). Armstrong achieved the landmark of the first Test century made with a local product, in the course of his 158 in the Sydney Ashes Test.

Crockett retired from umpiring six years later, becoming rather an institution. He and Test spinner Don Blackie would greet one another with a droll ritual. 'Owzat Rocketty?' Blackie would say, and Crockett would deliberately and solemnly raise his finger. The bat business, meanwhile, obtained a life of its own; the Shepherds Flat plantation was complemented by a factory in Charles Street, Seddon, near Footscray in Melbourne's industrial west. A visitor in July 1933 was surprised by the scale of the enterprise: 'There is constant cutting and replanting. The trees are cut down in the winter when the sap is down. They are felled by two experts. They first bare the beautiful white wood at the base. Then the crosscut saw goes in. To see those two men at work is to witness the poetry of effort. It is labour made beautiful ... The big fellow I saw come down cut up into four sections, each yielding twelve bat billets or forty-eight in all. Each billet is then roughly shaped into a bat blade and plastered with lime at both ends to prevent cracking during the seasoning process ... After the fourteen months' seasoning, the rough billets go to the Footscray factory, where they are shaped into the bat blades which every cricketer uses.'

When Crockett died of pleurisy in 1935, the firm was taken over by his son Jim, a wool classer who'd played district cricket for six seasons with Melbourne and Essendon. World War II then proved as significant in the company's history as had the first. Shepherds Flat churned out as many as 10,000 willow clefts in order to provide bats for Australian servicemen at home and abroad. When cane handles dwindled because Sarawak had fallen under Japanese control, a Crockett representative was flown to Balikpapan to buy cane from Dyak tribes on the Rajang River. *Sporting Globe*'s venerable Hec de Lacy once exalted R.M. Crockett & Sons as Australian cricket's unsung hero, for its ability to keep bats coming even in the war's darkest hours: 'The reward for all this work was the development of Australian service cricket to the highest plane even during the exacting years of the war. Young men who had entered the forces at 18 did not miss the development and coaching in cricket that would have been theirs in years of peace.'

Demand for bats took toll on Shepherds Flat. After the war, the firm's Charles Street factory relied increasingly on imported English willow and Borneo cane. But the firm flourished, particularly from association with Test players such as Lindsay Hassett, Peter Burge and Norm O'Neill. O'Neill recalls being approached after his record-breaking 1957–58 Sheffield Shield summer: 'I'd been using Slazengers that season, but Crockett got onto me and invited me down to the factory. The contract was £600, which seemed a lot of money.' He turned out to have underpriced himself: Crockett's O'Neill Dynamaster became a bestseller when O'Neill starred in his first Tests the following season. 'I should have asked for a percentage,' sighs O'Neill.

It is commonly reported, most recently in the *Herald Sun* in May 2003, that Crockett was 'the subject of a multinational takeover and died out in the 1950s'. The facts are more complex. While most of the Shepherds Flat plantation was felled in 1956, official filings suggest that this was while the firm remained in family ownership; not for another decade did R.M. Crockett & Sons come under the control of Slazenger. In any case, Slazenger was actually a subsidiary of dinky-di, true-blue Dunlop, then Australia's most compulsively acquisitive conglomerate.

It was a melancholy end to a remarkable enterprise once the last Crocketts left the board in August 1967: a voluntary wind-up was completed in November 1972. But thirty years after Crockett's felling, shoots are emerging from the undergrowth. When independent bat-manufacturer Lachlan Fisher set out his stall in 1989 after working for Maddocks Sports, his interest in the Crockett story was kindled by meeting Harry Preston, a veteran of the old firm and a staunch advocate of the merits of Australian willow. Like all Australian batmakers, Fisher is reliant on imported raw materials; Preston inspired him to open a nursery in Daylesford selling willow cuttings to farmers, with the intent of buying back the trees when they matured. 'In the south of Victoria, the dormancy period and growing season of the trees are very similar to those in England,' he says. 'And the weight, the performance, the grain of the bats are little different.'

Preston never saw his dream come true: he died in January 2003 of emphysema from a lifetime of inhaling cane dust while turning bat handles. But Fisher will shortly begin harvesting willow from a host of small plots around Victoria, mostly in Gippsland: each tree yields about twenty-five clefts. It may not be too long before traditional Australian steel is again reinforced by non-traditional Australian wood.

ABC Cricket Book 2003–04

BOOTS

Those Feet in Ancient Times

Fascinated by its twenty-six bones in a tangle of tendons and tissue, Da Vinci described the foot as 'a masterpiece of engineering'. It is a masterpiece on which cricket has done little to improve. Old photographs make you marvel that players managed to lift their feet at all, seemingly burdened by footwear of the kind that anchors deep-sea divers to the ocean floor. Fashion and technology favoured maximum strength and support. Almost as staggering as Warwick Armstrong's spinnaker-like shirt in the Australian Cricket Hall of Fame are his boat-like boots, of white kid leather with iron spikes, 32 centimetres long and 18 centimetres wide. Australia's heaviest captain took foot comfort seriously, confiding in his primer *The Art of Cricket* (1922) that whisky applied to the soles at teatime relieved tired feet; if that failed, presumably the rest could be taken internally at stumps.

There were some technical justifications to this ballasting of boots. Until the 1960s, cricket was governed by the back-foot no-ball law, based on where that foot landed rather than where it ended, with the result that most bowlers' actions featured a drag, cribbing as much as a yard on the full twenty-two. Thus Colin Cowdrey's famous rejoinder when asked why he'd not played forward to Australia's most stupendous dragger, Gordon Rorke: 'I was worried he'd step on my toes.'

The back-foot drag, it was held, required a boffo boot, usually with a steel toecap, an ankle-length cut and the architectural solidity of a Norman cathedral, something Frank Tyson evoked in a lyrical description of the boots worn by Harold Larwood during the Bodyline series: 'The sole of the right member has been virtually dragged away from the upper along the whole length of the inside of the boot; an indirect and silent testimony to the beautiful side-on action of the wearer. But the massive quality of the shoe is the really striking feature of the footgear ... The sole is at least a quarter of an inch thick and the heel an inch high. The uppers extend well beyond the top of the ankle, and a rough estimate of the weight of each boot would be in the area of two pounds.'

Two pounds? No wonder that, damaged as they were, Larwood's boots survived the tour better than he did. The Englishman left the field in Australia's second innings in the Sydney Test with a broken bone in his foot, an injury which became chronic and curtailed his Test career as surely as the Marylebone Cricket Club's queasy conscience.

It's arguable, in fact, that our former footwear fetishes did more harm than good. Where fast bowlers today complain of bad backs, foot and leg injuries were once equally common. No one shared the fate of the tragic Trinidadian Donald Eligon, who died in June 1937 from blood poisoning originating in a misplaced nail in his boot, but many famous names felt an incapacitating pinch. Bill Johnston blamed the cartilage damage that ended his career squarely on a bad pair of boots: long stops that stuck in the ground in a game at East Molesey in May 1953, causing him to wrench his knee. Tyson suffered abrasion from twisting inside his shoe so severe that his doctor said he would end his career with a left leg effectively fifteen years older than the right. Thirty years ago this week, Dennis Lillee limped out of a Melbourne Test with a bruised right instep. The sight of his receding figure, shoe and sock in hand, so galvanised Mike Denness's Englishmen that they won the game by an innings.

Even then, though, times were changing, and shoes emerging which complemented rather than counteracted the foot's flexibility. In January 1970, the nabobs of the New South Wales Cricket Association informed players by letter that the only 'regulation' cricket boot had six spikes in the sole and three in the heel. They were objecting to new low-cut, lightweight Adidas shoes, where the ankle was free to do as nature intended, and which obtained their grip from rubber heels and angled wedges. The association considered the shoes unsafe and unsound, enforcing the diktat by dishing out a one-month suspension to their chief promoter, state skipper John Benaud. When the ban was repealed after a month of ridicule, the 1970s and '80s became decades of half spikes, ripple soles, and light nylon instead of dense leather.

The NSWCA was right to suspect that the trend would have an effect: groundsmen learned that the new shoes burned the chlorophyll in the leaf of their grass, while spinners found pitches, scuffed rather than scarified, lasting longer. But for these belated concessions to comfort, cricketers of all capabilities have had cause to be grateful – even those such as myself. Australia's fastest bowler of the 1930s, Ernie McCormick, once said that it was time to retire when you took off one boot, then the other boot half an hour later. With modern shoes, I find it barely takes twenty-five minutes.

Age February 2005

BOXES

Protection Racket

There is a shrewdly observed moment early in Scott Hatcher's tragi-comedy *A Horse Named Resurrection*, which closes tonight after a season at the Carlton Courthouse Theatre, when one of the two cricketer protagonists casts a furtive eye down the front of his trousers, then heaves an exasperated sigh. On the night I attended, at least, the cricketers in the audience distinguished themselves at once by their rueful and sympathetic laughter. Few who've played cricket for any length of time fail to experience the annoyance of having absent-mindedly attired in boxer shorts, rather than the Y-fronts necessary to provide a snug mooring for their protector.

The other cricketer in Hatcher's play resolves the dilemma swiftly, chivalrously debagging and surrendering his own under-garments with only the mildest grunt of annoyance: a gesture that comes to contrast, as the play continues, with his essential lack of generosity in all other matters. Yet Hatcher, a stalwart of Barnawatha North CC in addition to his works theatrical, may also have revealed one of those cricket understandings no less profound for being unspoken. It can be a hard, cruel, unsparing game, fostering rivalries and animosities, bad blood and bad faith … but no one should ever have to play without their box.

A cricketer and his box have a special relationship. No item of protective gear provokes such stifled amusement; yet no item would a cricketer be less inclined to part with, or indeed to share, puberty usually marking the end of innocence when one begins to guard one's own guard and keep it for purely personal use. Share underpants? At a pinch. A box? Forget it. The relationship, more-over, abides: one seldom has to dispose of a box; more often they simply stray, destined to meet us again in heaven with all the odd socks. Few ever materialise for purchase in cricketana sales. Bradman baggy greens seem to abound, but no Bradman pro-tector has come to light, despite his feeling tribute in *The Art of Cricket* (1958) to 'these confidence producers'.

One famous auction at Brighton in Sussex twenty years ago, according to *The Wisden Book of Cricket Memorabilia* (1990), offered for sale 'a box worn by Brigadier Michael Harbottle for almost three decades' – a special relationship indeed. Opportunity to ascertain its market value went begging, however, when a family member bought it at the last minute for £50, 'presumably unable to face the future without the family heirloom'.

The protector's insertion has tended to be a private moment. 'This necessary expedient for protecting the vital parts has come into general use of late, but the modest nature of many cricketers make it a delicate matter to mention,' wrote G.D. Martineau in his potted history of cricket accoutrements, *Bat, Ball, Wicket and All* (1950). 'It is bundled politely away into the depths of the cricket bag, and there are awkward moments in some village pavilions which, having no dressing room, drive the wearer of the "abomi-nable belt" to assume it behind a hedge.' Yet there is also some-thing inherently democratic in that, junior variants aside, boxes are almost all of the same size. It is just as well that pornography found a use for Dirk Diggler; cricket had no place for him. Joel Garner pushed the envelope, as it were, sufficiently.

No cricket accessory so essential has a history so obscure. Next year, we know, marks the sesquicentenary of the first unambiguous reference to a 'private guard' – as it was referred to in an advertise-ment in the 1855 edition of *Lillywhite's Cricket Guide*. More specula-tive scholars, however, cite references four years earlier: the citation in Rev. James Pycroft's *The Cricket Field* of 'a cross-bar India-rubber guard', and a cryptic advertisement for a 'body guard' which so completely protected the person from injury 'that the most timid can play without fear'. A handkerchief down the front of a long jacket apparently also served protective purpose – from which might perhaps be derived the expression 'a discreet veil'. But not everyone in Victorian England was running round dressing highly suggestive piano legs. By the 1880s, protectors had overcome the prudes, and were being freely advertised. There is something enjoyably candid about an 1890 promotion for 'Palmer's Patent Groin Protector' at 7s 6d.

No cricket injury, of course, is quite so visibly incapacitating, yet causes such mirth and companionable feeling, as the blow to the box. The twin sensations among witnesses to mishaps, of identification and relief, are never more pronounced. When England's David Lloyd tells the famous story of having his protector turned inside out by Jeff Thomson at the WACA thirty years ago, there is seldom a dry eye in the house. Look at pictures of the Aussie slips cordon at the time, and there weren't too many then, either.

Some cricketers, legendarily, have scorned protection. The free-spirited Australian Jack Gregory apparently found them uncomfortable, while the Springbok opener Eric Rowan admitted in a documentary history of South African cricket a few years ago that he went bare into battles with Lindwall and Miller because it 'made me concentrate'. As it would. Or perhaps he kept forgetting the correct underpants.

Age December 2004

STUMPS

Woodhenge

Were you to encounter stumps in ignorance and out of their cricket context, it would be hard to know what to make of them. Somewhere to dock your bicycle? Maybe a trellis for climbing plants? Woodhenge, worshipped by very small druids? Oh, look at these detachable rococo features on top: nifty! For a cricketer, of course, the very sight of them makes the sap rise, especially when they are disintegrating after being hit by a ball and emitting perhaps cricket's most compelling sound, known colloquially, if macabrely, as the 'death rattle'.

The stumps connect us to cricket's bucolic origins. Their name and cylindrical shape remind us that bowlers first took aim at trees. The most detailed early description, circa 1700, involves two sticks connected by a crosspiece, 2 feet wide and 1 foot high, not unlike a farm gate. Since flipping ninety degrees for cricket's first set of laws, then acquiring a third peg in the middle, the stumps have grown steadily from 22 inches by 6 inches to their present size of 28 inches by 9 inches, while one bail has become two, accommodated atop the stumps in grooves.

The rationale for these grooves is not immediately obvious. If the purpose of the wicket was simply to provide something to break, the bail could be a flat piece of wood reposing on flat-topped stumps, heavy enough to withstand the wind but susceptible to every impact. It seems, though, to be a little jest from time immemorial, first ordained in the 1744 code, when there were only two stumps: 'The Bail hanging on one Stump, though the Ball hit

97

the Wicket, it's Not Out.' The laws of cricket for bowled, hit-wicket, run-out and stumped still add this minuscule possibility of remission: it is not sufficient to hit the stumps; a bail must be dislodged.

A cricketer who plays for any length of time will be reminded of this from time to time. In club cricket, the rare but recognisable phenomenon of the stumps being glanced without the bail's disturbance seems to happen about once every couple of seasons, never failing to spread mystification, then chagrin, through the fielding side, and to elicit from the batsman a guilty smirk. Demanding that the bail fall seems a vestige of the culture of capital punishment, like the mercy traditionally granted a prisoner at the gallows when the rope broke or the trapdoor malfunctioned. Mind you, there are also cases of moral balancing, where the snick on the stumps is mistaken for an edge and the batsman has to depart anyway: something equivalent to the euphoric reprieved prisoner having the misfortune to walk in front of a bus.

A reprieve is the subject of one of cricket's best photographs, from the First Test of the Bodyline series, which shows a ball delivered by Bill O'Reilly nestling against the striker's stumps that has lacked the force to complete the job. The image's focus, though, is less the ball than the preternatural calm of the observing batsman, Herbert Sutcliffe, not a hair of whose brilliantined head is out of place. At the time, he had scored 43, and the match was as delicately poised as his wicket; the famously nerveless Yorkshireman ploughed on to 194, underpinning a decisive 164-run lead. Sutcliffe's attitude has become the first and last word on him. Bat held casually in his right hand, his majestic impassivity mocks the exasperated fielders round him. Bob Wyatt, the non-striker, recalled, 'The bails wobbled and started to fall off and then settled back into their grooves as if to say: "No, this batsman is Herbert Sutcliffe."'

I first saw an instance of the aforementioned moral balancing in a Melbourne Test thirty years ago: a batsman wafting at the air but being adjudged caught at the wicket because of an audible nick that, on reflection, could only have been a stump brushed. Poor Geoff Dymock was collecting a pair, too, and had cause for remonstrance with the cricket gods, whose discussion you could almost hear:

'Sutcliffe?'

'No, Dymock.'

'Well, what are you waiting for? Fire 'im.'

Stumps serve purposes other than targeting, if not so elaborate as nurturing honeysuckle or parking bicycles. Close of play is, of course, 'stumps'. The ceremonial lifting of the bails indicates a break in play. In Lord's' renowned weathervane, Father Time is doing the job during a spell from grim reaping. The stump in international cricket, meanwhile, now both accommodates a camera and acts as a hoarding. It's a wonder, really, that the wicket hasn't become a single billboard of 252 square inches sponsored by CUB, so that every time it's knocked over you feel provoked to grab a beer. But perhaps the most remarkable alternative use is already behind us, when a youth in rural Australia took up a stump to hit a golf ball. That stump's misfortune was a glad tiding for all others: no one, in due course, would leave stumps safer than Sir Donald Bradman.

Age November 2004

PADS

Legs Eleven

Last Sunday, I played a bush game with a very good cricketer who hadn't played seriously for about seventeen years (and probably still hasn't, seeing it was only with me, but you get my drift). Bats and gloves, he mused, seemed not to have changed. But pads! His last pair, the traditional cane and cotton encased in buckskin, had been cumbrous and heavy; those he'd just borrowed, miracles of compact lightness, seemed barely there.

I was reminded again that modern pads seem to have less in common with the pads I've been wearing most of my cricket life than with my first pads, cut from cardboard, secured to my seven-year-old legs by rubber bands, and making a fetching ensemble with my mother's gardening gloves. They reflect, nonetheless, cricket's punctuated evolution these two hundred years past, answering the same problem as the original pads. These were stimulated specifically by the transition from underarm to overarm bowling between 1827 and 1864, through the intermediate round-arm stage. Games of the era, with a rock-hard ball on unkempt pitches, were nasty, brutish and short; pads, originally bits of board and sack, formed part of the quest to prolong them.

'It was not so much the speed of bowling but the fly-about uncertainty of it ... that gave rise to padding,' wrote Rev. James Pycroft in *The Cricket Field* (1851), although pace certainly concentrated the mind. One important figure in the pad's history probably never buckled one on. Before nurturing a love of God in his congregations as rector of Edgefield Holt, Rev. Walter Marcon put the fear of God into a generation of batsmen and wicketkeepers, bowling round-armers so fast and full that he required as many as three long-stops. 'Mr Marcon did not trouble about the length of the ball,' recalled W.G. Grace. 'He aimed at the wicket, and the ball flew straight from his hand to it without touching the ground; and nearly every time it hit the bottom of the stumps, the stump was smashed.' If the leg impeded the ball's progress it suffered similarly: he broke at least one opponent's leg.

When Marcon was playing for Eton, one Harrovian came out to bat wearing two pads on each leg; Marcon still clean-bowled thirteen of fourteen victims. It was when he was at Oxford, precipitating in one game as many as 90 byes, that his keeper John Marshall had 'leggings made to order of prodigious thickness'. And it was at Marcon's peak in the early 1840s that the Nottinghamshire cricket-craftsman Thomas Nixon, after initially experimenting with cork, first fashioned pads using the Malayan malacca and rattan cane that he is also credited with introducing to bat handles.

Cane is the poor relation among cricket's raw materials – willow and leather tend to hog the limelight – but it has been profoundly important. The Confucian poets and philosophers who exalted cane's combination of strength and flexibility as a spiritual metaphor would have appreciated its application to cricket, where it exhibits similar qualities, lending bats their elastic spring, and absorbing and spreading the impact of the ball that beats the bat and strikes the leg.

Pad use did not become universal overnight. In his primer *Felix on the Bat* (1845), Nicholas Felix recommended 'longitudinal socks' of linen inside the legs of trousers; betraying that this wasn't completely effective, he also recommended a 'phial of sweet oil' to treat bruises. The first batsman depicted wearing a pad, on his left leg, can also lay claim to being among the worst named: Yorkshire's George Nixon Duck.

Some obscurantists echoed Rev. Frederick Beauclerk, who thought pads acceptable at practice 'but how unfair for a bowler if allowed in a match'. As late as 1883, I.D. Walker captained Middlesex wearing no pads. And in the early 1890s, according to 'A Country Vicar' in *Cricketer* magazine, Shropshire's H. Richmond was known for performing a veritable striptease: 'He came in wearing pads and gloves. As his score progressed he discarded, first, his pads; then his gloves; finally, his sleeves! The last were made to button to his shirt.' But the ambition to do more than simply survive and slog, and the advantage of freedom from injury that they conferred, eventually grew too strong for batsmen to resist.

Once the bare cane was clothed during the Edwardian era, then reinforced with horsehair and other materials, innovation was restricted to quaint variations like the pneumatic pads inflated with a foot-pump for the 1930s millionaire cricket nut Sir Julien Cahn by his chauffeur. Pads were noticed usually only for failing to fulfil their function: Len Hutton recalled that he knew his fast bowling tyro, Frank Tyson, was something special fifty years ago when he saw a pained Australian batsman unstrap a pad to rub his leg.

Not until about twenty years ago did science's stealthy advance resume. Only older batsmen now recall the abrasion of the back of the ankle from the bottom buckle before the introduction of velcro; likewise, only older keepers remember the days before Rod Marsh and Kookaburra pioneered the cut-off look when you only needed to heft batting pads round in your kit. Nowadays, furthermore, there are guards for bits of your anatomy that you didn't even realise were exposed. Equipment manufacturers, after all, are capitalists as well as technologists. The lighter the gear, the more one can comfortably wear, and the more they can feasibly sell.

Age November 2004

SCORES AND STATISTICS
The Moving Finger

For many years at my club, the Yarras, our longest serving player, Hicksy, found veteran status a mixed blessing: he liked being venerable, disliked that only he could remember his best days. There evolved, in particular, a standing joke about his claim to have scored 99 in a semi-final back in the mists of time, of which no trace could be found in club records, for Hicksy's batting talents seldom seemed to justify his confidence that the scorebook had simply gone astray.

As far as I was concerned, of course, the fewer the club scorebooks in circulation the better. Blast those statisticians, never letting a story get in the way of a good fact! After all, how can mere scratchings on a sheet explain the value of that score of 4 last season – on a bumping pitch, in blinding light, if you don't mind?! Yet I sympathised with Hicksy – either robbed by the passage of time, or in the grip of some weird hallucination – and reflected again on how integral to cricket are its record-keeping processes.

Records are a precondition for modern sport. Without scoring, games perish even as they are played: by 'keeping' score, we cheat their fundamental transience. When we talk of cricket history, in fact, we are by definition describing that which is documented. It's possible, for example, that centuries were compiled before John Minshull's 107 for the Duke of Dorset's XI against Wrotham in August 1769, but they went either unscored or unretained.

What we know of scoring suggests that its fundamentals have remained very constant. Minshull's innings is even documented in the running style still favoured, with the runs from each stroke pressed against each other so that they read back like a cipher: 12131223 ... The way we have kept scores, furthermore, sometimes tells us a historical tale. Confirming the prejudice that cricket has always been a batsmen's game is the fact that it wasn't until 1836 that bowlers received recognition for wickets other than bowled, and until 1840 that bowling analyses were systematically kept.

As individual cricketers captured the public imagination, so did pressure grow to track their personal prodigies. The ball-by-ball scoring system which differentiated the deliveries faced by each batsman was popularised from 1893 by John Pendlington, a businessman, Shakespearean scholar and cricket devotee, who first used it in a game between the Australians and C.I. Thornton's XI at Scarborough. He presented the fruits of his work to Dr W.G. Grace, who was apparently delighted, as though admiring the likeness of a portrait.

By this time, too, scores had been pressed into service as the raw material for statistics. The most striking feature of the inaugural averages table in *Wisden Cricketers' Almanack 1887* is the class distinction it preserves, for amateur gentlemen and professional players are segregated. But that was not so much an artefact of snobbery as a recognition that it was principally to the latter that averages mattered. Statistics, in time, undergirded the economics of county cricket. Professionals were aiming to ensure new contracts by hitting numerical targets, such as 1000 runs in a season, and for fifties and five-fors, which translated into financial bonuses called 'talent money'. The story is told of the original nob, Lord Hawke, upbraiding his unruly Yorkshire opening bowler George Emmett: 'Do you know, Emmett, that you have bowled 48 wides this season?' Emmett replied, 'Throw me t' ball, yer Lardship, and ah'll soon 'ave me talent brass.'

Jeremiahs were unimpressed, believing statistics gave rise to selfishness. Frederick Gale lived up to his nom de plume, 'The Old Buffer', with a withering denunciation of 'the average mania' in his *The Game of Cricket* (1888): 'With some of the world a place or two higher in the batting list gives additional lustre to the professional's fame, and of course he is anxious to retain it; for, say what you please, there is much analogy between actors and the stage, and between professionals and public cricket-grounds. The danger is if a batsman is putting his average before winning the match in which he is engaged ... In every sport under heaven the unselfish man is the best man.'

The other criticism of averages was that they were a coarse measure of excellence, and often misleading. 'Nowadays, far more notice is taken of batting averages than is good for the game,' griped the Australian captain Monty Noble in *The Game's the Thing* (1926). Worcestershire's stalwart Fred Root took 1512 first-class wickets at 21, but you'd never know from his *A Cricket Pro's Lot* (1937) because he scorned a records section: 'There are no tedious statistics here, for averages are an abomination to real cricket.'

Noble could hardly have anticipated that a personality would shortly arise to put such aesthetic namby-pambiness to flight. By mass-producing runs on an industrial scale, Donald Bradman brought numbers to the fore. Only the Don could justify a book like B.J. Wakley's *Bradman the Great* (1958), in which the scores in his 234 first-class matches are pored over in such fetishistic detail that one expects to find on the last page that they form the Da Vinci Code.

Those of us without B.J. Wakleys at our beck, of course, cannot take permanence for granted – although, just occasionally, chance takes a hand. Last season, the Yarras' clubrooms were broken into. Beer was filched from the fridge, which seemed to place everyone under suspicion, but the thieves also busted the place up looking for money, which just as quickly put us in the clear: every Yarras player knows we're broke. One place the burglars searched was an old filing cabinet, locked for years, keys long lost. And as we studied the damage, it disgorged an artefact of priceless significance: the Yarras scorebook for 1980–81, revealing R. Hicks as the unlucky but proud compiler of a match-winning 99. Hicksy, these days, is a far happier man. Designation 'all-rounder' restored, he will occasionally remark that some of his best friends are bowlers.

Age November 2004

THE TOSS

Chance, Luck and Destiny

This winter marks the centenary of one of cricket's greatest floods of fortune: the tide in the affairs of the Hon. F.S. Jackson, a consummate all-round cricketer who topped the batting and bowling averages while leading England to a handsome Ashes triumph. But that wasn't all. Into the bargain, Jackson won the toss in all five Tests: the first of only four occasions on which it has happened in rubbers between England and Australia. Jackson's summer stats against rival Joe Darling, in fact, were seven–zip, for luck also smiled on him in two tour matches.

The story is told that Darling came to his last engagement proposing to toss Jackson in 'the Graeco-Roman style'; that is, choice of innings should be decided by wrestling. It was, as Darling's team-mate Frank Laver recalled, to no avail: 'The coin was thrown in the air and head was called, but Jackson was so sure of winning that he did not even look to see which side the coin was showing. He walked to his dressing room looking ashamed ...'

No wonder Darling favoured alternative dispute-resolution; no wonder Jackson felt a little shamefaced. These things aren't meant to happen. When, in Tom Stoppard's play *Rosencrantz and Guildenstern Are Dead*, Guildenstern is spellbound by the fall of a coin which has in ninety consecutive instances come up heads, confounding his unchanged call of tails, he decides that malign forces must be at work. 'The equanimity of your average pitcher and tosser of coins,' he says, 'depends upon a law, or let us say a probability, or at any rate a mathematically calculable chance that ensures that he will not upset himself by losing too much, nor upset his opponent by winning too often. This made for a kind of harmony and a kind of confidence. It related the fortuitous and the ordained into a reassuring union which we recognised as nature.'

Anyone knowing ought of mathematics will remonstrate that the tosses of a coin are independent events, and that even after ninety heads the odds on Guildenstern calling correctly remained fifty-fifty. But cricketers are with Guildenstern: no skipper expects to win every toss; one simply expects not to lose more than one's share. There is probably more upset caused by consistent misfortune at the toss, feeling as it does like a discouraging omen, than satisfaction from regular fortune, it being the workings of mere chance.

Most skippers have talismanic tossing beliefs, either holding fast to a nostrum such as 'tails never fails', or trusting in a lucky coin like Warwick Armstrong in his American dollar or W.G. Grace in his gold sovereign. It is said that Grace won many a toss with the latter, which featured Britannia on one side and Queen Victoria on the other, by employing the call: 'It's a woman!' There may also be other agents: Douglas Jardine won the toss at Adelaide in January 1933, after a bad streak, when Maurice Leyland gave him 'a miniature black cat'. But, of course, winning tosses is not the only measure of luck. At the end of his first series as captain, Richie Benaud complained to Sir Donald Bradman about the coin he had given him before the Gabba Test: 'This is not much good – I haven't won a toss with it.' Bradman replied, 'No, and you haven't lost a Test with it, either.' Benaud used it for the rest of his career.

Others have favoured still quainter habits. England's tour match against a Combined XI at Perth in October 1962 began with the curious sight of one captain, Ted Dexter, leading his team into the field, and the other, Barry Shepherd, chasing him. It transpired that Shepherd had, on winning the toss, told his counterpart: 'Well, you take the blade.' Dexter had interpreted this as 'We'll take the blade,' presumed it local parlance for 'We'll bat,' and marshalled his men for a spell in the field, not learning of his misapprehension until he and men were halfway to the middle.

The charms of the toss, alas, are under threat. Like so many other features of international cricket, the ritual is being hemmed in by the game's steady industrialisation. In days of yore, the captains walking out to determine choice of innings was the first time the spectator glimpsed any of a game's dramatis personae. The arena before the first morning of a Test today is like the Flinders Street Station forecourt at rush hour. Coaches deliberate. Bowlers bowl at single stumps. Batsmen enjoy endless throw-downs. Fielders dart about energetically. Ex-players promenade in search of some reflected glory, however pale and diffuse, just to remind us that they are special, and that we, poor plebs, are not.

Sometimes these activities can be quite instructive. Pakistan's warm-ups during the recent Test series were as doleful and desultory as the cricket they subsequently played. More often, though, these routines instil a sense of workaday humdrum, with the players made to seem as mechanical as the figures on a Subbuteo table. Their eventual entrance is shorn of all ceremony and drama.

At least the toss has not been improved on by the sale of naming rights, or by a Coincam, or enlivened with a Hawkeye animation of the coin's rotation in the air, with an ad for *CSI* in one corner of the screen and a 1800 number in the other on which you can order a limited edition print of Inzamam calling heads named 'The Big Tosser'. The toss remains, too, that most elemental of contests: one over which nobody has any control, where all are equal. While nominally it is simply a procedure to decide choice of innings, it is on another level a homage – a nod to the mischievous gods of a game over which, for all its skill, blind chance exerts such influence.

Age February 2005

WICKETKEEPERS
The Gloved Ones

It used to be said that the best wicketkeepers are the ones you don't notice. No longer. Ian Healy is both very good and very noticeable. One minute you're watching him prostrate himself in front of Mark Taylor at first slip to intercept a dying edge, the next you're hearing his laconic drawl over the pitch microphone: 'Bowled, Shane.' If he's not roller-skating wide of leg-stump to arrest a stray delivery, he's chiding a delinquent outfielder for a sloppy throw, all the while preying on the batsmen's concentration like a dripping tap.

After almost a decade, Healy's at the top of his profession. A recent poll in the English magazine *Wisden Cricket Monthly* selecting a putative World team to play Mars – in the event of sentient cricket-playing life being discovered there – nominated Healy as the custodian of the gloves. And he's done it his way: if experience has worn away a few of the rough edges he brought into Test cricket, it hasn't curbed his talent for encircling opponents by word as well as deed. In the tightly wound mechanism of Australian fielding, there's no missing who's the mainspring.

Healy makes it look a little easy, in fact, which is something he's aware of and resists. He quotes in his new autobiography some sage advice from Bert Oldfield, Australia's courtly and unobtrusive stumper for eleven years: 'If you get a chance make sure you let people know what goes into your skills. If you make a good leg-side stumping don't just dismiss it as routine. Tell them how you practice for it and how you couldn't sight the ball behind the batsman's body and had to snap into action very quickly to pick his pocket before he had his foot down. Tell them how hard it is.'

For there is no overstating the pain that comes with wicket-keeping's pleasure. Healy's gnarled and malformed fingers testify to the punishment of his diurnal duties. The regular hamstring pain and operations for varicose veins that Healy has undergone verify wicketkeeping's physical toll. And who cannot wonder at the unflagging attention span he brings to the task? Imagine standing at a bus stop without a timetable, waiting for a bus that may come in a minute or in six hours. No task in cricket requires such patience and alertness in equal measure.

*

Australian wicketkeepers have been pathfinders for their profession. Our inaugural gloveman, Jack Blackham – recently elected to the new Australian Cricket Hall of Fame – was the first to wave away his long-stop, then as fixed a part of cricket as the scorer. And three-quarters of a century of crouching keepers owe their bad backs and taut hamstrings to Sydney undertaker Hanson Carter: immediately after World War I, Carter decided to get down on his haunches as the bowler came in, and was immediately imitated.

After World War II was perhaps the greatest of them all. Pictures of Don Tallon show him as an archetype of the sinewy, sun-dried northerner. Yet so silken were his skills that, even at the end of his career, his hands were soft and prehensile. Standing back, he took some of the most indelible catches of the century: one famously skidding on his left elbow at the Oval in 1948 to catch a full-bladed Len Hutton leg-glance. Standing up, his stumpings were as subtle as a light tap on the shoulder in a crowded room: he only ever removed one bail, and the stumps never needed adjusting.

Sometimes he seemed faster than the naked eye. Alan Davidson recalls Tallon executing a stumping in New Zealand so fleeting that it went unrewarded. 'Not out,' said the umpire. 'You didn't touch the bails.' Tallon held up his glove, containing one ball and one bail, but still the umpire was unimpressed: 'You must have had it in your hand before he bowled it.' Says Davidson, 'Tallon was unreal. He was so well named it wasn't funny.'

Tallon's Queensland successor, Wally Grout, was thirty before he was called to the national colours. But he served five Test captains over his nine-year career, and team-mates remember his flair for the inspirational dismissal that spurred the team to greater heights. Brian Booth and Bill Lawry cite one from the last ball of the first day of a Test against Pakistan at Karachi in October 1964: Khalid Ibadulla caught off McKenzie for 166. It was the last match of an eight-month tour, but Grout skidded to his left to make the take. 'We'd been out there all day in this incredible heat and dust,' says Booth. 'Most of us were thinking about how nice it would be to get off the field. And Wally goes yards down the leg side. Probably the best wicketkeeping catch I've ever seen. The only problem was that, whenever Wally did something like that and you complimented him, he'd say, "Yeah, but you shoulda seen Don Tallon."'

Grout jealously guarded his inheritance, observing the creed 'Never give a sucker an even break.' The title of his autobiography, *My Country's Keeper* (1965), betrays the pride he took in his position. Indeed, Grout may have taken his spirit of self-sacrifice too far. For many years, he kept mum about a heart condition that would take him to an early grave at forty-one. Barry Gibbs, then secretary of the Queensland Cricket Association, recalls taking Grout to see a doctor about his heart in 1964: 'The prognosis was that, if he wanted to live to a ripe old age, he should stop playing immediately. He wouldn't, of course, and that's the way he wanted it. But you could tell that Wally was suffering. He'd come in at the end of a day keeping for Queensland or Australia and he'd be grey in the face – puffing a cigarette, mind you – and he'd sit there motionless for three quarters of an hour or so.'

Grout died within three years of retiring, but he had time before the end to take to lunch his Queensland successor, John Maclean. Maclean in turn invited Healy to lunch when the latter was selected for Australia in September 1988, and the current

Australian keeper intends doing the same for the gloveman who succeeds him. A close-knit freemasonry, these wicketkeepers.

*

'Unless you have been a keeper,' Healy says in *Playing for Keeps*, 'it's difficult to understand the keeper's lot. In your entire career you might speak to 10 people who fully understand the job. We love talking shop ... what sort of gloves we use, what type of work we are doing, what problems we are having and why we are having them.'

Only a keeper, for instance, can understand what a dangerous job his can be. Broken fingers are only the start of it. Beamers are a menace: full-throttle full tosses from Wes Hall and Neil Hawke twice broke Wally Grout's jaw. So, too, the batsman of extravagant flourish: witness Healy himself, coshed by Sherwin Campbell during the recent Second Test against the West Indies at the SCG. Even scattering bails can pose a danger: from Hanson Carter, who lost an eye keeping to Stan McCabe in 1932, to England's Paul Downton, whose left eye was so badly damaged from a John Emburey delivery in 1990 that he had to retire.

And there is indeed a vast reservoir of wicketkeeping lore, from England's Herbert Strudwick, who recommended rinsing the hands in a chamber-pot daily in order to harden them, to the South Australian Gil Langley, who took a safety pin everywhere he played after tearing his trousers in his first Sheffield Shield match.

Alan Knott was perhaps the most assiduous of recent wicket-keepers – almost anally retentive – and some of his mannerisms give an insight into what a top-line keeper must consider. For a start, Knott was fanatical about his fitness: he never ate cheese and meat at the same meal, took honey with his tea, scorned golf as a recreation because it did not provide enough exercise. And he had a manicurist's mentality about his hands, sprinkling water on them before taking the field, and keeping his fingernails long in the belief that it might save him from fingertip fractures.

Knott became renowned for his calisthenic bending on the field between deliveries – toe touches, pelvic rotations, spinal stretches, everything but Burpee jumps – and there was method in his madness. Orthopaedic surgeon Bill Tucker had told him, after his first season for Kent in 1965, that his hamstrings might prevent his playing after the age of thirty. The public, too, saw only a fraction of the Alan Knott Workout Class. Every day when on tour, Knott would stick an alarm clock set for six in the morning under his pillow (where it didn't disturb his room-mate's slumber), so that he could greet the dawn with a half-hour regimen of extensions and protractions. And at the end of every season, he would return to Tucker to be manipulated under anaesthetic. With such constant dedication, he played eleven years past the doctor's deadline.

Knott designed his own gauntlets, kneading the rubber facing constantly to keep it supple, and always taking them home at the end of a day's play lest the leather stiffen in a cold dressing shed. Inside them he wore two pairs of chamois leather inners, lined with plasticine just below the base of the third and little fingers, and fixed in place with sweatbands so that they did not unravel if he removed the gauntlet to throw. Knott took three pairs of boots to every day's play, one for each session. Each pair would have a different pattern of spikes on the sole, so that throughout the day the pressure would be spread evenly over his feet. He experimented briefly with rubber soles, but eschewed them after slipping and failing to reach a catch offered by Sunil Gavaskar at Calcutta.

When Knott entered the game, most keepers kept in the pads they batted in. To his mind, that was not good enough. He bought a pair of junior batting pads so that the flaps still covered the knees but did not rise far above them, and customised them by razoring off the second strap and binding them to his calf with elastoplast; while still tight, the elastoplast 'gave' where the strap did not. 'A freak,' said his captain, Mike Brearley. 'And probably the best wicketkeeper of the modern era.'

*

The wicketkeeper a decade or so later is a little more fortunate. Cut-off pads were introduced to the game by Knott's Australian peer, Rod Marsh, and Dermal Pads (AKA 'fat pads') can be worn inside the gloves for extra protection. Webbing on gloves between thumb and forefinger, too, has survived various legislative efforts to kill it off. It's surprising, though, how little really has changed about wicketkeeping and the fastidious characters drawn to it. Healy is noted in Australian ranks for the neatness of his apparel and care of his kit: gauntlets, pads, inners, boots and wristbands. 'I've often roomed with him and found him cleaning his shoes at 11 p.m.,' Craig McDermott recalled. 'On the Pakistan tour in 1988–89, he used to say that cleaning his shoes was the highlight of each evening.' On the road he is renowned for his solitary subterranean practice habits. He can often be found wearing his inner gloves in hotel car parks, flicking a golf ball against the wall at demanding angles to sharpen his footwork and reflexes.

The unflappable South African Dave Richardson – at thirty-seven the oldest international keeper, and a qualified attorney who represents his team on contractual matters – also has a practice ritual all his own. He pegs markers at the extremity of his reach and has team-mates hurl the ball at them, fifty one way, fifty the other. Pakistani Rashid Latif videos hours of cricket from Star TV, and astonished Healy when they dined together in Karachi in October 1994 by quoting the Australian's career back to him, chapter and verse.

Jack Russell is a singular figure in English ranks, addicted to running (six miles a day), tea (twenty cups a day), Weetabix (soaked in milk for exactly twelve minutes and eaten with honey) and his oils: he is a painter accomplished enough to have been invited by the Dean of Gloucester to render the Gloucester Cathedral on its 900th anniversary. He is the lightest man in English first-class cricket – he weighs 9.5 stone, about half an Ian Botham – and easily the most patriotic: on England's recent tour of Zimbabwe, he had his wife hold the telephone near to her TV set, in Chipping Sodbury, so that he could hear the Queen's Christmas Message.

A disciple of Knott's, Russell shares the Kent keeper's fastidious customs of kit care. He has kept in the same sunhat since 1981, washing it twice a season, and it still has the scorch marks from when it caught fire in an oven in the West Indies, where he had put it to dry. On the county circuit Russell carries a toolkit of needle and thread to repair his gloves – he has used only two pairs in sixteen years – and a portable tumble-dryer for drying his togs. He has even planned his own funeral: an aficionado of military history, he says that he would like his coffin to be drawn on its final journey atop a British tank from World War II, to the tune of 'Wandrin' Star' sung by Lee Marvin.

The unkind might say that Russell's old hat has ceased to give him necessary protection from the midday sun. But as he put it after achieving a Test record eleven dismissals against South Africa at Centurion Park in December 1995: 'It's getting there that matters, not how you get there. I've managed to reach a certain status in my sport because of my individualistic streak, not despite it.'

*

Judging a good wicketkeeper is among the hardest of all selection tasks. Batsmen make runs, bowlers get wickets, but a wicketkeeper can't take catches if the chances don't come. They also serve who only squat and wait.

One clue is to see how long he stays low: generally, the longer the better. Ian Healy is an object lesson, never rising until he has summed up a delivery's line and length. Another barometer, according to Australia's last keeper-captain, Barry Jarman, is how well the gloveman handles work down the leg side. He says that some keepers, especially when they are short on confidence, stealthily creep a couple of feet wider than usual of off-stump: that way they don't have to stretch so wide to their right, and nobody blames them if they don't get a glove on those leg-glanced half-chances. 'I was always dirty on keepers who stood a yard outside off-stump,' Jarman says. 'My reasoning was that you could have nine fellas in slips but only two behind square on the leg side, so the keeper had to act as the first leg-slip.'

Concentration on each delivery is paramount. While keeping, Jack Russell will incant the mantra 'Ball ... hands; ball ... hands', not because English is his second language, but to ensure that he is in line with every delivery. A key index of attentiveness, too, is how well a keeper copes in the final session of a day's play. Fielders' minds can wander as time ticks away, but a keeper's must not. Wally Grout's attention span was limited in the early stages of his career, and he attributed his improvement to an observation of team-mate 'Slasher' Mackay. 'You're the best keeper in the world, Wally,' said Mackay. 'Before lunch.'

A further factor for the last two decades, thanks to the rise of one-day cricket, has been how well the keeper can bat. Before Healy routed his critics this season with a rash of runs in the first two Tests, a vocal minority favoured his abdication in favour of West Australian Adam Gilchrist, a competent stumper, but a superior left-hand striker. Similarly, Jack Russell has often played second banana to Alec Stewart, a steady stopper who hits the ball with alacrity.

The classification wicketkeeper-batsman is a handy one to attain, but a hard one to retain. Sooner or later – as with all-rounders – one faculty seems inevitably to suffer. Even the bell-wethers of the business have struggled to sustain their batting form. Jeff Dujon made his first 2000 Test runs at an average of 38, but for the remainder of his career averaged just 25. Rod Marsh's initial 1500 Test runs came at 37, his last 2000 at 22.

The problem for Joe Keeper is effectively two-fold. Not only does he frequently come to the crease tired, but he also usually has only the tail for companionship. Some even slough off the gloves to further their batting ambitions, like West Indians Clyde Walcott and Rohan Kanhai in the 1950s, and New Zealander Adam Parore in the last few years.

On one hand, it's obvious that today batting ability in a keeper is an essential rather than accessory. On the other, a keeper played for his batting can be as distracting as an actor cast on his looks. Sri Lanka's smurf of stumping, Romesh Kaluwitharana, made a spectacular century in his first Test against the Australians, at Colombo in September 1992, but cost his team the next match by twice failing to stump Australian centurion Dean Jones while he was in single figures. The preferences for batting back-stops like Stewart, Wayne Phillips and Taslim Arif have almost always been defensive gestures, signs of weakness, and hence regressive.

*

If one of the first questions asked of a promising keeper today is 'Can he bat?', not much later it will be enquired 'Can he chat?' Inspired by Marsh and Maclean, Healy believes a team with a quiet wicketkeeper is 'like a band without a conductor'. And, up to a point, this is true. By gingering fielders and bowlers, a loquacious wicketkeeper can set a tone of on-field hostility that augments their attacking threat. But not every keeper is comfortable in such a role: South African Richardson, for instance, makes it a rule never to speak to batsmen. And not everyone can sustain such an effort. England brought Steve Rhodes to Australia two years ago on the grounds that his personality, more extroverted than Russell's, would increase the vigour of their efforts. But Rhodes's form with the gloves was so mediocre that, by the end of the tour, he was as quiet as Marcel Marceau.

Healy also tells a story, against himself, of keeping to Sri Lanka's worldly Asanka Gurusinha four years ago. Peeved at the Guru's unsuccessful cross-batted efforts to lay a stick on Greg Matthews, Healy quipped, 'Any danger of playing straight?' When Gurusinha got the message and began pointedly playing down the line, with far greater assurance, Mark Taylor observed, 'Any danger of you shutting your mouth?' Careless talk, it seems, can cost runs.

Inside Sport February 1997

COACHES

Running the Show?

Cricket's formative trends are often only to be understood in retrospect. So it is with coaching. Twenty years ago, after an unsuccessful tour of New Zealand, the Australian Cricket Board appointed Bob Simpson as the first full-time coach of the national team. Today, the role in every country is crucial, controversial and often rather precarious: eight of the ten Test nations have changed theirs in the past three years, some several times.

When it comes to surveying the rise of the coach, however, the first cause for wonder is not the twenty years in which they have been a phenomenon, but the preceding century in which they were not. Every other sport kneeled at the altar of the coach, manager or guru; in cricket, despite a technical rigour and complexity that begat so many instructional books, the captain remained all-powerful, and the game, as it were, was learned without formally being taught.

There have been figures called coaches in first-class cricket for many years, but they tended in olden times to be sinecured former players responsible for duties such as managing net practice or taking care of the team's equipment. Tom Emmett's métier as 'coach' of Leicestershire was crushing judgements: 'Who told thee thou could laik at cricket? Why, ah've two lasses at home; I'll bring 'em o'er this afternoon and if they don't shape better than some of thee, then off they go to Yorkshire by the next train for more practice.' W.T. Grayburn was 'coach' at Surrey when Jack Hobbs joined a century ago, but Hobbs learned nothing from him. 'As a matter of fact, I have never had one hour's coaching from anybody in my life,' he recalled, 'and the reason why I emphasise this point here is that I am a natural batsman, entirely self-taught.' When the venerable Charles Lawrence retired at the Melbourne Cricket Club in 1900, he was not replaced. 'In the Melbourne nets alone there are on a brilliant summer evening sometimes a hundred players hard at it,' noted the former Australian captain Tom Horan on the eve of World War I. 'Yet never once since Charlie Lawrence left have I seen an attempt made to coach a young bowler at the nets.'

In Australia, in fact, coaching was identified with a restraint on the flowering of innate ability. 'In Australia, boys learn by watching each other and any grown-up cricketers who they see,' wrote Fred Spofforth. 'The result is individuality, and their natural ability is not dwarfed by other people's ideas.' A hundred years ago, Dr Leslie Poidevin saw cricket as bred in the Australian bone: 'There's something marvellous about a young Australian's devotion to and aptitude for the game. He gets no "coaching". He merely takes a bat and it seems to be "in him" to know what to do with it.' Part of the legend to giants of the Australian game like Donald Bradman and Bill O'Reilly was their flouting of orthodoxies. O'Reilly recalled being the recipient of coaching advice at the Sydney Cricket Ground nets within the hearing of Charlie Turner; Turner sidled up and told him to take no notice, confiding that he had profitably ignored coaches' advice all his career. When, in 1929, the New South Wales Cricket Association mooted employing a professional coach, ten former Test players put their names to a letter objecting 'that the natural Australian freedom of style might be sacrificed by the introduction of orthodox teachings'.

There was certainly no question of a Test team having a formal, full-time coach. If players had something to learn, they did so from one another rather than from a formally appointed authority. When Neil Harvey struggled to come to terms with English conditions on his first tour in 1948, he sought advice from Bradman via his room-mate, Sam Loxton, and received the oracular counsel: 'Hit the ball on the ground and you can't be caught.'

Probably the first individual to take on coaching tasks with a national team was Ken Barrington, in his managerial roles on England's winter tours to India (1976–77), Pakistan and New Zealand (1977–78), and Australia (1978–79 and 1979–80), when he combined administrative responsibilities with technical guidance and selection duties. So popular was Barrington that England's players insisted on his reappointment when the Test and County Cricket Board initially excluded him from the party for a tour of the Caribbean – the tour on which, at Bridgetown in February 1981, he so tragically died. Barrington took on his tasks, however, because he was Barrington rather than because he was coach. He was not replaced on his death, and Australia's decision to appoint a full-time coach twenty years ago was in the face of considerable scepticism. The first man offered the job, Ian Chappell, declined because he doubted the role was necessary; the second, Bob Simpson, said he regarded it as a finite appointment, and foresaw making himself redundant; when England appointed Micky Stewart to a similar role later the same year, he was designated not 'coach' but 'team manager'.

The impetus for the appointments of Simpson and Stewart was simple: failure, and a resultant dislocation in leadership. In five years, Australia had had four captains and England, six; the latest appointments, Allan Border and Mike Gatting, were bearing their burdens uneasily. Simpson ascribed the need for his job to the 'diminishing role of the Australian captain and the almost total destruction of peer influence within Australian cricket' after the sudden professionalisation of the game in the wake of World Series Cricket. In an environment of constant comings and goings, he became the face of continuity. The creation of the roles also reflected the trend to specialisation in numerous occupations: how could a captain be responsible for technical supervision and physical conditioning as well as pre-match strategy and on-field tactics? This was not so much a case of cricket pioneering as cricket catching up and aligning with other sports; in the United States, coaches like Knute Rockne, Vince Lombardi, Tom Landry, Bobby

Knight, Yogi Berra and Nick Bollettieri have been as famous as any athletes.

The other factor in the rise of the coach, generally ignored, is television. Instant then slow-motion video replays made it possible to study technique up close, over and over again. Brian Booth, an Australian captain of the 1960s, has recalled that he went through his entire career and saw himself bat for only one delivery: by chance, he once saw himself being bowled on a newsreel. Ricky Ponting, the present incumbent, has been able to watch every ball of his career as often as he has wanted, on television and on the screen of his laptop. It is one thing to tell a player he is doing the wrong thing; it is quite another to be able to show him. The role of replays has expanded from the analytical to the motivational, for Test cricketers today routinely prepare for playing by watching footage of their earlier successes: a means of reminding themselves of what they are capable.

Bob Simpson was a coach of a conservative disposition, but conservatism in his time was a form of revolution. He stressed basics such as fielding and running between wickets, and preached the gospel of hard work to a team, at first, averse to it: 'In many cases, the work ethic was non-existent … What was worse, they did not seem to want to match up. Instead, they treated the whole training exercise as a bit of a joke, in order, I believe, to disguise the fact that they couldn't hack it.' When Australia won the 1987 World Cup as rank outsiders, their strength was perceived as a dedication to detail, and a vindication of the idea of an off-field taskmaster.

Micky Stewart, a player of less ability than Simpson but similar discipline and determination, brought an NCO's gruffness to his role. Some captains were more at home with his religious devotion to physical preparedness than others. David Gower, an agnostic, deplored Stewart's 'soccer-manager style of bullshit'. Graham Gooch, a true believer, recalled that they 'debated and discussed things endlessly and never seriously fell out about anything'.

Both Simpson and Stewart also constituted a buffer between their captains and an increasingly demanding media. Had

Australia and England been led by more assertive and publicly confident individuals during this period, the growth of the coach's role would not have been nearly so conspicuous. As it was, from the early 1990s, all countries came into line by appointing officers titled either 'coach', 'team manager' or 'cricket manager', at least for tours: India had Bishen Bedi then Ajit Wadekar; New Zealand, Warren Lees then Geoff Howarth; Pakistan, Mudassar Nazar then Intikhab Alam; the West Indies, Rohan Kanhai then Andy Roberts; South Africa, Mike Procter then Bob Woolmer. The thought put into each appointment varied – Procter was chosen four days before South Africa commenced its return to international cricket at the end of 1991 – and likewise the perceived difference to team performance. But the appointments occasioned so little fuss that it must be assumed Test cricket had by then developed a coach-shaped hole. International cricket was ready for the national coach; whether the national coach was quite ready for international cricket was another matter.

Cricket is a game that measures almost everything. But how was the coach to measure the value he was adding to his team by anything other than the banal ledger of wins and losses, or the subjective gauge of observation and anecdote? After all, when Yogi Berra was once asked what made a great baseball coach, he replied simply: 'A great ball team.' The 1990s became, accordingly, a period of considerable experimentation. The experiences of Kapil Dev with India and Viv Richards with the West Indies suggested that getting the right coach was not as easy as appointing a great player, but nor did astute captains, in England's Keith Fletcher and New Zealand's Geoff Howarth, make off-field masterminds. The reign of Ray Illingworth did little for the cause of a single supremo with selection as well as training responsibilities; in fact, apprehension about the consolidation of too much power in one individual saw Simpson lose his role in Australian team selection. But the ambit and job security of other coaches, particularly in Pakistan, were too circumscribed for them to have much impact: Wasim Raja enjoyed a tenure of just on two months.

Emerging interest in innovation was embodied in Bob Woolmer, who ran South Africa's team in conjunction with sports scientist Tim Noakes from the University of Cape Town, and John Buchanan, with a degree in Human Movements from the University of Queensland and a Master of Arts in Sports Administration from Alberta University in Canada. Not all Woolmer's innovations, however, occasioned admiration, particularly the earpiece with which he fitted captain Hansie Cronje at the 1999 World Cup; the later revelation that his players consorted with match-fixers without telling him also suggested imperfect communication. With a first-class batting average of 12 and an affinity for consulting jargon, Buchanan has never convinced Ian Chappell: 'If I had a son, the last bloke in the world I would take him to for cricket coaching would be John Buchanan.'

The individuals most closely identified with significant improvement have been three hard-working sweats who made the most of limited abilities in their playing days, and who were likewise capable as coaches of wringing extra from talent at their disposal: Dav Whatmore in Sri Lanka, John Wright in India and Duncan Fletcher in England. All came from outside their respective cricket systems. All won reputations for meticulous preparation and close relationships with their captains: Whatmore with Arjuna Ranatunga, Wright with Sourav Ganguly, and Fletcher with Nasser Hussain and then Michael Vaughan. The deadpan Fletcher, a former skipper of Zimbabwe whose coaching spurs were won at unfashionable Western Province and Glamorgan, has been perhaps the chief surprise packet. Nasser Hussain has admitted nothing but surprises in the early stages of their partnership: 'I thought I would be starting off as the senior partner with the perceived upper hand in our relationship because I was the one who had played a lot of Test cricket ... I thought he would be coming to me saying "What's he like?", "What's that one like?" How wrong could I have been! I soon realised that Duncan knew everything about everyone!'

Trends in coaching have been governed by cycles of success, with the perception that any success is somehow a vindication of the coaching model. For the last few years, with Australia all-powerful, Australian coaches have been the vogue: a fashion followed in New Zealand (Steve Rixon), the West Indies (Bennett King), Zimbabwe (Carl Rackemann, Geoff Marsh), Sri Lanka (Dav Whatmore, Bruce Yardley, John Dyson, Tom Moody), Bangladesh (Trevor Chappell, Whatmore again) and, most significantly, India (Greg Chappell). During the 2005 Ashes series, England was perceived to have gained an advantage from the work of Fletcher's specialist batting and bowling coaches, Matthew Maynard and Troy Cooley. 'We can learn from England,' said Ricky Ponting on returning home. 'They were well managed, well skilled and had planned well. It's a pity that we didn't have any expert coaches to help our guys out.' Look out for Australia, and other countries, taking care to avoid that pity in future.

Coaching at cricket's top level may also become more individualised, with the rise of personal coaches for the provision of one-on-one advice. The phenomenon of life-coaching, a combination of psychotherapy and management consulting for a social group known as 'the worried well', has swept the United States in the last five years. Executive coaching, in particular, is the country's second-biggest growth industry, behind jobs in information technology, with about 40 per cent of *Fortune 500* companies now using them; according to one CEO, Bob Nardelli of Home Depot, executives without coaches 'will *never* reach their maximum capabilities'.

The Australian batsman Michael Clarke arrived on the international scene with his own coach cum manager, Neil D'Costa, a former coach of Western Suburbs and Northern Districts in the Sydney Grade competition. D'Costa had been Clarke's mentor since Clarke was seven, with a broad brief to prepare him not only for sport, but for life: when Clarke was twenty, for instance, D'Costa sent him to live with the Socceroo player Aytec Genc, in order to learn about the quotidian reality of being a professional sportsman. When Clarke learned he would make his Test debut at Bangalore in October 2004, his first act was to fly D'Costa in to share the achievement – a heart-warming moment. The obvious question, however, is what might happen to a player given conflicting advice by national and personal coaches.

What is clear already is that coaches in cricket meet similar fates to those in other sports when they are perceived to be failing: Bangladesh has had no fewer than seven coaches in its short period of international cricket. Because results are expected fast, coaches are striving to move faster. The honeymoon period between Chappell and his captain Ganguly, for instance, ended almost as soon as it began, on their first tour in September last year. And while coaches have so far circulated freely, Woolmer and Whatmore coaching two countries, how long before sovereign interests intrude? After Woolmer went from Warwickshire to South Africa, he received a Christmas card calling him a traitor to England and advising that he would 'rot in hell'. What would happen if one country became so set on another's coach as to poach him on the eve of their meeting in a series? The old saying is that not much new happens in cricket. Many of the ramifications of the rise of the coach, however, can only be guessed at.

Wisden Cricketers' Almanack 2006

WISDEN AND AUSTRALIA

The Yellow Press

It is often argued that 1864 should rank as the dawn of cricket, and the year has much to recommend it. On 10 June, overarm bowling became legal, thus completing bowling's 'march of intellect' from underarm innocence: in the opinion of Sir Donald Bradman, 'possibly the greatest single change in the development of the game'. Representing South Wales Cricket Club against the Gentlemen of Sussex at Brighton a month later, a clean-shaven, fifteen-year-old William Gilbert Grace notified the game of his talent with 170 and 56 not out. His batting would revolutionise the way cricket was played, and his personality the way it was organised and watched.

That we know so many years later how many runs Grace scored in that match, meanwhile, reflects 1864's third development of significance. The publication of the first edition of *Wisden Cricketers' Almanack* was more than the minting of a distinguished imprint; it manifested the emergence of a record-keeping instinct in the game, now taken for granted, but intrinsic to its senses of continuity and context. The idea of records was a precondition for modern sport – and a compelling one. 'What is a record?' asks Allen Guttman in *From Ritual to Record: The Nature of Modern Sports* (1978). 'It is the marvellous abstraction that permits competition not only among those gathered together on the field of sport but also among them and others distant in time and space.' In records and the games from which they are derived, a two-way process is at work: a Test match is meticulously recorded because it is important, and is important because it is meticulously recorded. Since the dawn of the age of quantification, one might say that sport has harboured a variation of that conundrum about the proverbial tree in the forest: does a game take place if no one is around to score?

First acquaintance with *Wisden* doesn't evoke proverbial trees so much as literal ones: all that paper, all those pages. Its draft and displacement today are partly an outcome of tradition: in two dimensions, *Wisden* has remained unaltered in 140 years. Cricket's spread and sophistication, meanwhile, is indexed by *Wisden*'s third dimension, its fourteen-fold expansion from the 116 pages of its first edition to the 1632 of its most recent. And while the pace of change in cricket today seems so great, it's worth noting that most of *Wisden*'s growth actually occurred between 1882 and 1922. In the year of Australia's first Test victory in England, *Wisden* came in at only 224 pages; in the course of reporting eight consecutive Australian victories at English expense forty years later, the almanack scraped 1000 pages. *Wisden* may be classified as the most English of books about the most English of games; nodding to Kipling, Rowland Ryder once described it as 'the thin yellow line'. But its fortunes have been inseparable from the rise of international cricket in general and Australian cricket in particular. Indeed, it is difficult to think of another overseas book that has documented Australian striving in *any* field of endeavour so exhaustively and approvingly.

A mischievous soul could go further, and argue that Australians are likelier to read *Wisden* closely than the English. *Wisden* is published in the northern hemisphere amid the pleasurable distractions of the cricket season's commencement; when *Wisden* navigates its way south a month or two later, it arrives as a blessed relief from winter and wall-to-wall football. And such is its transporting charm, *Wisden* might actually be better appreciated at a remove from its place of publication. In England, the name *Wisden* has authority. Away from England, it has resonance; it conjures up names, people and places. I once asked Ron Archer why he'd acclimatised to English conditions so quickly on his first tour, making a century in his first innings at Worcester in May 1953. He explained that he'd devoured his grandfather's *Wisden*s so avidly as a child that it felt like he'd played in England before. When the firm John Wisden & Co marked its centenary, the encomium it liked most was from Australia. Prime minister Robert Menzies, whose almanacks were obtained by minions at Australia House in London for forwarding to Canberra in the diplomatic satchel, stated simply, '*Wisden* and cricket are synonymous.' Responded Lord De L'Isle: 'Let this message from Australia be the tribute of the whole British Commonwealth at once to a famous cricketer, to the great enterprise, and to the game of cricket wherever it is played.' Even here, the word *Wisden* is regarded as proverbial for comprehensive and compendious. In greeting Peter Coleman's history of Australian censorship, *Obscenity, Blasphemy, Sedition* (1962), forty years ago, Ross Campbell described it as 'a *Wisden* of banning'.

Wisden, though, doesn't need articulated tributes; readers pay their own annual homage by trusting it as the authentic record of cricket's preceding year. Collecting it has a lore of its own. One renowned bibliophile, Yorkshireman Karl Auty, spent most of his life in Chicago; his favoured nocturnal ritual was reaching down to the set of *Wisden*s he kept beneath his bed and choosing a volume at random, which he would then pore over for hours. The almanack has even palliated hardship and horror. Cricket historian Harry Altham recalled being distracted from the death around him on the Western Front by the obituaries in his 1916 *Wisden* of W.G. Grace and Victor Trumper, 'feeling no real sorrow for W.G. passing Homeric and legendary into Elysian fields, but an almost personal pain that Trumper's gallant spirit and matchless grace should have been called so early from the world it enriched'. And possibly the most famous single almanack is a manhandled 1939 *Wisden* owned by the journalist E.W. Swanton, rebound in remnants of gas cape, glued with rice paste and thumbed by thousands of internees in a dozen different Japanese prisoner-of-war camps along the Burma–Siam railway. Visitors to its glass case at

Lord's can still discern a fading Japanese censorship stamp on the top left of the title page. It indicates that the volume is 'not subversive'.

*

Wisden has, distantly but diligently, followed and featured Australian cricket over the last 140 years; more subtly, the coverage of Australian cricket has both reflected and contributed to *Wisden*'s fortunes in that time. Before studying the game through *Wisden*'s eyes, one should understand a little about the institution itself.

It is a cliché to say that John Wisden could not have foreseen how his little annual would prosper and his name be perpetuated. On the contrary, his objectives were probably short-term. A professional fast bowler, Wisden had been in various sporting enterprises throughout his career, including the joint management of a cricket ground at Leamington, secretaryship of the Cricketers' Fund Friendly Society, the first cricket tour to the United States and Canada in 1859, and latterly a tobacconist cum sporting-goods depot off the Haymarket in London, subsequently relocated in Leicester Square. In starting his almanack, Wisden was doing little more than imitate the rival Islington firm Lillywhite Brothers & Co, which had promoted its business for the fifteen preceding years with an annual *Cricketers' Guide*. The rivalry between *Wisden* and the succession of annuals bearing the Lillywhite name has been largely ignored by historians, content simply to know who won. But it was a competition with some intriguing fluctuations.

John Wisden and Fred Lillywhite had been in business together between October 1855 and December 1858, but their relations had soured in the early 1860s, after Wisden succeeded Lillywhite as secretary of the Cricketers' Fund Friendly Society. There is a hint of mischief about Wisden's move to set up in competition with his erstwhile partner, and more than a hint of malice in the brief biographical note about Wisden in Lillywhite's guide of 1865: 'Was a "good 'un", but now "does nothing" for his county, England, or any other eleven, in fact, devotes his time to do [sic] a "deal of good" for promoting the manly game, for which he spends a vast amount of "coin".'

Such remarks about Wisden and others – the great George Parr he described as an 'able manager ... when out of his bedroom' – cost Lillywhite's guide the patronage of the Marylebone Cricket Club; he was felt to have 'exceeded the fair limits of criticism upon cricketers'. But the first *Wisden* – AKA *The Cricketers' Almanack for the year 1864 being the Bissextile or Leap Year, and the 28th of the Reign of Her Majesty Queen Victoria* – wouldn't have caused Fred Lillywhite much heartache. A messy book, its scores surrounded with such factual bric-a-brac as winners of the Derby, Oaks and St Leger, a potted history of China, and the rules of pastimes like Knur and Spell, it seemed destined for a short life. One can only admire the inventiveness of its compilers, or sympathise with their desperation, as they bulked their book with digressions into popular history like: 'The graces of the modern tea table were quite unknown to the country folk, although that favourite beverage, brought by the Dutch to Europe, was introduced into England by Lords Arlington and Ossory in 1666.'

These divertissements were a temporary measure: the graces of teatime would prove no match for the Graces of the green. But working out how to treat cricket in the antipodes would challenge *Wisden* some years yet. The first game in Australia that *Wisden* reported, the initial Melbourne engagement of H.H. Stephenson's trailblazing Englishmen with a Victorian XVIII on the first three days of 1862, was in a loose-knit grouping under the heading of 'Extraordinary Matches', which also included Shillinglee's feat of dismissing the 2nd Royal Surrey Militia for 0, and an encounter between Sixteen of Sheffield and Sixteen of the Country Round Sheffield in which all the contestants were aged sixty or over. Fred Lillywhite, meanwhile, showed his experience: by slightly delaying the publication of the *Cricketers' Guide*, he managed to accommodate the scores of matches being played in Australia by the team that George Parr was leading there, while the tour was in progress.

The first *Wisden*s were cobbled together – so far as is known, and much is not, many of *Wisden*'s records having been incinerated during the Blitz in 1940 – by the journalist W.H. Knight, in collaboration with his printer, W.H. Crockford. Initially, they concerned themselves purely with scores, abjuring commentary, perhaps wary of antagonising Marylebone as had their rival: 'We, of course, make no comments upon the matches, leaving the cricketer to form his own opinion with regard to the merits of the men, since a great many of our readers are at least equal, if not superior, to ourselves in arriving at a right judgement of the play.' As their publication was far from spacious, they were also apt to condense those scores that did not absolutely demand complete recapitulation; thus, disappointingly, were the deeds of Charles Lawrence's 1868 Aboriginal visitors pared back to a puny page.

Australian cricket and cricketers infiltrated those early almanacks stealthily. One of Lawrence's team, Johnny Cuzens, was the first antipodean inclusion in *Wisden*'s 'Births and Deaths' section: his death on 22 March 1871 was recorded in the 1872 edition. The second inclusion was also a death, that of Victoria's Richard Wardill on 17 August 1873, which made the 1874 edition – only to vanish rather mysteriously from the next edition, perhaps when it was learned that he had drowned himself in the Yarra after being exposed as an embezzler.

While *Wisden* was improved annually throughout the 1870s, there remained little sense of order or continuity about the almanack. Knight reported the matches played by Australia's first representative touring team in 1878 in voluminous detail, but scattered them throughout the almanack under the subsections on each county. George West, the cricket correspondent for *The Times* who succeeded to *Wisden*'s editorship on Knight's death in August 1879, drew the matches played by the team of 1880 together in their own chapter, but was much lighter on the detail, pleading limitations of space. Most bizarrely, *Wisden* ignored altogether what is today regarded as the very first Test, at the Melbourne Cricket Ground in March 1877; it disposed of the entire tour, in fact, in a few perfunctory lines.

Why this occurred can only be speculated. It wasn't easy for *Wisden* to keep tabs on the early English visits to Australia. Because the undersea telegraphic cable linking Australia with Britain after 1872 was prohibitively expensive for all but short items, *Wisden*'s compilers would for many years depend on seaborne copies of colonial newspapers such as the *Australasian*, the *Leader* and the *Sportsman*. But circumstantial evidence suggests that *Wisden*'s lapse had a commercial cause. The captain of that English team in Australia was James Lillywhite Jr, a scion of the famous family, and the tour coincided with another phase of chilly relations between the Wisden and Lillywhite camps. *Wisden* had issued the frankly dubious claim to have 'in circulation outstripped all its rivals, old and firmly established as some of them are'. *John Lillywhite's Cricketers' Companion*, which had absorbed the old *Cricketers' Guide* on Fred Lillywhite's death in 1866, scornfully counterclaimed 'an infinitely larger sale than any other annual work on the game', and damned statements otherwise as 'not founded on fact'. The contrast between the 1878 editions of the two annuals was, then, most marked: while James Lillywhite Jr reported extensively on the tour and the inaugural Test in *Lillywhite*, *Wisden* studiously looked the other way.

Whatever the case, *Wisden*'s failure to even acknowledge the match must have seemed more and more embarrassing as Australia's famous 45-run victory sedimented into the bedrock of cricket history. In 1930, editor C. Stewart Caine even made what looks like an attempt to justify the almanack's Homeric nod, observing airily that the forthcoming season marked Test cricket's golden jubilee, 'for although the representative games played in Australia by James Lillywhite's team in 1876–77 and by Lord Harris's team in 1878–79 are in these days counted as Test matches, none of those encounters should strictly be so regarded'. Lillywhite's team was dismissed as 'a financial speculation', Harris's as 'merely an amateur combination'; the Oval match of 1880 – which *was*, of course, in *Wisden* – should thus be accorded the status of the first 'real Test'. But no move was made to adjust the almanack's record section, perhaps because Caine's statistician, Sydney Southerton, was actually the son of James Southerton, who had been one of Lillywhite's players. And a scorecard of the inaugural Test was finally published in the 1978 edition, where it was bracketed with the scorecard of the Centenary Test. In the meantime, *Wisden* had completed a neat double-blink by largely overlooking the first one-day international in January 1971, also at the Melbourne Cricket Ground, granting it only a potted score and scorning to run a match report.

Mistakes? By *Wisden*? They do happen. One might as well acknowledge *Wisden*'s fallibility at the outset: some claims made for the almanack, as Rowland Bowen remarked, 'differ only in degree from those which the fanatical devotees of some religions make for their own revealed books'. But having said that, *Wisden*'s ignoring of the inaugural Test looks less like a mistake than a deliberate oversight; it is a pregnant silence, exemplifying the organic and arbitrary nature of cricket's growth, how its forms have been more or less arrived at, rather than invented or decreed. It's a reminder, too, that Bismarck's famous advice about sausages and laws – how one should never watch their making, lest one's respect for them diminish – sometimes applies equally well to cricket records.

*

When John Wisden died a bachelor in April 1884 he left, paradoxically, an orphan. With no son to inherit his sporting-goods business, the future of the almanack was especially clouded. The last *Wisden* in the eponymous founder's lifetime was still markedly inferior to the competition. When Hon. Ivo Bligh's Englishmen reclaimed the still-warm Ashes in 1882–83, what had become *James Lillywhite's Cricketers' Companion* allotted the tour twenty-three pages, prefaced with a feature by Bligh himself. *Wisden*'s coverage ran without a covering article, and began on a page facing a calendar for the year 1844: a rather congruous misprint.

Step forward Henry Luff, the late John Wisden's manager, who acquired the firm and perforce the almanack from the executors of the estate. Only twenty-eight, Luff was a shrewd businessman: he would broaden the company's activities from straightforward retailing to manufacturing and branding as well. And he was also a believer in the almanack. When Billy Murdoch's Australians won their first Test match in England at the Oval in August 1882, for instance, it was Luff who arrived the next morning at Covent Garden's Tavistock Hotel to painstakingly transcribe the ball-by-ball record of the game from the visitors' own scoresheets. 'And,' he stated proudly, 'they were printed ... exactly as they were set out in the scoring book.'

The almanack resumed uncertainly under the new regime. George West succumbed to a 'long-continued indisposition' – the cause of which has never been explained, though his was a sociable nature – and the 1886 edition appeared a whole year late. But this seems to have convinced Luff that *Wisden* should be run by full-time specialists (today, it would be called 'outsourcing'). The Cricket Reporting Agency was a small news-agency by the standards of giants such as Reuters, Havas and Wolff. With its editorial oversight, however, *Wisden* ceased to be principally a promotional vehicle for its founder's athletic equipment and emporium, and became a force in its own right.

The Cricket Reporting Agency was chiefly the doing of three young brothers: Charles, Sydney and Edgar Pardon. That they were young – at the agency's founding in 1880, Charles was thirty, Sydney twenty-five, and Edgar twenty – is often overlooked. In fact, their vitality was probably fundamental to their success. At a time when Australian visits to England were still regarded with some severity, as intrusions marring the more congenial contours of county cricket, the Pardons relished them. Edgar's first act on leaving school, for example, had been to follow Dave Gregory's 1878 Australians round the country, while Charles Pardon had turned his writings on the 1882 Australian tour for *Bell's Life* into a book, then collaborated on another book describing the 1884 Australian tour with Sydney, Edgar and C. Stewart Caine. Indeed, Geoffrey Moorhouse believes that there are grounds for regarding Charles Pardon as 'the first great cricket reporter'.

Though Charles Pardon's editorship spanned merely the four

editions from 1887 to 1890, he accomplished much. The births-and-deaths pages were overhauled and expanded by that crick-eting Herodotus, F.S. Ashley-Cooper, who also introduced a statistical section, 'Some Cricket Records'. *Wisden*, for the first time, commissioned portrait photographs and prose appreciations of the season's leading cricketers, the forerunner to its annual 'Five Cricketers of the Year'. 'Six Great Bowlers of the Year' in the 1889 edition – including three Australians, in Charlie Turner, John Ferris and Sammy Woods – proved so popular that *Wisden* sold out, necessitating a reprint – another first. Even Charles Pardon's untimely death in April 1890 left *Wisden* a legacy: the short death notice for him in *Wisden* 1891 foreshadowed the first of more than 10,000 obituaries to appear in succeeding editions.

The coverage that *Wisden* lavished on Anglo–Australian cricket was perhaps its greatest advance, and point of product differentia-tion. In this, Charles Pardon and his brother Sydney, who suc-ceeded him, were far-sighted. English counties would not establish a Board of Control for Test matches until 1899, and the Maryle-bone Cricket Club not take responsibility for tours of Australia until 1903, but *Wisden* both sensed the growing importance of Ashes cricket and contributed to it. In the almanacks from 1887 to 1900, *Wisden* devoted 486 pages to reports and scores from Aus-tralian tours of England and English tours of Australia; its cov-erage dwarfed that of *Lillywhite*, which allocated the same games 281 pages. John Wisden & Co also dealt closely with Australian teams in England. Henry Luff was generous in tending their equip-ment needs, and they were generous with their names; even when the company was acting as agent for a triangular bat, Australian captain Percy McDonnell was prepared to offer an endorsement. Australian managers and scorers never failed to pay their respects at the Cricket Reporting Agency in Fleet Street. Sydney Pardon was so impressed by the 1893 Australians' teenage scorer that the agency took him on at the end of the tour: Sydney Southerton, a former ship's steward who had obtained his commission with John Blackham's side after meeting them aboard the *Liguria* en route to

England, spent the rest of his life at *Wisden*, being known as 'Figure Fiend' for his astoundingly retentive memory.

Wisden's interest in cricket in Australia also grew. It began printing scores from Australian intercolonial matches in 1887–88, while *Lillywhite* persisted in the eccentric tokenism of printing averages for the East Melbourne Cricket Club in Melbourne's pennant competition. Not that *Wisden* was in any sense a globalist; on the contrary, it cheerfully acknowledged its parochialism. In toasting English success against the 1886 Australians, Charles Pardon commented: 'As, without the least ill-will towards the Australians, we in England are chiefly concerned with the prosperity and popularity of the game within our own border, it would be mere affectation to pretend to be anything but contented with the general net result of the last Australian tour.' Sydney Pardon, said C. Stewart Caine, 'mourned over any England failure', having been raised 'in an atmosphere that presumed the superiority of the Englishman in every walk of sport'. But this allegiance, always tactfully expressed and never mutating into partisanship, probably resonated with the times better than overt impartiality, tapping into the evolving sense of rivalry between England and Australia. For an Australian to have his portrait in *Wisden* – as in the 1890s did John Blackham, George Giffen, Syd Gregory, Hugh Trumble and the Trott brothers, Albert and Harry – was to make it in front of the audience that mattered, as much a source of colonial satisfaction as the Royal Academy hanging Arthur Streeton's *Golden Summer: Eaglemont*, or London critics' acclaim for Tasma's *A Knight of the White Feather* and Melba's *Lucia di Lammermoor*.

By the turn of the century, meanwhile, *Wisden*'s own rivalry had been resolved. Its 1900 edition was its largest yet, its robust 650 pages encompassing the previous year's successful tour by Joe Darling's Australians, and elevating Darling, Clem Hill and Monty Noble to the 'Five Cricketers of the Year' pantheon. *Lillywhite* followed two months later, a slighter 350 pages; it was destined to be that publication's last edition.

*

The first Australians to arrive at Lord's in May 1878 did so 'in such a quiet and unpretentious way' as to pass unrecognised; the mistake was not repeated as they left that evening having routed MCC and Ground, W.G. Grace and all, by 9 wickets. Dave Gregory's men sent £100 of their tour-takings to a fund for the bereaved in the loss of the *Princess Alice* (a Thames pleasure steamer which sank at the cost of 700 lives); the Australian team's donation of its prize money to the Sydney bushfire appeal in January 2002 was, like so much in cricket, far from a unique gesture. Welcome to a world in which English fielders at the Sydney Cricket Ground are distracted by the blue of Australian skies then confronted by 'a field of snow', in which an English captain maims himself in a shipboard tug-o-war and a Middlesex supporter dies while spectating, where boundaries at Lord's bounce 'through the fanlight of the billiard-room door' and where a match at the Oval is stopped to allow photographs to be taken. Welcome to *Wisden*.

Introduction to *Endless Summer: 140 Years of Australian Cricket in Wisden* (2003)

OBITUARIES FROM WISDEN
The Passing Parade

It's been said that, not being an especially religious people, the English devised cricket as a vision of the eternal. The game's vocabulary certainly provides regular intimations of mortality. A 'dead bat' is a useful accessory; a 'dead ball' is provided for in the laws; 'dead Tests' are not unknown. Batsmen can enjoy 'lives', but learn to dread the 'lethal' delivery; that is, when they have not first 'self-destructed' after a 'rush of blood'. To be captured plumb LBW is to be 'dead in front'; to be bowled is to hear the 'death rattle'. To bat as a match or innings concludes is to be 'in at the death'; to bowl at the same time is to be delegated 'the death overs'. Then the 'post-mortems' begin.

Death of the permanent rather than the passing kind, furthermore, has long been a salient feature of *Wisden Cricketers' Almanack*. Since inaugurating the custom in 1892, cricket's biggest and yellowest book has published more than 10,000 obituaries, covering the great, the good, the conventional, the heterodox, the remembered and the forgotten. Over time, in fact, *Wisden*'s annual chronicle of death notices has acquired quasi-institutional status, its glimpses of the love of cricket in all its varied forms somehow a source of vitality and regeneration. Forty years ago, in one of the loveliest of cricket essays, Ronald Mason cherished a Cheshire nurseryman called Frederick Hyland, an 'inconspicuous embodiment of obscurity' who had attracted the attention of cricket's record angel by spending two overs on a first-class cricket field representing Hampshire in a rain-ruined game: 'He retired, after the fashion of all good philosophers, to cultivate his garden; but by his ten wet minutes on the first-class field he had as irrevocably joined the ranks as W.G. had, whose playing life in that region spanned forty-four years. In the sight of the eternities in and beyond history, forty-four years and ten minutes are as one: Frederick J. Hyland, cricketer and nurseryman, may, in the sight of all us envious idealists beyond the pale, stand kin to Grace in honour. Of his kind is the game given its enduring strength and fascination.'

Hyland is one of the 250 or so entries in *Peter the Cat and Other Unexpected Obituaries*. His kind is the book's subject: men who squeezed cricket into their lives rather than their lives into cricket. Some of them are men who achieved high office: five kings; one British prime minister; two Australian prime ministers; governors of Canada, Australia and the Windward Islands; two Lords Chief Justice; ministers of defence and labour; a field marshal; a president of the Board of Education; a director of the Bank of England; and a member of the International Olympic Committee. But mostly it attests the breadth of cricket's appeal. To be found are not merely the president of the Football Association, the president of the Institution of Mechanical Engineers, the secretary-general of the International Planned Parenthood Federation, the US cultural attaché to Italy, the Chief Psychologist at the Directorate for the Selection of Personnel at the War Office, the chief of staff for the UN peacekeeping force in Cyprus, the chairman of selectors for the British equestrian team, the head porter of Trinity College, the Indian ambassador to Paris, and the honorary weedkiller at Lord's; but also a music hall artiste, a monk, a missionary, the father of the English bar, the father of English socialism, a distinguished art critic, a learned Arabist, an expert on Roman pottery, a self-made textile magnate, a long-distance driver, a designer of missile nosecones, a biographer of de Gaulle, a producer of *ITMA*, and a star of *Doctor Who*.

Then there are the frankly unclassifiable, such as Gwynfor Evans, whose threat of a hunger strike was instrumental in expediting Welsh-language television, and Kenneth Gandar-Dower, who represented Cambridge at six sports, flew a private plane to India, became a noted big-game shot, and introduced a team of Kenyan cheetahs to London where they set speed records on its greyhound tracks – this in a life ended by war at thirty-six.

Wisden, of course, is primarily a book of records, and shows in these obituaries its uncanny sense of them. Achievers may be found not only of such esoteric sporting accomplishments as the only man to score a hundred and a try at Headingley, and the only man in history to be out for a duck in a county match at Stourbridge six weeks after receiving an FA Cup winner's medal; but also the setter of a world benchmark for grouse-shooting, the rider of 250 winners for the Queen Mother, and a hunter involved with thirty-three packs of hounds. The father of the game in Russian Lapland is honoured; likewise Belgium's favourite cricketing Australian.

Nor are the distinctions merely those of a sporting nature: commingled are the founders of *Drum* and of the *Whakatane Beacon*, descendants of Oliver Cromwell and of a man who rescued Charles II, survivors of the force that successfully relieved Cecil Rhodes at Kimberley and the column that arrived too late to save Gordon at Khartoum, commander and casualty at the Battle of Jutland, a survivor and a victim of the *Lusitania*, the inventor of the slips cradle and of the 'Aerial' fishing reel, winners of the 1911 Cairo Grand National and of the deck quoits 'Ashes', the British Army's youngest general and the British Museum's oldest ticket holder, the model for Bobby Southcott in MacDonnell's *England, Their England*, and the author of a Pindaric ode on the 1981 Headingley Test; holders not just of the Victoria Cross, but of the White Eagle of Serbia and of the Russian Order of St Stanislaus with Swords, too. Perhaps the rarest distinction of all is surviving a *Wisden* obituary, like Archibald Fargus, who missed a train and thus his date with death at the Battle of Coronel; and Andrew Newell, whose disappearance turned out to have been deliberate but temporary.

Wisden does not tell us everything. Sometimes it is painfully discreet. 'Of the faults of private character that marred Pooley's career and were the cause of the poverty in which he spent the later years of his life,' it remarks of Ted, 'there is no need now to speak.' Five murder victims are included, but the death by hanging of the one murderer, Leslie Hylton, goes unmentioned; nor did *Wisden* strive to do justice to the writers P.G. Wodehouse, Rupert Brooke, Samuel Beckett, Terence Rattigan, R. Warren Chetham-Strode (whose *The Guinea Pig* became the first film to use the word 'arse'), and E.W. Hornung (acknowledged as 'a keen cricketer' but not, mysteriously, as the creator of Raffles, the Amateur Cracksman). *Wisden*'s detailing of death, however, is sometimes surprisingly unflinching. One can admire the chivalry of Dr C.T. Aveling, who died 'answering the appeal of a nervous lady for help', lament the haplessness of Donald Eligon, who succumbed to blood poisoning from a nail in his cricket boot, or wonder at the waste of Paul Brookes, who bowled Bradman as a sixteen-year-old and perished of wounds seven years later.

Bradman? Though this is not a selection concerned with the giants of the game, they exert a subtle gravitational pull. W.G. Grace makes his presence felt through the many lives he touched: his devoted batmaker, his last surviving grandchild, a fielder whose hand he shook, an umpire whose decision he ignored, a batsman whose identity he challenged, a famous whip who drove him to a match, a journalist who dismissed him for a duck, another journalist who wrote a book about him saving the world from the Martians, and even one perverse enthusiast who nonetheless 'never took the trouble to see W.G. Grace play'. It is the fame of great players, moreover, that contributes so much to the cricket fever with whom so many of the subjects in this book were stricken, and which endures even in these less reverent times. Nobody could be more deserving of *Wisden*'s tribute than the individual in *Peter the Cat* most recently born: twenty-eight-year-old fireman Jeffrey Wornham. 'As a boy,' reported the almanack, 'he spent much of the summer dressed in whites on the off chance that he might find a game he could join.' Wornham's approach to school was linear: 'spring term to prepare for cricket, summer term to play it and autumn term to relive the matches'. Nothing much changed in adulthood: he had spent much of the winter's day that he died knocking in a new bat, and mourners at his funeral last year heard the strains of the signature tune for cricket on the BBC, 'Soul Limbo'. Above all, this is a book about the enduring appeal of cricket which a person such as Jeffrey Wornham personifies. *Vita brevis*, for sure, but *cricket longa*.

Introduction to *Peter the Cat and Other Unexpected Obituaries
from Wisden Cricketers' Almanack* (2006)

LIFE STORIES

AUTOBIOGRAPHIES

In Their Own Write

Steve Waugh stares from the cover of his new autobiography with all his trademark intensity, gimlet eyes and grim features framed by his baggy green and upturned collar. Thought this was just a book, eh? No way, mate. This is a contest. The 800-page *Out of My Comfort Zone* is not exactly a ticket to reading pleasure. It invites the judgment attributed to Lord Beaverbrook, who is said to have sent on, unopened, a big biography of his fellow press baron Lord Northcliffe with the dismissive note, 'It weighs too much.' But survival of the fattest is a plausible new approach to an old challenge: after all, one way to command attention in this overcrowded market is simply to take up all the available shelf space.

And it *is* overcrowded. By an inexact count of my own book-shelves, 127 senior cricketers, coaches, umpires and administrators of the last two decades have written, initiated and/or endorsed 174 works of autobiography or approved biography in that time. This includes diaries, but excludes unauthorised volumes such as Don Mosey's *Botham* and Alistair's McLellan's *Botham: Hero or Villain*, works of instruction such as Botham's *Cricket My Way*, works of opinion like *The Botham Report*, and novels such as *Deep Cover* by Ian Botham and Dennis Coath; in fact, inclusion of all those works ascribed to the Beefmeister would so have skewed the figures as to have rendered them meaningless. Nor does it count franchise-extenders such as *The Matthew Hayden Cookbook* and Glenn McGrath's forthcoming *Barbecue with the Master*, even if the latter will probably afford deeper personal insights than his 2003 *World Cup Diary*.

These days, the barriers to entry are low indeed. In the book-review section of the inaugural edition of *Wisden Australia*, the essayist and poet Jamie Grant commented satirically on the sheer volume of player product: 'Can *The Paul Reiffel Diaries* be far away?' The short answer was no. Compelled to review Paul Reiffel's auto-biography *Inside Out* in *Wisden Australia*'s second edition, Grant commented merely that it had 'made satire impossible'. Accordingly, I will refrain from making jokes about *I, Blewett* and *Where Did Our Love Go?*

And while it may seem odd to describe anything to do with the genteel world of print as ruthless, selling books, unlike cricket, is essentially a zero-sum game. The person who buys your rival's work will probably not buy yours. Phil Tufnell famously commented that every time he peered down the other end of the pitch he saw someone trying to end his career; now he need look only to the end of the bookshop shelf. This is a business, more-over, of increasing stakes. Penguin advanced Steve Waugh a record $1.3 million for his musings; the lakhs of rupees chasing the signature of Sachin Tendulkar boggle the mind. Twenty years ago, Kapil Dev packed his life into the 104 pages of *By God's Decree*; by Waugh's standards, Tendulkar's book should outbulk *Wisden*.

This is despite the fact that cricket autobiographies are almost invariably disappointing. That Waugh's is the year's most eagerly awaited cricket book is easy to understand on one hand, but hard on the other. Waugh is a genuine giant of the game. Yet how many giants of the game have written interesting books, as distinct from books of interest because of who wrote them?

Autobiographies face, chiefly, two challenges. Cricketers are doers. Such opinions as they hold are seldom diverting or original. The insularity and fixity of purpose common among champions is likelier to lend itself to egotism and self-absorption than detached contemplation. As Ernest Hemingway summarised a giant of America's national pastime: 'Ty Cobb, the greatest of all ballplayers – and an absolute shit.'

If a cricketer has enjoyed sufficient success to justify an autobiography, moreover, he is arguably unlikely to have suffered the
kind of setbacks that might make his struggle worth reading:
Tolstoy's distinction between happy and unhappy families probably
applies equally to successful and unsuccessful sporting careers. The
classics of autobiographical writing emerge from inner turmoil,
like Augustine's *Confessions*, or are provoked by outside attack, like
Newman's *Apologia Pro Vita Sua*. In any meaningful sense, the vast
majority of cricketers are strangers to both.

The problem is an abiding one. A century or so ago, when
W.G. Grace was commissioned for his *Cricketing Reminiscences and
Personal Recollections*, the religious affairs journalist of *The Times*,
Arthur Porritt, was recruited as amanuensis. Porritt found Grace
a closed book, and their routine became depressingly familiar.
Porritt would ask Grace how he had felt during a particular
innings. The Doctor would be puzzled. Felt? Why, he hadn't felt
anything: 'I had too much to do to watch the bowling and see how
the fieldsmen were moved about to think about anything.' Grace
even chided Porritt for using the word 'inimical', remonstrating
that team-mates would ask: 'Look here, W.G., where did you get
that word from?' Porritt persevered only with the gravest difficulty.
'Often I left his house in absolute despair,' he recalled. 'Once, at
least, I asked leave to abandon the enterprise.'

Ben Bennison, the former sports editor of the *Daily Telegraph*
who helped Don Bradman fashion his first autobiography, *Don
Bradman's Book* (1930), had similar reflections: the mighty Australian gave little away. 'A more serious young man or one richer in
power of concentration I have not met,' Bennison recalled in his
own memoir, *Giants on Parade*. 'Cricket was his profession, and his
unswerving purpose was to reach the top. He loved the roar of the
crowd and rejoiced in his triumphs, but quietly, as will a business
man chortle over a big deal.'

The other challenge is more recent. Cricketers' lives now follow
a very familiar trajectory. If they have talent, they are usually
spotted early, and funnelled into a system with countless others

more or less exactly like them; their ambitions, influences and experiences will not deviate far from the norm. If they prosper, their lives will become public, and their careers will be minutely reported: anyone sufficiently interested in a player's autobiography to buy it, indeed, will probably already know as much about that cricketer as they need to know.

Steve Waugh is the quintessential example. He has already published ten tour diaries; it is not as though *Out of My Comfort Zone* fills a yawning gap in the public record. His exchanges with Curtly Ambrose at Port-of-Spain ten years ago (page 354) and with Herschelle Gibbs at Headingley in 1999 (page 535), for instance, largely recapitulate narratives on pages 103 of Waugh's *West Indies Diary* and 195 of *No Regrets*. If Waugh's autobiography justifies its advance and sells in the numbers anticipated, he will have accomplished the incomparably rare feat of selling the public his story not once but twice.

So, what's the point? For the player, there's usually some satisfaction in telling his story without interruption, especially if he suffers from the sense of feeling 'misunderstood'. Even Bradman experienced such pangs. His *Farewell to Cricket* (1950) – which he wrote apparently unaided, having been ghosted by William Pollock of the *Daily Express* in his earlier *My Cricketing Life* (1938) – contained a thirteen-page gripe headed 'Critics'. Methodically enumerating slight after perceived slight, it included even a heartfelt defence of his abstinence from alcohol. But typically, it is controversial cricketers who feel the need to give their side of the story. 'Unfortunately, my aggression has been misunderstood,' griped Javed Miandad in *Cutting Edge* (2003). 'It has been misconstrued as something negative and troublesome ... As far as I was concerned, cricket was war and I was at war whenever I played.' And what could be negative or troublesome about that?

The cavalcade that accompanied Steve Waugh's retirement, too, is an exception. Most careers ended peremptorily. But if a cricketer is denied final fulfilment, there is consolation in having the last word. The chapter in Michael Slater's new autobiography, *Slats*, that describes his final omission is entitled simply 'Misunderstood', and blames variously his captain, his vice-captain, his marriage, his medication and his mobile phone for his predicament; lack of runs was, presumably, too obvious an explanation.

In line with the confessional trend of the culture, in fact, cricketers are taking increasingly to public brooding on their personal travails. Phil Tufnell set the standard by filling his *What Next?* (1999) with hair- and headline-raising misadventures. 'In my time I've been arrested, spent a night in the cells on three separate occasions I can remember, and been hit over the head with a half brick by a man I sincerely believe wanted to kill me for my treatment of his daughter,' he announces. 'I've been married twice, divorced once from a girl whose subsequent choice of employment was prostitution, and I've been accused of all sorts of antisocial activities with all sorts of materials, *some of which I didn't even do*.' Hard to believe, really.

There are limits to this. Slater's mea non culpa was ghosted by an Australian rock journalist, Jeff Apter, and reads at times like one of those self-mortification memoirs beloved of showbiz figures, lacking only a visit to the Betty Ford Clinic. Nasser Hussain, in *Playing with Fire* (2004), and Graham Thorpe, in *Rising from the Ashes* (2005), have adopted incendiary titles to convey the unsuspected depth of their passions; their books are certainly edgy, but ultimately rather joyless. On the other hand, there is something quite moving about the straightforward struggles with self-doubt of Steve James in his *Third Man to Fatty's Leg* (2004), in which Tufnell himself appears with a typical mot. 'I can't wait to get a game against Glamorgan this year,' he sneers. 'They must be crap if you can get a game for them.'

The main purpose of an autobiography today, however, is not so much to tell a story, set a record straight, or bid a dignified adieu, but to create an image or market presence that stakes out one's commercial territory. If you don't create an authorised product, the theory runs, someone else will create an unauthorised one. After all, as Kin Hubbard once observed, 'After a fellow gets famous it doesn't take long for someone to bob up that used to sit by him at school.' To vary the traditional graveside oration, the player that is born of cricket hath but a short time to cash in.

Since perceiving that they have a market value, players have become increasingly proprietorial about the particulars of their lives. With careful management, they are being told, by the Australian Cricketers' Association among others, that one's stories can mature into a future meal-ticket; as such, they are not to be surrendered lightly or freely, not even by your mates. In his recent biography of Waugh, *The Waugh Era* (2004), Greg Baum reports sadly: 'A senior Australian player refused to contribute to this book because it was unauthorised. Seemingly, to his mind, there should be no biography, just autobiography and hagiography. Or perhaps there should just be money.'

A telltale trace of the trend is the proliferation of the tautologous title *My Autobiography*, pioneered by Charlie Chaplin and Benito Mussolini, but these days circulating most freely in sport, whether the books concern football (Robbie Fowler, Patrick Vieira, Terry Butcher, Ian St John), rugby (Jason Robinson, Bill McLaren), golf (Bernhard Langer, Peter Alliss) or snooker (Jimmy White); Sir Alex Ferguson made authorial authority trebly clear in his *Managing My Life: My Autobiography* (2001). For the 'My' is more than a frivolous affectation; it is a reassertion of ownership. Before embracing *My Autobiography* as a title for their memoirs, Ian Botham, Garry Sobers, Dickie Bird and Shane Warne had all been the subject of unauthorised biographies; their message: 'This is the genuine article. Beware of imitations.' Warne has gone so far as to say that he wishes it were illegal to write a book about someone without their permission, and has declined to answer enquiries from his latest biographer, Paul Barry.

This counts no less for the humble striver. The surprise media star of the last few Australian summers has been Kerry O'Keeffe, an undistinguished cricketer whose self-mocking schtick as a commentator is to pretend that he was even less distinguished: a soi-disant 'straightbreaker' whom his team-mates held largely in contempt.

The '70s drinking and sledging stories with which O'Keeffe has made his name, and which bulk out his recent autobiography, *According to Skull* (2004), provide an antidote to the po-faced ponderousness of Channel Nine.

O'Keeffe is no Ranji Hordern or Arthur Mailey, true artists of whimsical self-deprecation. His writing is an uneasy mix of silliness, scatology and sentimentality, and the effect is wearing off even now; his efforts to branch out into stand-up comedy are more painful than an over of long hops. But where publishers tend to see us as hanging on the every word of a Waugh or a Warne, O'Keeffe is a reminder that the best-seller is not always to the swift, nor the sequel to the strong.

Cricinfo February 2006

DONALD BRADMAN AND STEVE WAUGH
Public Privacies

'Did you hear about the old man who turned 100?' asked Sir Donald Bradman in a cheerful note to the journalist Rohan Rivett in October 1968. 'They asked him what it felt like. He said wonderful – I haven't an enemy in the world. The buggers are all dead.' That's our Don: twenty years retired and still thinking in hundreds, eh? This century, it turned out, was one he could not overhaul: he was 92 when he died on 25 February 2001. But the job was done; the buggers *were* all dead. Bradman remains, to use Christine Wallace's words from her new book *The Private Don*, 'the best-ever player in the best-loved sport in the most sports-loving nation in the world'. Wallace's book attests another quality: he remains a sporting media property without compeer.

The Private Don offers a new perspective on Bradman. It is not – thank Don – yet another recitation of the Greatest Story Ever Bowled To. It distils instead a twenty-four-year correspondence between Bradman and Rivett, Rupert Murdoch's first editor of significance at the *Adelaide News*, then inaugural 'editor emeritus' (a phrase Rupert allegedly coined when he sacked Frank Giles from the *Sunday Times*: 'E means you're out, meritus means ya deserve

---

Review of *The Private Don* by Christine Wallace (Allen & Unwin), *The Waugh Years: The Making of a Cricket Empire 1999–2004* by Greg Baum (ABC Books) and '*One Who Will*': *In Search of Steve Waugh* by Jack Egan (Allen & Unwin)

it'). This isn't the Don we know; it covers Bradman's long twilight years in suburban Adelaide, when he was cricket's number one administrator rather than its foremost personality, and also Rivett's financial adviser. Wallace seeks to know Bradman by applying Plutarch's wisdom that 'very often an action of small note, a short saying, or jest, will distinguish a person's real character more than the greatest sieges or the most important battles.'

It's a good idea; it also has problems. Bradman's famous domestic contentment, *The Private Don* suggests, was no fond illusion: in his personal life, nothing much happened. Nor was Bradman given to illuminating retrospective judgments: there are no warm stories here about admired contemporaries, or mellow reflections on former days. This is actually an intriguing absence, although Wallace seems oblivious to it. She accepts Bradman's self-description as 'a simple country lad [who] wanted nothing more than to play cricket for fun and as a joy and recreation and loved the simple life in the country with birds and animals' without demur or even comment; yet it is surely an idiosyncratic conception of cricket that mentions 'birds and animals' rather than team-mates.

The tone of the letters is a mix of the friendly and the formal. Rivett was an instinctive liberal who travelled widely, Bradman a natural conservative who scarcely left home: there is a fair bit of gentle political sparring along these lines. Rivett was a keen cricket enthusiast, Bradman the game's greatest practitioner: many exchanges, as you'd expect, involve the former proposing and latter disposing. In some sections, Wallace goes a long way on very little: the pages spent trying to decrypt Bradman's financial advice and political musings seem largely pointless. The small notes, short sayings and jests turn out to be little more.

Only twice does Bradman drop his guard: once in sorrow, once in anger, both at perceived insults. The most moving sections of *The Private Don* concern Bradman's relations with his son John, whose childhood was blighted by polio and whose adolescence was prolonged by depression. Bradman, solicitous and forbearing to begin with, steadily soured; when John flirted with the '60s counterculture and even grew a beard, father and son became irreconcilable. Finally, in March 1972, feeling the pressure of his patronymic, John Bradman became John Bradsen.

Bradman could make nothing of his son's antagonism towards 'the system, the establishment or something'. And to the name-change he would return again and again: it was 'a deep wound which I will have to bear silently until the end', evincing 'an apparent hatred of the legacy I have given him in my name and a detestation for all the things I believe in and stand for'. Bradman was convinced that 'eventually the full magnitude of the heart break he has caused will dawn on him', although also that 'I shall carry this cross to my grave'. There is something touching about these passages: it is a generational conflict that might have befallen any family of the period. But the limits of Bradman's empathy are also rather starkly revealed. Quick to lament the burdens of a fame which, to a degree, was of his own making, Bradman would not countenance John's complaints about a reflected renown which was not. It is a strange failure of imagination.

Bradman reserved his most crimson rage, however, for when former team-mate Jack Fingleton sent Rivett a copy of a new book he'd written with the suggestion, a little cheeky, that he review it. Catholic Fingleton and his coreligionist Bill O'Reilly were famously agnostic where Bradman was concerned, the roots of their dis-agreement lying in Bradman's *sauve qui peut* response to Bodyline in 1932–33, but there is something rather disproportionate about the force of Bradman's response to a transaction that does not directly concern him. The letter's fury survives Wallace's rather clumsy paraphrase: 'Bradman wrote to Rivett that, honestly and without bias, Fingleton's letter reeked to him of jealousy, bigotry, envy and ego. Bradman thought it outrageous that Fingleton should ask Rivett to write a review. This was something of an over-reaction on the part of Bradman, who went on to say that it was unsurprising Fingleton was not better known as a cricket writer in Australia at the time. He ridiculed Fingleton's comment that he wanted his "cobbers" in Canberra to know about his new book, saying he was glad Fingleton had some cobbers there: he only knew, he said, of one Fingleton had left in the cricket world and that, claimed Bradman, had to do with things in common other than cricket. He was presumably referring to Bill O'Reilly.'

This is a most peculiar letter. Fingleton was, to be sure, an ambitious, brittle man with sometimes jaundiced views, but no cricket library worth the name is without *Cricket Crisis* (1946) and *Brightly Fades the Don* (1949). And 'Things in common other than cricket'? This isn't easy to reconcile with Wallace's confident closing judgment that the correspondence contains 'no whiff of the anti-Catholicism which has been an undercurrent of criticism promoted by his knockers'. It would be unwise, however, to invest too much significance in the content of *The Private Don*. There is simply not enough of it. Wallace's researches began for a feature article published in the *Australian Magazine* earlier this year; a feature article, frankly, is what they should have stayed. They reveal only that behind the private Don lay … another, even more private Don.

Steve Waugh, little less private a man than his distinguished predecessor, seems equally determined to remain so. He declined to co-operate with either cricket historian Jack Egan or journalist Greg Baum, whose new books have recently joined the growing pile concerning him and his era. This does not represent an insurmountable handicap. If anything, the opposite is the problem: Waugh's period is so exhaustively documented and recorded, not least by himself in his tour diaries, that *One Who Will* and *The Waugh Years* bog down in recapitulating recent and all-too-familiar history. Thus sentences like this from Egan: 'In Melbourne, on a wicket described as "sub-standard", West Indies made only 280, Australia replied with 242, then Richie Richardson, with 122 scored in six and a half hours, guided the West Indies to 9 for 361, leaving Australia with 400 to win.' Egan's book, unfortunately, doesn't rise far above this, and the personal tangents his book takes add nothing to it: who cares that he's read *Beyond a Boundary* or toured India with the Grey Kangaroos? There are, additionally, some strange omissions in it: Australia's progress in the group games in the 1999 World Cup, when Waugh's captaincy was under intense scrutiny, is skated over in nine lines; Australia's defeat in India in 2001, possibly the best Test series of modern times, is glanced at in two pages.

Baum's book, fortunately, flowers in its second half, where he discusses Waugh thematically rather than chronologically. Baum, readers of the *Age* will know, is a gifted phrasemaker and a sharp observer; he has an appealing touch, even, of Waugh's own gruffness. He might have let himself go a little further and developed points at which he hints. 'Boorish, threatening and disruptive crowd behaviour was to become a constant of the Waugh era, and also a mark of the times,' he comments at one point, perhaps suggesting a relationship. 'Cricket has not had a technology debate like golf and tennis but maybe it needs one,' he muses later, moving on before it has quite sunk in. But he is admirably even-handed, and also draws wickedly accurate distinctions. Watching Waugh's Australians swan round at 2002's Laureus Awards, Baum confides: 'It was hard to escape the feeling that this was not so much sportspeople getting Laureus awards as Laureus awarding itself sportspeople.'

Waugh's views, meanwhile, await his own autobiography. He also still thinks in hundreds. Egan informs us, in fact, that contemporaries call him 'Fairy Bread': 'He only deals in hundreds and thousands.'

Australian Book Review November 2004

FRANK TYSON
A Dear Diary

One of the hoariest of cricket's truisms – after the ones about it being a funny game and catches winning matches – holds that what goes on tour stays on tour. I'm not sure how well that holds up today. What goes on tour stays there for the time it takes to whip up a tour diary, pose for the cover and get Ricky Ponting to write the introduction. Frank Tyson is more circumspect. He has decided on a stay-on-tour moratorium of fifty years, which gives it a somewhat more stringent security classification than cabinet papers, and a status a little less important than documents covered by the Official Secrets Act. Quite rightly, I think you'll agree.

I'm here today to launch *In the Eye of the Typhoon*. I do so gladly, and I'll do so briefly. In Frank's book, he recalls how any player in the England team of his day who found himself being earbashed at a function emitted a mayday signal to team-mates by sticking his finger in his ear. If I go on too long, feel free to revive this tradition and let me know.

Having Frank write on the 1954–55 tour is like having Spofforth write on the Oval Test of 1882, or Warwick Armstrong talk us through the Ashes of 1921. Ah, let's not undersell him: it's like having Phar Lap confide his impressions of the 1930 Melbourne Cup. And if Phar Lap has retained his youthful good looks, Frank is a great deal more erudite and informative.

In the Eye of the Typhoon is an incalculably valuable book. For one, it's a time capsule. On page 8, in an image from the *Chronicle and Echo*, we see a besuited, betrilbied young Tyson standing solitarily at Northampton station. He could be a young soldier in mufti. He could be a film-noir gumshoe. But he's a young cricketer waiting for his train to London, without agent, ghost-writer, life coach or spiritual guru in sight. Though the fanfare was minimal, the sentiments were somehow more spontaneous and authentic.

Trains figure as prominently in Frank's book as planes would today. Frank tells us that on the train from St Pancras to Tilbury, supporters had graffitied encouragement: 'Good luck Len' and 'Stick to it, Boil.' Cricket graffiti is, alas, today a thing of the past. The last example I can think of dates from 1989 when, during the Poll Tax riots, someone scrawled on a wall the legend 'Thatcher Out'. It was noted that another anonymous hand had added 'LBW Alderman'.

To read Frank's book is to be transported back to an era when travellers from Melbourne to Sydney swapped locomotives at Albury after a midnight meat pie in the refreshment rooms. Nowadays going to Sydney merely entails pretending an IQ fifty points lower. *In the Eye of the Typhoon* is, furthermore, not merely the narrative of a cricket tour, but a story about the joy of being part of a hearty, happy and successful team. It proves, I think – if it needed proving – that cricket is the most companionable game of all. Certainly more socially rewarding than a game of golf involving right-handed Frank and left-handed Brian Statham, whose dialogue, Frank tells us, once they had teed off with their respective slices, consisted of occasional grunts of 'See you on the green', followed by long solitary walks.

The centre of this unit is Len Hutton: shrewd, tough, taciturn and yet, at times, strangely vulnerable. Colin Cowdrey once told a story about Hutton's performance at his first Australian press conference, in Perth, and how his underkill caught the local press completely unawares: 'We've got a chap called Tyson. But you won't have 'eard of 'im, 'cos 'e's 'ardly ever played.' Now we learn that while the *Orsova* was en route, Hutton had taken Frank aside, along with Cowdrey, Peter Loader, Jim McConnon and Keith Andrew, and confided that they couldn't expect to play a major role in the series. Have you ever heard of such a thing, consigning five members of a seventeen-man squad to oblivion?

Nowadays, he'd probably be sued, or chastised by a sports psychologist for damaging his men's self-esteem, even as Frank was sent off for counselling. Frank tells us that it redoubled his determination to make a contribution: I wonder whether this wasn't Hutton's intention all along. At perhaps the crucial moment of the tour, immediately after Australia's colossal First Test win, we see Hutton in a different context, calling half a dozen players into his room to tell them that he was completely confident of winning the series. This grand old Duke of York only had seventeen men, but he treated hills with a similar contempt. My favourite Hutton story, however, concerns Frank joining him at Eden Park when England was 7-down and still 36 runs in arrears on the first innings against New Zealand: 'Stick around for a while, Frank. We may not have to bat again.' The only thing more startling about this assertion is that it was right. England obtained a lead of 42, and bowled NZ out for 16 fewer. The Kiwis have improved since then, though on last Sunday's evidence, perhaps less than was thought.

We all know how famously fast Frank was on that tour. Ron Archer once told me that he was caught at slip off Frank in Sydney not because of an edge, but because Frank hit his bat so hard it turned in his hand. For his own part, Frank recalls being clocked by the Royal Aeronautical College at 89 miles per hour – this, he modestly adds, was without warming up and while swathed in sweaters; he nobly refrains from adding that it was in Wellington, where the commonest balls have nothing to do with cricket but are those frozen off brass monkeys.

I dare say Frank bowled about as fast as a man could fifty years ago, but I wouldn't want to overstress the importance of his speed. A 95-miles-per-hour half-volley is still a half-volley, as anyone who's watched Brett Lee bowl for the past couple of years would tell you. In Len Hutton's *Fifty Years of Cricket*, he makes the startling report that Frank and Brian Statham bowled not a single bouncer in the Adelaide Test. The most important bouncer of the 1954–55 series was bowled at Frank, not by him: by Ray Lindwall, in Sydney. It was the cricket equivalent of taking aim at one's foot and blowing off both kneecaps. We all know what followed, and now we can read about it as though it was just yesterday.

Ladies and gentlemen, I thank you for keeping your fingers from your ears for long enough to hear me out. It gives me great pleasure to hand over to this remarkable book's remarkable author.

Speech at the Melbourne launch of *In the Eye of the Typhoon*
by Frank Tyson (Parrs Wood Press), November 2004

IMRAN KHAN AND KEPLER WESSELS
The Tiger and the Tough Guy

As the captain of Sussex County Cricket Club seventeen years ago, Tony Greig had an eye for talent. Pakistani Imran Khan and South African Kepler Wessels were then little-known quantities, but Greig fostered both and promoted them to places in Kerry Packer's World Series Cricket spectacular. Despite that shared upbringing, there would seem few more antithetical performers than charismatic Khan and cadaverous Kepler. And while they've both attracted devoted biographers, these two books are profoundly different. Imran is an Eastern creature under a Western microscope, while Wessels has been packaged by and for loyal patriots.

Imran, a Pathan from Lahore educated at Oxford and living in London society, has always straddled cultures, and not always with ease, especially if one is to judge by the furore that Ivo Tennant's biography has touched off in England by its confirmation that the fast bowler tampered with a ball while representing Sussex. The salient paragraphs are a minor component of this book, but they are central to the portrait Tennant paints of an athlete only apparently at one with the environment of his game and chosen circle. Tennant's book is also notable in that, unlike Imran's own autobiographies, it examines his romantic entanglements, which the cricketer has previously treated with some disingenuousness. Tennant cites the introduction to a 1982 newspaper article by a woman

----

Review of *Imran Khan* by Ivo Tennant (Witherby) and *Kepler: The Biography* by Ed Griffiths (Pelham)

journalist: 'Imran Khan is worried in case I portray him as a sex symbol. This is possibly why Imran is stretched across his hotel bed wearing only a petulant expression and a pair of tiny, black satin shorts.'

Imran was a naif when first chosen to tour England as a teenager in 1971. 'His first ball delivered in new kit and boots sailed past Aftab Gul's nose,' reports Tennant. 'This would have been almost forgivable had Aftab not been batting in an adjoining net. Apologising profusely, Imran tried again. His next ball hit a spectator on the head.' Ten years later, however, Imran was the best fast bowler in the game, with a mastery of all its arts, and a batsman to contend with. Ten years after that, he was the guru of the Pakistan team, destined to purloin the World Cup from under England's unsuspecting nose. Is he finished? So it would seem. It transpires that Imran, after retiring, dreamed the same comeback dream six or seven times. Then he awoke in the middle of it, realising that he would not play again. 'The dream had turned into a nightmare,' reports Tennant. 'He would have hated to make another comeback. He has not had that dream since.'

Ed Griffiths, the sports editor of South Africa's *Sunday Times*, has done an exhaustive job chronicling the kaleidoscopic career of Wessels, capped by Australia twelve years ago, then captain of his country for the last three. He has interviewed everyone from Allan Border and the brothers Chappell to a whole XI of present-day Proteas, and the anecdotes testify to an iron will first exhibited in childhood, and an impulsiveness beneath the taciturn exterior. Griffiths describes, for instance, the decision Wessels reached twenty years ago to choose cricket over tennis, reached not after calm deliberation or wise counsel, but in the middle of an important tennis match: 'He stormed off the court, straight past his speechless father, and emerged from the dressing room not long after brandishing his racquet. All the strings had been cut. He had found a pair of scissors in the dressing room and slashed wildly at the racquet head. That was it. He had made up his mind. He would stop playing tennis.'

That staccato style is also characteristic of Griffiths. When Wessels faces Joel Garner, for example, it's pure Sergio Leone: 'Garner would have to be faced alone. Wessels knew that. One on one. Garner with the ball. Wessels with the bat. One winner. One loser.' And this. Happens. A lot. Again and again. Kepler walks into town. He's tough, lean, mean etcetera. He's the man for the job. It looks like a long shot. Kepler pulls it off. Then he goes to the bar and orders a glass of milk. And like one of Wessels' batathons, *Kepler* can be heavy going. This is Wessels A–Z and, with the sheer density of the material and Griffiths' obvious awe of his subject, it's pretty wearying to realise you're at R and already know what's in S.

Still, there are worse ways to occupy your time while flaked in front of the football this winter than with the tiger and the tough guy – or, if you prefer, the cheat and the mercenary. You can fantasise of Imran galloping in from one end, Wessels dead-batting at the other, with Greigy as their agent and Kerry Packer as their impresario.

Australian June 1994

IAN BOTHAM

Look at Me

'Who writes your scripts?' Graham Gooch famously asked Ian
Botham during a 1986 Test at the Oval. As well he might. Botham,
if you recall, had been languishing suspended all summer, after
having confessed in a tabloid to smoking the odd joint, but with his
first ball equalled Dennis Lillee's record for Test wickets.

Had it turned up in a script, the life of Botham might well have
been rejected on grounds of implausibility. At times in *Botham: My
Autobiography*, even the subject seems to have trouble believing the
fates that befell him. 'I set off on England's winter tour ... determined to put the nightmares of the last couple of years behind
me,' says one characteristic link. 'And I succeeded – those nightmares were replaced by even bigger ones.' Botham famously cultivated panto as an alternative career, and this book seems to betray
its influence. No sooner is one crisis averted than the reader is
tempted to call out: 'Look out behiiind you!'

This is not the first time the story has been retailed. Since Bob
Farmer's on-the-spot *Ian Botham* fifteen years ago, there have been
versions of the story – from Dudley Doust, Don Mosey, Peter Roebuck and Frank Keating – and Botham has been richly caricatured
as a cricketer and character. This book looks authoritative, and is
certainly presented as the last word and story-straightener. It turns
out, however, to be simply another caricature, and a sad, petty,

---

Review of *Botham: My Autobiography* by Ian Botham (HarperCollins-
Willow)

awful book. Socrates said that the unexamined life was not worth living; it is certainly hardly worth reading. 'I have always found it difficult to admit to mistakes,' Botham allows at one point; he owns up to being 'selfish, aggressive, tyrannical, chauvinistic and hot-tempered'. But that's just a throat-clearing exercise. In the next breath, he claims that this has been integral to his success.

Critics? The hell with them: 'I learned from a very early age that if you worry about what people write in the press, you will never get out of bed in the morning.' Yet at least a third of *My Autobiography* is taken up with newspapers, the scandal-mongering and suing thereof. The critical cricket influences of his life – such as his Somerset skipper, Brian Close, and England captain Mike Brearley – are squeezed for space by Botham's lawyer, Alan Herd, and his tabloid amanuensis, Chris Lander. And far from distancing himself from that milieu, the whole effort seems geared to producing the kind of extracts that are grist for Fleet Street's mill, including barroom blah to better George Best and clunking anecdotes about the likes of Elton John and Mick Jagger.

The Botham story should be marvellous. On his 1966 tour of England, Garry Sobers did everything except keep scores. A ten-year-old boy from Yeovil who only stopped bowling when he wanted to bat decided there was no cricketer he more wanted to emulate: not Barrington, not Graveney, not even Fred Trueman, but a West Indian whose sole inhibition seemed the time available to impose himself on the game. The boy Botham matured into the wonder of his age, batting with a swagger, taking wickets with outrageous fortune, and lounging at slip one minute before leaping to interception the next. He did not, however, become Sobers. With Sobers, you said: 'Look at him.' Botham said: 'Look at me.' Botham was always a cricketer of disproportions: superabundant abilities, outsized aggression, overpowering appetites. When the talents began to fade, the other qualities remained.

The last five years of his Test career were a long, slow, unedifying fade. In his last twenty Tests, he added just 600 runs and 30 wickets to his record, at averages of 20 and 50 that reversed those attained in his first twenty Tests. England chose him in the same way that Napoleon chose lucky generals, but his reputation everywhere else diminished. In the multitude of statistics Botham left, one above all betrayed his style: no bowler had conceded as many as 10,878 runs. 'Nothing would be more horrible to him than playing as a grumpy old professional at 38,' Roebuck once wrote of him; in the end, Botham only just beat the deadline.

For Roebuck, Botham reserves the nastiest lines in *My Autobiography*, setting on him like a mugger in a dark alley. 'Throughout my career at Somerset, I had always thought there was something a bit odd about Roebuck,' he decides. 'And he was a very hard man to talk to – unless, of course, it was he who wanted to do the talking.' You would never guess that Botham was actually collaborating with Roebuck on a biography, *It Sort of Clicks*, when relations between them soured, during what is here called 'The Somerset Mutiny'; for these purposes, Roebuck is simply a pathetic nobody with a chip on his shoulder.

Why this flair for vendettas? Perhaps it was because he was so comprehensively bested by the *Mail on Sunday* in 1986, during his first legal skirmish, that he grew obsessed with Fleet Street and its works: there was nothing like a setback to stimulate his competitive juices. He loathes past-player critics: 'I find it very sad when former great players have to resort to cheap shots in newspapers to keep their egos alive. If I felt that was happening to me, I think that would be the time to blow my brains out.' But, of course, even as he took them on with such crusading zeal in later years, Botham was never above accepting the tabloid shilling and using the media to pump his personal profile. And now that the script is finished, how else to live on but as one of the bores he so reviles?

Australian October 1994

VIV RICHARDS

Ready for His Close-up

'You're a long time retired,' cricketers say. And it's no wonder that many postpone the dread day as long as possible. It's hardest of all for the genuinely great: how else to replicate the stimulus of performing at the highest level, and the narcotic of adulation? Consider the case of Vivian Richards, perhaps the greatest of all post-war batsmen. This is his third book about himself; there's also been an authorised biography. It is subtitled 'The Definitive Autobiography', though what this means is unclear: in no sense is it an advance on those previous works, and in some respects it is a regression.

For a start, it's incredibly sloppy: by my count, at least seventeen names have been spelled incorrectly, including several rivals and colleagues of long standing. Worse still, many stories have been carelessly garbled; the chapter on World Series Cricket, for instance, is a farrago, conflating incidents from at least four separate seasons. This is, of course, the publisher's fault, and it has let Richards down appallingly: half an hour with some *Wisden*s would have corrected 90 per cent of the errors. But perhaps it was simply falling in with Richards' own often muddleheaded thinking.

Some sportsmen achieve clarity and perspective when their careers conclude. Richards, alas, isn't one of them; he still craves recognition as the biggest, baddest, meanest dude in town, sometimes to the point of self-parody, and at the expense of coherence. This is particularly apparent in a garbled chapter on 'sledging' –

Review of *Sir Vivian: The Definitive Autobiography* by Viv Richards and Bob Harris (Penguin) cricketspeak for the verbal intimidation of opponents. Richards admits to having once tried to knock Dennis Lillee over while going through for a run, then to trying to 'work Dennis up' because 'I honestly wanted to fight him.' Richards would also 'gladly have fought' Craig McDermott, because of McDermott's lack of 'real manliness'. And, were he pitted today against Glenn McGrath, notable for his on-field volubility, Richards would think nothing of physical retaliation: 'I ... would be like a desperate rat and I would trample all over him.' But just when Richards seems about to advocate the replacement of batting gloves with boxing gloves, he comments: 'The authorities must do something about it before this aspect of the game turns into rollerball.' Huh? He then contends that when the game 'starts to become physical, that is when it is dangerous'. Finally, however, he concludes that he'd still like to flatten McGrath.

If the opinions in the book are superficial and sometimes contradictory, the anecdotes are even worse: flat, familiar, banal. Richards played with some of the greatest cricketers in history, but you'd hardly know it; they are here rarely more than names, unaccompanied by insight or understanding. The only glimpse Richards gives of himself, meanwhile, is unconscious. In the concluding chapter, concerning his future, he recounts his brief tenure last year as coach of the West Indies on tour in New Zealand. The team was conclusively thrashed, and Richards was overlooked when a full-time coach was appointed; the job went instead to two former teammates, Roger Harper and Jeff Dujon. Richards' indignation remains white-hot. His rivals for the job were not real men; some 'as players ... used to run away from fast bowling and had hearts the size of peanuts'. He awaits the inevitable recall: 'I am an individual who is ready to put himself forward to help in whatever capacity, physically or morally, to do whatever needs to be done.' On the other hand, he might also go into politics: 'Our people need inspiration, and that I can give to them if and when I am called on.' To paraphrase Norma Desmond, he's still big: it's the cricket that got small.

Sunday Age October 2000

DIARIES

And Then … Nothing Happened

'Keep a diary,' said Mae West, 'and one day it'll keep you.' Cricketers took a while to catch on, but in the last ten or fifteen years have twigged that journals of tours or seasons can indeed be nice little earners, particularly if success or controversy is part of the raw material. As in so many matters, Steve Waugh was the trendsetter, his daily musings about 'mental toughness' and 'mental disintegration' a motif of the era of Australian dominance. The Australians' Ashes defeat has been ascribed to the absence of Steve Waugh as captain, but might also be chalked up to his disappearance as lucky diarist: only one of his ten diaries involved a Test series defeat, and that Indian series five years ago appears purely as a prelude in *Ashes Diary 2001*.

Cricketers, of course, have been chronicling their capers since they started touring. But to an era of congested cricket calendars where one takes a day at a time and is only as good as one's last performance, the diary is ideally suited; given the sheer repetitiveness of so much touring life, it might even serve as a means of distinguishing one day from the last, and documenting the passage of time. The diary has also fundamentally reshaped the cricketpublishing market, for sales of diaries have proven inversely proportional to those of old-fashioned tour books. The days when bookshop windows at the start of the cricket season would be festooned with journalistic descriptions of the last are long gone. These days the players play the game and call it, too.

The Ashes of 2005 were celebrated in countless ways, but it was the dramatis personae who shifted the product. Michael Vaughan's *Calling the Shots* was the season's hot ticket, with its breathless revelation that Kevin Pietersen is nicknamed 'KP'. The counter-story was Ricky Ponting's *Ashes Diary*, a rather diffuse book starting in June 2004 with Tests against Sri Lanka and ending with forty pages of pedestrian 'player profiles', at the end of which the Ashes appear not to have been lost at all, merely mislaid.

The cricketer's diary, these reminded us, has two faces. It is straightforward, requiring perhaps a few notes every evening ('Got up. Made century. And so to bed.'), but also speculative. When a publisher commissions an autobiography, it is usually of a known quantity, and can be guaranteed to include a preordained sequence of events. When a publisher signs a cricketer to generate a diary, both become hostages to fortune. In Ponting's book, it is almost as though the tide of events turned too late to rethink the generally triumphal tone, leaving sentences only slightly more nuanced than: 'Now that we had ~~won~~ lost the Ashes, I was ~~completely stoked~~ utterly devastated.'

It was ever thus. The first player's book on an Ashes series, Ranjitsinhji's *With Stoddart's Team in Australia* (1898), was likewise written in the shadow of 1–4 defeat – or, as the author put it, of 'imperfect success'. Worse was the fate of South Africa's Roy McLean, able to document a successful series against England in *Pitch and Toss* (1957), then obliged to report his own loss of form and omission against Australia in *Sackcloth without Ashes* (1958).

When the old-fashioned player narrative began to be supplanted by the new-fangled diary in the late 1970s, the challenge became more sharply defined. Doling out action by day was simple; it could also end up proving Edna St Vincent Millay's philosophy that life wasn't one damn thing after another but the same damn thing over and over. In 1979, Bob Willis's *Diary of a Cricket Season*, narrating the season of 1978, and Geoff Boycott's *Put to the Test* and the joint production by David Gower and Bob Taylor, *Anyone for Cricket?*, doing the same for England's Ashes win of 1978–79, all suffered the same malaise. The Tests described, won from a puny

New Zealand and a Packer-plucked Pakistan and Australia, were not much to write home about, and little more entertaining to consume in diary form. The interesting segments of Willis's book had nothing to with on-field action; they described tensions at Warwickshire over the renewal of the contract of Packer signatory Dennis Amiss. Willis's position is a perfect specimen of the hypocrisies of the time. Delighted to be able 'to exploit my commercial potential as England's only genuine pace bowler', Willis was nonetheless vehement that Amiss 'could not have his cake and eat it' and 'should not be picked for Warwickshire again'; not surprisingly, he describes Amiss as 'oddly bewildered', and how their relationship 'faded with a dreadful inevitability'. The other books did not even have this dimension. Once the novelty wore off, Boycott's book savoured of retrospective self-justification, Taylor and Gower's of self-conscious merriment.

Nonetheless, the genre had taken root, and somewhat better lay ahead. Indeed, the sequence of county-cricket diaries published in England over the next decade represent some of the best writing of the period, and the keenest observations of the lot of the professional cricketer: most notably Brian Brain's *Another Day, Another Match* (1981), Peter Roebuck's *It Never Rains* (1983), Graeme Fowler's *Fox on the Run* (1988) and Jonathan Agnew's *Eight Days a Week* (1989). All were players striving to stay at the top of the first-class game; Fowler and Agnew were also in the lower reaches of international cricket. The diary structure suited their theme of personal struggle, each day subtly informing the next, moments of hope making the disappointments survivable, setbacks taking the edge off successes.

Brain, a wily seamer who wound up at Gloucestershire after sixteen years at Worcestershire, was in his fortieth year when he penned his autumnal book, fortified with 'twenty fags, a couple of pints of lager a day and a prolonged diet of cricket talk', and motivating himself with admiring glances at his durable skipper, Mike Procter: 'God, if he can keep going, so can I.' Brain's voice was tinged with severity: he complained that Derek Randall 'plays to the gallery too much', and that David Gower 'makes my blood boil'. But it was the passing of contemporaries that he noticed. There was Mike Harris at Notts: 'The game looks much harder for him now and I hope to goodness I get out of it before anyone says the same about me.' There was Basil D'Oliveira at Worcester: 'Dear old Bas just couldn't accept that the years were catching up on him ... I shan't hang around long enough for my fellow pros to feel sorry for me.' There was his own era: 'I didn't see one batsman walk in the 1980 season. They stand there, look at the bat if it's LBW, and take an eternity to drag themselves away from the crease, all the while looking back at the umpire.' *Another Day, Another Match* was seasoned with the sensation that there would soon be neither.

In mid-career, Roebuck saw the grind differently. *It Never Rains* was like the story of a troubled romance, an *odi et amo* with cricket as the most capricious of partners: 'Why was the game so easy yesterday? Why is it so impossible today? ... It's a cussed game. It can show you glimpses of beauty in a stroke perfectly played, perhaps, and then it throws you back into the trough of mediocrity.' It was a brave and honest book, for it candidly revealed the writer's periods of despondency: 'For some reason I seem unable to last from April to September without a bout of morose self-examination.' On his most morose day, indeed, Roebuck found himself too melancholy to write at all.

The same fate befell Fowler in *Fox on the Run*, although the nadir of his fortunes was three days of rain at the Second XI match involving Lancashire and Surrey in August 1985, at the end of which he asked simply: 'What was I doing in Banstead?' A fair question, because Fowler had made a Test double-century six months earlier in India. The diary showed, though, that even then he was finding the going tough: 'I try to keep my feelings repressed, which is the way to cope through tours anyway. I never allow myself to look forward to anything, because that means you can never be disappointed ... It is a strange existence, strange to have to catch your emotions, bottle them and throw away the bottle, but it helps you to cope.' The unease manifested itself physically, for Fowler complained constantly of injuries: wrist, groin, back, ankle, skin and finally neck. 'I'm twenty-seven years old and becoming a physical wreck,' he mused. 'Sport seven days a week really messes you up.'

When he sustained a serious injury, Fowler found out how much. Deserted by form and fortune, the diary became both confidante and curse: 'I haven't really written much about the last three weeks of the season because I was so depressed; if I had done, it would have sounded suicidal.' Yet his attachment to cricket ultimately proved stronger than to others in his life. In his last entry, he described moving out of the matrimonial home to share with a team-mate: 'All I want to do now is concentrate on cricket. And that is what I am going to do.'

Statistically, Agnew had the best season of all four diarists, bowling himself to the brink of Test selection, and *Eight Days a Week* became the story of dealing with one's best being not quite enough. Most clearly of all his contemporaries, Agnew revealed the sacrifices, accommodations and compromises of the county circuit's habitués: 'In reality, players end up doing all kinds of dead-end jobs to see them through the winter, assuming they can get a job at all. Les Taylor has worked in a quarry in the past, but last winter he was on the dole. So was Peter Willey. I spent one winter driving a lorry … and almost killed myself when the steering failed on a steep bend … Another year I knocked windows together for a local manufacturing company. It was so boring.'

The county circuit has lately been revisited by Justin Langer in *From Outback to Outfield* (1999), Ed Smith in *On and Off the Field* (2004) and Mark Ramprakash in *Four More Weeks* (2005). But the cricketer's diary is another species propagated in England that has proliferated in Australia. Geoff Lawson's pioneering *Diary of the Ashes* (1989) was a low-key offering spiced with the writer's flair for terse, astringent judgments, like his observations of the initial press conference: '"Do you think you can win?" "Many people say this is the worst ever Australian team to come here. Do you agree?"

"Will the team be drinking a lot of XXXX on tour?" What sort of answers do they expect? "No, I don't think we can win. We've just come here for a holiday."' It is now notable mainly for having inspired Steve Waugh to take the plunge in *Ashes Diary* (1993) when Australia next toured: the basis of a series so successful that Ponting has now taken up the threads, while Glenn McGrath and Mark Waugh have also dabbled.

Perhaps because Australian hegemony was so prolonged and pronounced, or because of his own exhaustive conscientiousness, Waugh's diaries became less and less interesting as he became more and more famous. His earnestness could be inadvertently amusing – in his first book he described going to see a film which was 'a true story about a man who was abducted by aliens' – but the comic wasn't his natural vein. He tended to cautious, measured, largely uncontroversial calls, like one on his flash new team-mate of 1993: 'Dealing with the media was the biggest and most difficult adjustment I had to make when first selected in the Test team, at the age of 20. Hopefully, Warney is better prepared to handle it than I was.'

The question arises, indeed, why the outstanding Australian cricketer of his generation has not produced his own travelogue. Perhaps it demonstrates that Tallulah Bankhead's judgment of actresses – 'Only good girls keep diaries; the bad girls never have time' – applies equally to cricketers. But, considering *News of the World*'s vigilance, maybe a Warne diary isn't strictly necessary, either.

Cricinfo Magazine June 2006

MATTERS OF HISTORY

SIR ABE BAILEY

Cricket Imperialist

'So little done, so much to do.' The last words of Cecil Rhodes' crowded life remain a popular injunction to action and commitment; yet to few can they have meant so much as his protégé, Abe Bailey. Bailey's first action on Rhodes' death was to begin the acquisition of the plutocrat's Rhodesian ranch, Rhodesdale. He consummated his devotion by naming his first-born Cecil, which doesn't seem so remarkable until you realise she was his daughter; his second-born took Rhodes' second name, John.

Bailey's hankering to emulate his mentor was so public that *Vanity Fair*, limning him as a 'Man of the Day' almost a century ago, succinctly headlined the portrait 'Rhodes the Second': the subject did not demur. The profile was replete with his prophesies – mostly grandiose and unfulfilled, like forecasts that Rhodesia would 'become the great state in South Africa', and the Karoo 'the garden of South Africa'. Bailey's chief legacy, it turned out, was then in the making, even if it seemed at the time one of his least accomplishments: the Imperial Cricket Conference, forerunner to the International Cricket Council.

For Bailey belongs in that long tradition of wealthy cricket patrons, beginning with the Dukes of Cumberland and Richmond, extending from nobs such as Lord Sheffield and Baron Plunkett to serious businessmen such as Sir Arthur Sims and Sir Julien Cahn, with modern equivalents in Sir Ron Brierley and J. Paul Getty, who more than make up for deficiencies in playing by apparently bottomless moneybags and enthusiasm. The stern, shrewd, acquisitive

Bailey was kept busy by much besides his mining and pastoral empire: he played polo; he spent lavishly on bloodstock; he became a vigneron; he owned the *Rand Daily Mail*. But nothing obsessed him like cricket: he felt he owed it something, and perhaps he did.

Several versions exist of how Bailey, a merchant in Queenstown who had made and lost a fortune by the time he was twenty-one, was rescued by a cricket exploit after his business exploits turned sour. Walter Hammond, who, like Sir Pelham Warner, was on several occasions his guest in South Africa, relates in *Cricketers' School* (1948): 'He made some money, lost it, and got into rather low water. Then he heard of openings for adventurers in Australia, and bought a ticket to sail from Cape Town for the Southern Continent. That ticket took the very last of his money. Just before his ship was due to leave, Bailey agreed to play in a cricket match in Cape Town. He was the best bat in the side and knocked up a sparkling 114. An onlooker who had won a number of side bets on the result of the match was so delighted that he went round to the team's dressing room and presented young Bailey with a cheque for 100 pounds as a reward for pulling the match out of the fire. A hundred pounds was power to Abe Bailey and he immediately cancelled his passage to Australia, invested his 100 pounds in some land on the Rand, sold the land shortly afterwards at a big profit, and began again to amass that elusive fortune. This time he succeeded … Sir Abe Bailey never forgot that amazing turn of fortune, whereby a century scored in a chance match in Cape Town set his feet on the royal road to millionairedom.'

Once his own modest playing days were ended, Bailey set himself to repaying the debt many times over. While watching the English XI under Major Warton demolish a Johannesburg XXII in January 1889, Bailey commented tersely to Bernard Tancred, the best South African batsman of the era: 'We must set ourselves to beat the Englishmen on equal terms.' That they did, and little over fifteen years later, was due in no small part to Bailey's deep-pocketed benefaction of Transvaal cricket, from recruiting George Lohmann as coach to his employment as personal secretary of Springbok captain Frank

Mitchell. It was only Bailey's bankroll, for instance, that lured Australia to South Africa in October 1902; likewise was the national team's successful visit to England eighteen months later underwritten, at considerable expense, by a Bailey guarantee.

These indulgences were shoehorned into a life devoted to commerce, where he became the most daring of mining speculators, and nationalism, where he was a politician of dubious instincts. As captain of the first touring team that Bailey financed, for instance, Lord Hawke arrived in Johannesburg in January 1896 to be told: 'Mr Bailey is not here. He is in jail.' As indeed he was, having – like the other members of the Reform Committee – been taken into custody for their succour of the Jameson Raid.

Bailey's work involved some improbable expenditures, for he was famed for thrift to the point of meanness. 'It can be truly said that there never was a Christian who deserved to be an Israelite more than the Queenstown lad,' said rival speculator Louis Cohen, 'whose snub nose should have been a hooked one of alarming proportions'.

It also entailed some improbable commitments, such as Bailey's advocacy of the inclusion of the Coloured fast bowler Krom Hendriks for South Africa's first tour of England, and his promotion of the Coloured all-rounder Buck Llewellyn as coach at the Wanderers Club. These stances were particularly unlikely, given that Bailey was otherwise the basest of racists, crudely derogatory of blacks ('I am for the white race being on top of the black'), Indians and Chinese ('The Asiatics were the white ants of South Africa, destroying the foundations of our institutions and the roots of the livelihood of the white race'). But the promotion of South African cricket was, for Bailey, a cause with its own rules and parameters, and the excuse for a gaiety rather absent from the rest of his life. 'He would always discuss cricket with the most delightful glee,' recalled Hammond of his quondam host, 'and with almost professional knowledge. I believe he studied reports of every ball that was bowled and every stroke that was made in Tests in which South Africa was involved, and he had an amazing memory.'

The impetus for the ICC was South Africa's unexpected 4–1 home triumph against the MCC just over a century ago, master-minded by its googly quartet – two of whom, Reggie Schwarz and Ernie Vogler, were actually on Bailey's personal payroll. Bailey seized on the breakthrough to begin agitating for a tri-cornered summer of cricket in England involving the hosts, Australia and South Africa. When Australia proved disinclined to share the lime-light and the gate, he urged the South African Cricket Association's meeting of March 1908 to 'press for the creation of the Imperial Board of Control as soon as possible': the association's English envoy, Ted Wynyard, also employed at Bailey's expense, was duly instructed 'to urge the formation' of an Imperial Board 'by all means within his power'. And when it finally met for the first time, on 15 June 1909, with a further meeting on 20 July 1909, the upshot was a long-term commitment to a Triangular Tournament three years hence.

In the interim, time did not deal kindly with the effective team South Africa had assembled. Routed 1–4 in Australia in 1910–11, they were a fading force by the time 1912 rolled around. Bailey con-tributed a gushy chapter to the lavish panorama *Imperial Cricket* (1912) that Plum Warner edited to mark the tournament, but oth-erwise kept his own counsel as South Africa lost five of its six Tests in a dank summer barely worth the name. The Australian Board of Control indulged in some gratuitous I-told-you-so-ing in its annual report: 'The Triangular scheme proved, as was anticipated, a failure, and as it cannot possibly be carried out in Australia or Africa, will doubtless not be heard of again for many years to come'. But if triangular cricket was off the agenda until rediscov-ered by another plutocrat of less philanthropic bent, Kerry Packer, the ICC endured, even if it is fair to say that it never again made the mistake of being too far ahead of its time.

From 1912, Bailey was increasingly resident in England, either at his rural seat in Surrey, or a city mansion in Bryanston Avenue, where Winston Churchill was a frequent visitor: one of Bailey's sons later married one of Churchill's daughters. He was newly a

KCMG, and recently remarried, almost a decade after the death of his first wife, to Mary Westerna, the twenty-year-old daughter of the notorious Anglo-Irish rake Baron Rossmore. Their union yielded five children, although Sir Abe was a distant, distracted husband, and Lady Bailey eventually took secret flying lessons in order to 'get away from prams'. In March 1928 she informed Sir Abe that 'I have felt the need for a change of scene and interest lately', and promptly flew solo from Croydon to Cape Town, then back. When her record for the journey was broken, she took it back, her husband indulging her with generosity equal to that he showed toward South African cricket – albeit with somewhat greater bemusement. By the 1930s, Lady Bailey's fame probably eclipsed her husband's: she was an aviatrix to rank with Amy Johnson, Louise Thaden and Lorres Bonny.

At Sir Abe's death in August 1940, aged 75, the world was very different from that in his mentor's day; a newly formed political force, the Herenigde National Party, would within twenty years have severed South Africa's imperial ties altogether. The old man had not, in fact, become Rhodes the Second. Though rich beyond the dreams of avarice, he had left no mark on politics, little on society, little on the culture. Bailey's own last words might well have been: 'So much done, so little to do.' His sixth child and third son, James Richard Abe, born in October 1919, would be more relevant to South Africa's future, returning from a career as a wartime pilot to the scarcely less hazardous role of founding proprietor of *Drum*, the first South African magazine of significance to give a voice to black journalists. At least in cricket, though, Sir Abe Bailey's ambitions had fructified: from *this* little, much more would flow.

Cricinfo September 2006

THE ASHES

A Most Peculiar Grail

The contest for the Ashes, cindery symbol of Anglo–Australian cricket supremacy, doesn't appear to have much to recommend it. It does not determine cricket's world champion. It is not played for cricket's largest purse, and no trophy changes hands. It is not even cricket's oldest international rivalry: that honour belongs to the United States and Canada, whose annual matches date back to 1844. Yet, after 116 years, the Ashes remains cricket's most prestigious brand name, to Australia's captain Mark Taylor 'the most glittering prize in world cricket'. As Australian leg-spinning cynosure Shane Warne puts it: 'I still think it's the best series to be involved in. There's still something a bit special.'

In England, which hasn't held the Ashes for almost a decade, fans high and low fantasise about their recovery. The British broadcaster Lord Bragg wrote recently of dozing off at the screening of an Ingmar Bergman film after a particularly galling Test defeat. Prodded awake, he interrupted Liv Ullmann's monologue with a startled 'Bloody Australians!' In Australia, even the most vocal nationalist is mute before the Ashes' apolitical, monocultural might.

The origins of this peculiar totem are humble: part journalistic hyperbole, part colonial high spirits. Responsible for the former was Reginald Shirley Watkinshaw, AKA Brooks, a dissolute Fleet Streeter destined to die young from what a contemporary described as 'the canker of self-indulgence and irresponsibility'. In August 1882, when the fifth Anglo–Australian Test ended in a breathless

7-run victory for the visitors, the twenty-seven-year-old secured immortality of a sort by inserting a death notice in London's *Sporting Times* 'in affectionate memory of English cricket', with the addendum: 'The body will be cremated and the ashes taken to Australia.' The high spirits were supplied some months later in Australia by a twenty-three-year-old aristocrat, Ivo Walter Francis Bligh, who had come as captain of an English touring XI. Bligh was a mediocre cricketer, and his performances in the series would be retarded still further by injuries sustained in a shipboard tug-of-war en route. On arriving in Adelaide, he referred jestingly to his objective as the 'recovery of the ashes'. The notion so captivated some Melbourne society belles that they subsequently awarded Bligh a dark red pottery urn and velvet bag containing something sooty, which since 1927 has remained in the custody of the Marylebone Cricket Club at Lord's.

Quaint, really. Yet even in their inception as an incentive for the gentleman's game, the Ashes began a lingering association with controversy. Watkinshaw's whimsicality was still two days away when England's W.G. Grace cunningly ran out Australian Sammy Jones as he strayed from his crease to examine a mid-pitch divot. Team-mate Tom Horan expressed the visitors' indignation: 'I do not think it redounds much to any man's credit to endeavour to win a match by resorting to what might not inaptly be called sharp practice.' Six months later, England's Richard Barlow accused Australia's Fred Spofforth of 'unlawfully putting spikes in his boots to cut up the turf' during the Sydney Test. According to the *Sydney Sportsman*, Spofforth retaliated with 'a blow which knocked Barlow over the seat'.

A return to the Spofforth school of dispute resolution seemed in prospect fifty years later when Douglas Jardine's Englishmen took the Ashes from Bill Woodfull's Australians in the so-called Bodyline series. England's Harold Larwood and Bill Voce so inflamed Australian sentiment with their life-threatening speed on a leg-stump line that, had World War II begun six years earlier, Anzacs might have marched off demanding Jardine's trial for war crimes. For many cricket historians, Woodfull's icy words to England manager Pelham Warner at Adelaide are as familiar as the Gettysburg address to American patriots: 'There are two teams out there. One is trying to play cricket, the other is not. The game is too good to be spoiled. It is time some people got out of it.'

The Ashes' thrall is mysterious. It can't be anything to do with the physical trophy, a striking case of less being more: the urn is not quite 11 centimetres tall and labelled with a sorry specimen of Victorian doggerel. It's not even clear of what its sacred soot is composed: ball, bail, stump or firewood. The historian Bill Mandle has proposed that cricket took root in Australia in the late nineteenth century because it was the only area in which the colonials could match themselves against the mother country – and thus dispel fears of white degeneracy in 'a country of blackfellows'. Advocates of Federation, in their campaign to unite the colonies politically, liked to remind them of their success in combining at cricket. And that Australia could achieve cricket supremacy when so much of its culture was derived and diluted lent the fledgling nation cachet throughout the first half of the twentieth century. As the novelist and republican gadfly Thomas Keneally has written, 'Cricket was the great way out of Australian cultural ignominy. No Australian had written *Paradise Lost*, but Bradman had made 100 before lunch at Lord's.' Even more puzzling is why this sporting *folie a deux* retains its power now that Australian culture has matured, English cricket has ceased to be a benchmark, and tradition is so often seen as an impediment to progress. Perhaps devotees, in an age when sport is rarely afforded the luxury of being just sport, enjoy the permissible anachronism of a contest for the sake of contest. One can't quite tell why it matters. It just does.

Time Asia November 1998

BODYLINE

Imperfect Tense

In the chronicles of cricket, England's 1932–33 tour of Australia is regarded in ways not dissimilar to the death of Marilyn Monroe. The diplomatic backdrop against which the 'Bodyline' Tests unfolded mean it will always reek to some of cover-up and conspiracy. The 1983 television series, for instance, reconstructed English captain Douglas Jardine as a tight-lipped terrorist on a mission to administer an imperial rejoinder to those upstart cricketing colonials. At least this was actually more believable than the vision of his fast bowler Harold Larwood delivering a variant of leg-spin, which should have carried an Australian Cricket Board warning not to try this at home.

Fresh light on DJ, however, is as sought-after as new material concerning MM. Just as another figure always seems to be bobbing up having spoken to the actress "just before" her semisuihomicide (and after it, for that matter), an unpublished letter from the cricketer to the Inland Revenue is worth at least a feature article. And if you sold Jardine as much as a jar of linseed oil on the 1932–33 tour, start thinking about the lecture circuit.

Gilbert Mant was a journalist with the Reuters Wire Service who lucked onto the trip and ended up providing English newspapers with a fair proportion of their daily coverage of antipodean events in the next six months. He recalls being rationed a total 25,000 words but, as the story ran and ran, knocking out about 100,000.

Review of *Cuckoo in the Bodyline Nest* by Gilbert Mant (Kangaroo Press)

Eventually he was in quite good company: according to *Cricket and Empire* (1983) by Brian Stoddart and Ric Sissons, the press party at the Adelaide Test match alone generated a word aggregate of 140,000. Very few of Mant's words, however, involved direct quotes from Jardine. In fact, a frosty 'I see' was the extent of communication from England's captain. Mant communed with the team and could subscribe only to the Jardine judgment he once heard from batsman Maurice Leyland: 'He's a queer 'un.'

That doesn't necessarily ruin his memoir, *Cuckoo in the Bodyline Nest*. I'll be glad enough at ninety to write my name, let alone knock out over 150 pages of reminiscences on events six decades past. There's just about enough fresh anecdote here to keep a reader turning the pages, and Jardine – even silent – is a charismatic character. Mant paints one exquisite portrait of the cricketer during a shipboard concert by the actress Violet Vanburgh, sitting inscrutably in the centre of a saloon with his aquiline nose in a book.

Brief glimpses of other heroes also amuse and divert. The Rechabite spinner Hedley Verity has to secrete his ale when the Adelaide chapter of his abstinence league bail him up in a hotel bar. The incomparable Walter Hammond displays a Richard Nixon-like mastery of expletive when Mant asks him whether he was bowled by a full toss during the Adelaide Test. But in the end, it's not quite enough. There's a fair load of ballast in *Cuckoo* to stabilise it at slim hardback scale. Most of the Jardiniana comes from Chris Douglas's 1984 biography, Larwood's ghosted memoirs are heavily quoted, and you get hoary helpings of barrackers' jibes and the very familiar full texts of the famous cables between the relative administrative boards. There's even a five-page history of the Reuters service, and an eight-page Mant rant at Kerry Packer.

So when Mant says he was 'effectively muzzled as a journalist' when Reuters' boss, in 1933, demurred at his post-tour suggestion that he write a book on the matches, perhaps it was merely friendly advice. The course history has followed since means that

Cuckoo is probably more marketable today than it was sixty years ago. In the meantime it awaits some inspired scholar to reveal the extraordinary link between Douglas Jardine and Marilyn Monroe. Can't say too much.

Modern Times December 1992

THE CENTENARY OF LARWOOD

The Anti-Bradman

In the years after he settled in Sydney, the humble Kingsford home of Harold Larwood became a place of pilgrimage for English cricketers, especially those mandated by nature to bowl fast. They usually came away twice marvelling: at the patch of English patriotism to be found just 5 kilometres from the Sydney Cricket Ground, and at the seemingly frail figure who cultivated it. Had this diminutive, bespectacled pensioner *really* been the terror of all Australia?

Nor was this merely a matter of age. When picked for England, Larwood stood just 5 feet, 7 inches tall and weighed less than 11 stone, and seemed as likely to be source of controversy as Michael Ramsey, born the same day and destined to become Archbishop of Canterbury. One of Larwood's most vivid memories from the Bodyline tour of 1932–33 was overhearing a little girl quizzing her mother: 'Why mummy, he doesn't *look* like a murderer ...' Yet, as few in cricket cannot know, Larwood achieved a notoriety as Australia's Least Wanted usually confined to criminals; he competed for headlines with the likes of the Lindbergh kidnapper, Bruno Hauptmann, and the mobster Al Capone.

Reviewing his legend a century after his birth, one obtains a slightly different feeling, from a sense of cricket's abiding search for a statistical and aesthetic equilibrium between bat and ball. In his autobiography, *The Larwood Story* (1965), ghosted by Kevin Perkins, the Englishman pleads guilty to a degree of batsman-slaughter, but presents himself as acting in legitimate self-defence: 'They said I was a killer with the ball without taking into account that Bradman with the bat was the greatest killer of all.' Indeed, had Larwood not existed, it might have been necessary to invent him.

Larwood was born on 14 November 1904 in Nuncargate, a Midlands village that served a colliery at Annesley in the nearby Leen Valley. Although his origins have commonly been depicted as underprivileged, the mine was actually an enduring and not ungenerous employer, lasting until January 2000. Larwood's parents owned their own home, and his teetotal Methodist father, Robert, captained the colliery's cricket team, which at various stages contained Test-cricketers-to-be Bill Voce, Dodge Whysall, Joe Hardstaff and Sam Staples; at fourteen, Harold went down the mine as a pit-pony boy, and took to cricket with a will. The game, he would explain, soon became his 'reason for living'.

In June 1922, Larwood saw his first game of county cricket, heading to Trent Bridge for the day so that he might bask in the glory of his idol, Jack Hobbs. Instead, Hobbs was dismissed first ball by local boy Fred Barratt, who not only hailed from Nuncargate but had worked the same coal seams; at once, the seventeen-year-old Larwood saw a future teeming with possibilities. A year later, he left the pit behind when he trialled successfully for Nottinghamshire.

Tiny, earnest, polite, etiolated from his years underground, running in an improbable distance, he was nonetheless recognised at once as a pace-bowling prospect, at a time when they did not abound. On one occasion, Larwood greeted the Leicestershire tailender Hayden Smith with a searing lifter, followed by a short one that looped from the edge and was taken on the bounce in the gully. Seeing Smith retreat, fielders assured him that the ball had not carried. 'Oh yes it bloody well did,' replied Smith, continuing on his way.

Curiously, the first time they met, his future captain, Douglas Jardine, was well positioned to take Larwood's measure. It was at Folkestone in August 1926, where they were representing an England XI against the Australians; Jardine, standing in for 'Tiger' Smith, was keeping. Larwood took 7–95, including the wicket of top-scorer Warren Bardsley with a delivery knocking the bat from his hands, which hit the stumps as the ball lodged in Jardine's gloves. Though the umpire denied Jardine a catch by ruling the dismissal hit-wicket, the encounter impressed the Surrey amateur forcibly.

For a time, this was as close as the pair became. Larwood would tour Australia with Jardine a little over two years later, but both were men who observed the proprieties where player and gentleman were concerned. On the evening, in August 1932, of their famous dinner in the Piccadilly Grill Rooms with Larwood's fast-bowling pitmate, Bill Voce, and their Nottinghamshire skipper, Arthur Carr, the conversation was at first stilted and strained, before finding the common obsession of Bradman.

Though they 'didn't contribute much' as Jardine revealed his theory that Australians in general and Bradman in particular were vulnerable to pace bowling concentrated at leg stump, Larwood and Voce were immediately impressed with the thinking. Under Carr's captaincy, they had been experimenting with such methods all season, claiming almost 250 cheap wickets between them. Bradman's telephone-number scores, meanwhile, were the talk of cricket, and Larwood was one of many bowlers who'd found his line permanently crossed. Among Bradman's *Wisden*-busting 974 runs in the 1930 Ashes series, 137 had been from Larwood, pilfered from only 147 deliveries.

Larwood and Voce are sometimes depicted as clockwork toys wound by the English establishment, bowling the leg-stump line that Jardine demanded of them like obedient professional automata. This probably derives from Larwood's first published remarks on Bodyline, in the *Daily Express* in July 1933, to the effect that 'in bowling as I did I was merely carrying out the prearranged plan'. This impression is erroneous. Larwood better explained the dynamic of relationship, and his loyalty to Jardine, to Perkins: 'I wouldn't say I was told to bowl leg-theory. I was asked to do it and I complied. In any case, I was convinced that I wouldn't get many wickets any other way.' The motive was, in large part, redress: 'I had a score to settle with him [Bradman]. He had got on top of me. As a professional, any scheme that would keep him in check appealed to me a great deal.' Larwood was no deferential dupe. David Frith reports in *Bodyline Autopsy* (2002) that his favourite tune was Frank Sinatra's 'My Way': whenever he heard it, he would 'always smile and nod knowingly'.

The other reason why it is wrong to underestimate Larwood's agency is that leg-theory was an attack designed with his gifts in mind as much as Bradman's. Larwood seldom obtained swing: the handmade balls of the period had a small seam, and in Australia their poor-quality lacquer wore away within overs. His chief asset, after speed, was accuracy, and his most dangerous delivery a back-break; he seldom had batsmen caught in the slips cordon even bowling an orthodox line. George Hele's close-up appreciation in *Bodyline Umpire* (1974) is worth citing: 'Harold Larwood was not only the fastest bowler I have watched. He also had the most beautiful action. While he was running in behind me I never heard him. He glided towards the wickets until the last three yards. Australian fast bowlers dragged their right or left toes as they gathered themselves into the delivery stride; Larwood dragged his entire right foot and at right angles to his course. He placed a tremendous strain upon that foot and his ankle. I have not seen a bowler gain greater impetus from his left and guiding arm. From here came his exceptional speed and exceptional accuracy. There was nothing loose, untidy or wasted about Larwood's action. It was a copybook, classic and utterly direct.'

Too direct for Australians prone to walking in front of their stumps but leery of the hook – and too hot to hold. 'He's too fast for me,' confessed Alan Kippax after his first brush with Larwood: sentiments that would be echoed by many others before tour's end. Bradman's scheme of withdrawing to leg and flailing toward the depopulated off bespoke desperation rather than daring. When he hit what was his first first-class six at Adelaide, Bradman explained it succinctly: 'Oh, I wanted to hit one bowler [Verity] before the other [Larwood] hit me.'

It was Bradman who continued his career, of course, rather than Larwood, whose retirement was rudely hastened in order to soften Bodyline's bruises on Anglo–Australian relations, and whose future so unexpectedly lay Down Under. But Larwood had helped reduce Bradman's Test average from its high-water mark of 112.9 to 99.7, which is where it pretty much stayed, apart from a brief post-war reflation. And in revealing Bradman's mortality and fallibility, Larwood not only gave heart to other bowlers, but provided the nemesis necessary to the hubris of his story. The narrative of Sir Donald Bradman's career is still among cricket's most inspiring, yet it would not be quite so compelling without featuring, at some stage, a kind of anti-Bradman: the role Larwood fulfilled.

Had there been no Larwood to cut his output down to size, to choose but one example, Bradman would never have needed 4 runs to secure his 100 average at the Oval in August 1948, and would never have failed to achieve it in such astonishing circumstances. Larwood, then, by introducing to the Bradman legend a hint of the evitable, might be considered the personification of cricketing uncertainty.

Wisden Asia November 2004

BOYCOTT AND AUSTRALIA
Abominable Slow Man

Australians and Yorkshiremen are meant to have a strange affinity, both calling a spade a bloody shovel, equally contemptuous of traditional hoity-toity, plumb-in-the-mouth Pomminess. Hutton, Leyland, Trueman, Illingworth: bonny fighters all, and straight talkers, too. Where Geoff Boycott was concerned, however, Australians made an exception. Granted, he could play a bit. But about his version of that particular Northern obduracy, there seemed to lurk personal rather than communal ambition. Hell, let's call that shovel by its name: Boycott was a selfish prick. Even in his finest hour, his return to the colours amid England's 1977 Ashes win, Boycott limelighted unashamedly, being seen so frequently with his arms aloft that he should almost have glued on his bat labels upside down.

In great sportsmen, of course, often lurks a streak of selfishness. It is a dimension of that self-mastery they today call 'focus'. And Boycott the batsman was nothing if not focused. Over two months I spent following county cricket in 1985, mainly in the North, I watched him for what seemed like days. His batting, rationalised and regimented to the brink of automation, had by then a kind of austere beauty. I recall with particular vividness his last innings against Australia: an unbeaten 52 in a rain-ruined game for Yorkshire. I arrived early to find Boycott finishing a lap of Headingley, in his whites, wearing his cap. He then drafted two young seamers to bowl to him, not in the nets, but on an old pitch on the square. He regularly left wide deliveries which, because he was in the open, he had then to chase and retrieve. Not the slightest effort did he expend sticking his bat out to stop them: one wouldn't perpetrate such a solecism in a match, so why do it when training?

As he came out to bat, he withdrew a handkerchief from his pocket, and dangled it between thumb and forefinger to ascertain the wind direction. One half imagined that, like Arthur Shrewsbury, he had already ordered his seltzers for the next two drinks breaks; certainly, he batted like a man who had already played the innings in his mind. It was a cold, still, quiet day, with so little crowd noise that one could hear the Australians chivvying and gingering one another in the field: 'C'mon digger!'; 'Let's get up 'im, Billy!' But they were like bursts of disapproved noise in a library, in which Boycott went on peacefully swotting.

Yorkshire was then a weak side, captained by David Bairstow. Boycott seemed to enjoy the serenity of mediocre surroundings, carrying on at his own pace, almost in his own game. One afternoon at Harrogate's picturesque ground, for example, Yorkshire were set a tempting target. Bairstow seemed to hanker to chase it. I say 'seemed' because as progressively wilder strokes were essayed at one end, Boycott dawdled insouciantly at the other. Bairstow came out, thrashed around briefly, and was bowled, strutting off fretfully. Boycott proceeded to a tranquil unbeaten 64 in the eventual draw.

Australian objections to Boycott, though, did not really originate in his style; after all, Australians esteemed Ken Barrington, who shares with Boycott the ignominy of being dropped from a Test for slow scoring. Like his countrymen, if not perhaps his Yorkshire countymen, we were baffled by his thirty-month sulk in the 1970s, which meant, among other things, that he avoided Lillee and Thomson in harness. Boycott's disgruntlement arose from the spectacle of England being led by a Welshmen (Tony Lewis), Scot (Mike Denness) and South African (Tony Greig), but that cut no ice here. Australians can actually condone selfishness – providing your country enjoys the benefit of it.

Alpha July 2005

APPEALING

Fair Cheating All Round?

Growing up in Melbourne, Shane Warne's first cricket aspiration was famously to emulate his hero, Dennis Lillee. And if it turned out he lacked the speed, part of Lillee's game he certainly mastered: the appeal. The action photograph that Warne chose for the cover of his autobiography is not of himself flicking out a flipper or speculating about a slider: he is instead red-faced and roaring, bent backwards by the effort of demanding justice from an unseen and unfortunate umpire. It reveals a few too many chins to be a flattering portrait, but it's a faithful rendering nevertheless. Like his bowling, Warne's appealing has multiple dimensions, being enquiry, assertion, celebration, exhibition, denunciation and defiance all at once – and sometimes, also, an annoyance.

The appeal is cricket's elephant in the dressing room: a feature that is a huge part of the game's ritual, yet is routinely overlooked. Just occasionally, though, someone gets a glimpse of a trunk or an ear. So it has been this summer. After defeat in Melbourne, South Africa's coach Mickey Arthur described Ricky Ponting's Australians as 'masters' of putting pressure on umpires with their 'histrionics', and singled out Warne as first among equals. ICC match referee Chris Broad agreed that the Australians were pushing the boundaries of fair play, and spoke to both Warne and coach John Buchanan during the game.

Earlier generations saw it even more clearly, former umpire Lou Rowan branding Ponting 'a smart arse and a disaster as leader', and the conduct of his team 'an insult to former players and people associated with the game'. Remonstration with umpires was a particular vexation: 'I have got no problem with the bowlers especially wanting to have a chat with the umpire and ask about certain decisions that have been made. But let's just make it one question and one answer, and then get on with it … The ever-present and accepted practice of sledging, obscenities, excessive appealing, the questioning of umpires and the accompanying dissent leaves our Australian team quite correctly dubbed "the ugly Australians".'

Even Ponting's and Warne's first Australian coach, Bob Simpson, piled in, using his column in India's *Sports Star* to air a litany of complaints: 'While present-day cricketers promote the need for the spirit of cricket to be adhered to, many of them do not follow in action this norm, which they publicly endorse in words. This not only includes sledging but excessive appealing, disrespecting the umpiring decisions and using their well-paid, generally ghost-written columns to bait opposition teams and players. Public criticism of the opposition now seems to be part of the team tactics. All this reminds me of the behaviour of small children and the bravado they use to disguise their own fallibilities.'

Not surprisingly, Ponting was having none of that, lashing out at 'they': that indistinct group of antique jeremiahs whom Australian players loathe. 'It's another little niggly thing they are trying to have a go at us with,' he complained. 'We are out there appealing every time we think something is out. We don't think there's anything wrong and we don't think there's been any over-appealing in this game.' Justin Langer even channelled the Lillee spirit himself: 'It's indicative of his [Warne's] passion for the game. I remember as a kid watching Dennis Lillee appeal. It was one of the great sights of cricket. I used to run around as a ten-year-old, bowl and then appeal like Lillee. He [Warne] thinks it's out and he gives it a big appeal. To me that's just part of the game, part of the great theatre of the great Shane Warne.'

*

Historical antecedents, of course, are not legitimation in and of themselves. What would Langer think if an English cricketer put the bails back on the stumps after being bowled and refused to leave the crease because it was 'part of the great theatre of the great W.G. Grace'? But he is right to see appealing as embedded in the game – more deeply than is sometimes imagined. Appealing was first a custom, sometimes with quaint variations. When their XIs met in 1727, Charles Lennox, Duke of Richmond, and Alan Brodrick, heir to Viscount Middleton, made appealing illegal except for themselves. 'There shall be one umpire of each side,' stipulate the terms of the game, 'and that if any of the Gamesters shall speak or give their Opinion on any Point of the Game, they are to be turned out, and voided in the Match; this not extend to the Duke of Richmond and Mr Brodrick.' After all, rank must have its privileges.

The principle that a batsman cannot be given out except on appeal was then laid out in cricket's oldest existing set of laws, in 1744. No one seems clear why, but one possibility is that it is a precaution about giving umpires too much power: a vestige of the original habit of teams to appoint an umpire each. Comic interludes involving umpiring bias were a feature of the era, perhaps the best example being a match at Loughborough in 1781 where a Nottingham umpire gave a Nottingham man in as the Leicester umpire gave him out.

The appeal was preserved amid the great reforms of cricket in the first half of the nineteenth century that turned it into a symbol of restraint and rectitude, even though it was an invitation to offences against both. It is, to be sure, a strange archaism. 'Incidentally, why do we have appeals in cricket at all?' asked former Australian captain Bill Woodfull in his instructional text *Cricket* (1936). 'Such appeals are not found necessary in any other sporting activity, and I should like to see a trial given to the game without appeals of any sort.' The abiding tension was nicely expressed in a letter to London's *Daily Telegraph* in August 1959. Cricket, said the correspondent, was a gentleman's game that prided itself on observation of proprieties: '[So] why is it, then, that this game is the only one in which exists the most hair-raising, grass-withering yell that can be produced by the human voice?'

The writer's purpose was to propose that appeals should only be made by keeper and bowler 'in gentlemanly and gracious tones'. And for a time, cricketers tried to impose their own checks and balances. 'Howzat?' seems to have become the standard catch-all enquiry about 180 years ago: the earliest written reference is in *New Sporting Magazine* in 1833 ('Well thrown by Huddleston!' – 'How's that?' – 'Run out!'). Even in Australia, players tried to behave. In a match on Sydney's Domain in January 1857, for example, William Gilbert Rees of New South Wales was given not out after an appeal for a catch at the wicket by Victoria's George Marshall. He was then asked 'as a gentleman' if had touched it, confirmed that he had and was promptly given out. Rees' cousin W.G. Grace would not have made the same mistake.

Lillywhite's Cricketers' Guide insisted on a 'morality of appeal', and counselled: 'Do not ask the umpire unless you think the batsman is out; it is not cricket to keep asking the umpire questions.' The umpire himself had to stand apart. An appreciation by 'Quid' (R.A. Fitzgerald) in *Jerks from Short Leg* (1866) specified: 'An umpire should be a man – they are, for the most part, old women; and he should have a thorough initiation into the laws of the game … He should avoid conversation with the field, should be above all suspicion of bias, and free from all odours of the tavern.'

Such efforts, however, were no match for human nature. There is no limit on appealing and thus no disincentive to doing so; the temptation will always be to go up for anything. Concerted appealing in which every fielder joined, whether out of excitement or for effect, seems to have been a feature of the game since the 1880s. It encountered, of course, fierce denunciation. In his classic primer *The Game of Cricket* (1887), Frederick Gale scorned what he called 'snapping' at umpires: 'There is only one word, and a nasty one. This practice is cowardly and un-English … It is bad enough when wicketkeeper or bowler does it … but when the outfield take up the cry in chorus it is shabby work. We want better breeding very often in the cricket-field. Duelling was a cruel custom, but there was more chivalry about it than in cricket conducted this way.' But if you could not be given what you did not ask for, why die wondering?

Because it was a time in which there was great respect for rank and authority generally, however, the custom did not lead to anarchy. It may even have improved officiation. In her history of umpiring, *The Men in White Coats* (1987), Teresa McLean conjectures: 'Concerted team appealing meant that a number of first-class umpires developed thick skins which stood them in good stead when it came to pronouncing unpopular decisions.' 'Not out, young 'un,' was umpire Bob Thoms' well-known retort. 'And I'm not deaf either.' His colleague Bill Reeves had a range of responses: 'You've got more appeals than Dr Barnardo'; 'Have you had bird-seed for breakfast? You seem in good song'; 'Hit the wicket? It wouldn't have hit the sightscreen.'

The chief threat to umpiring standards in England for many years, in fact, was not the bullying appeal; rather, it was the bullying amateur. Australians touring England looked askance at decisions in which umpires shrank from giving out the star gentlemen cricketers of the era, like Grace, F.S. Jackson and C.B. Fry. Joe Darling recalled a game at Scarborough when Jackson was run out by yards from cover: 'The umpire, who was a former player, gave Jackson not out. This was bad enough, but what disgusted us was that Jackson turned to the umpire, who was standing at square leg, and told him it was a good decision. In other words, Jackson told him he approved of him giving not out when everybody on the ground, spectators and all, knew that he was clearly run-out.' Umpires felt a particular dread for giving out captains. Essex's Johnny Douglas once skited that the county captaincy was worth 200 runs and 30 wickets a season to him. 'I do wish he would keep his legs out of the way,' an umpire who had just given a popular county captain out told Worcestershire's Fred Root. 'That is the sixth time I have had to give him out LBW in consecutive innings.'

*

Over time, appealing has come to be seen as part of the game's drama, and a form of individual expression. Englishman George Duckworth would play with lozenges in his pocket, after an early experience where the persistence of his appealing reduced his voice to a squeak. Australian wicketkeeper Bert Oldfield, by contrast, was known for his polite enquiries: Neville Cardus said that his appeals to the square leg umpire were 'almost a request for information', issued 'as though addressing him reluctantly but on a strict point of order'.

Australians in general were known for razor-edged appeals: 'Owizee?!' In his autobiography, *The Gloves are Off* (1960), Godfrey Evans recalled the general antipodean attitude as expressed by its glass of fashion: 'I remember once when Don Bradman, fielding at cover point, saw the ball hit Denis [Compton] on the pad and up he went with his "HOWZAT" and he was told "NOT OUT". Denis, never loath to express a view, said to him, "Don, how could you possibly see from out there?" and Don answered, "I couldn't ... but it might have been out, mightn't it? That's for umpires to decide, not me!"'

Early West Indian teams, meanwhile, were noted for their simple, deep, euphonious enquiry of 'How?' In county cricket, varieties abounded. Tom Goddard of Gloucestershire was famous for the West Country burr of his 'How wuz 'er?' and for its persistence: seventy years ago, he appealed for LBW five times in 9 deliveries against Kent's Ian Akers-Douglas. Alec Skelding of Leicestershire once promised a nervous young Notts colt a run to get off a pair, then almost forgot himself when he got a nick to his first ball in the second innings. 'How's ...' began Skelding, before correcting himself, 'yer father?' The umpire smiled. 'Quite all right, thanks.'

Fervent and unrestrained appealing has also been recognised as increasing the potential that umpires will err under pressure. From time to time, efforts have been made to ease the umpire's burden. Sometimes this has been of players' volition: when England toured India in 1972–73, captains Tony Lewis and Ajit Wadekar agreed that their teams would reduce the clamour and constancy of their appealing for bat-pad chances. Usually it has been administrators. In 1982 it was England's Cricketers' Association announcing that it was 'totally against any action or gesture which puts unnecessary pressure on umpires' and urging members to 'make every effort to maintain the traditional standards and status of the game'. In 1993 it was England's Test and County Cricket Board officially condemning 'orchestrated and animated appealing by whole teams and open questioning of umpires' decisions'.

So what has changed, so that sixteen players and a coach have been charged with either excessive appealing or dissenting a decision in the last year, including a captain in Inzamam ul-Haq, who was suspended for a Test after charging an umpire? Partly, it is simply the mores: less inhibited, more aggressive. Appeals are not the only aspect of cricket that is more demonstrative: celebrating a Test hundred currently takes longer than some Twenty20 games; the fall of a wicket is now marked by scenes reminiscent of VE Day. The umpire today is no longer an individual of stature, but a lowly functionary, a lonely and isolated figure undermined by technology, second-guessed by referees, assailed by the media. And what do we do with the lonely and isolated these days? Why, we pick on them, of course.

The main development is that players no longer see the possibility that the umpire may err under pressure as a problem; they perceive it as an advantage for the seizing. What the professional foul is to football, so the 'professional appeal' is to cricket: all in a day's work. 'Guys, these umpires are under tremendous pressure,' Hansie Cronje told his South African comrades during their 1998 series against England. 'If it's close enough I want to hear appeals and I expect you to SCREAM the appeals.' The logic continues to appeal to Cronje's countrymen. Asked to respond on the recent remarks of his coach, Andre Nel commented simply that South Africa should heed the Australian example: 'I think they are very, very clever about the way they do things with umpires. They put a lot of pressure on the umpires and sometimes it counts in their favour. Maybe we can learn something from them in a certain way by doing this.'

Gradations of appeal have almost disappeared. Virtually every shout is at full spate. Slips cordons go up in magnificent unison. Nothing loops to short leg without the cry of 'Catch it!' No blow on the pad is unaccompanied by a crimson-faced cry: LBWs now account for more than 17 per cent of Test decisions, compared to less than 12 per cent in the 1970s. The ICC want us to get excited by the Power Play and the Super Sub, yet remain strangely oblivious to what might be called the power ploy, the mass celebration that takes place without regard to a decision, as though only umpire Helen Keller could demur, and the super sulk, the prolonged pout which follows most not-outs. Warne may be continuing in the great Lillee tradition as an appealer, but he is breaking new ground in his mime routines when decisions go against him, making the failure to grant an LBW look like the gravest miscarriage of justice since the conviction of the Birmingham Six.

Richard Tyldesley once joked of Roses matches, the traditional derbies involving archrivals Lancashire and Yorkshire: 'What wi' need is no oompires and fair cheatin' all round.' He didn't realise that fair cheating all round did not require the umpires' leaving. David Shepherd relates that after the Bangalore Test of 1998, Ian Healy was invited to dinner by his counterpart, Nayan Mongia, whose sulphurous appeal had cost him his wicket. 'Did you hit the ball when Shep gave you out?' asked Mongia. 'You know I didn't,' replied Healy. 'I didn't think you did,' commented Mongia. Oh well, pass the chutney …

*

Even the media seems inured to such episodes. In the 2003 World Cup final, a snick from Adam Gilchrist's bat travelled low to first slip Sourav Ganguly, the conviction of whose appeal was entirely undiluted by the obvious fact the ball had bounced six inches in front of him. Everyone looked slightly embarrassed, the commentators construed this merely as evidence of Ganguly's great competitive nature, and the next day's match reports almost entirely ignored it.

All of which may well suit us. Human life is full of hypocrisies, minor and major: stirring an ethical murk will suffice to obscure most offences. With appealing, in fact, it's easy. It's our job. We're just passionate. We're just competitive. They're doing it, too. It's good for the crowd. It's good for TV. And, of course, technology is the answer. Which is fine, if that's the kind of game we want. In the meantime, though, while we're still stuck with those burdensome, fallible humans rather than RoboBillyBowden, the players will have to deal with the consequences.

Is it a coincidence that standards of umpiring have declined as the persistence and petulance of appealing has increased? Is it a coincidence that members of the ICC panel often seem to enjoy a good first year, then steadily deteriorate from there? In his auto-biography *White Lightning* (1999), Allan Donald said he didn't think so: 'We players have to look closely at ourselves and take some of the blame. We all know the more times you appeal the greater the chance you have of getting lucky. So every team is at it more now than a few years ago ... The players have seen they can get away with it if they're lucky and they're happy to let the umpire take all the aggro if the decision is wrong.' Players are apt to complain that a bad decision could end their careers. Why are they so comfortable about bad decisions befalling their opponents?

Inside Sport February 2006

GLAMOUR

Eleven Magnificos

KEITH MILLER

'Nearly stumps pulled that time!' Thus did Keith Miller walk away from the wreckage of a fighter-bomber circa 1944. Not long after he was playing soccer with his comrades, and within a year or two was a Test cricketer with a similar unconcern for danger. If you could choose your own cricket attributes, you would always choose to emulate Miller: he hit hard, bowled fast, caught expertly, dressed well, caroused long, bet big and never looked other than a treat.

RANJITSINHJI

The Golden Age's greatest magnifico, and still cricket's most exotic personality, radiating ease at the crease and oriental wealth off it. Rewrote the rules of batsmanship by opening up the leg side as a scoring area, then enriched his legend by quitting the game for an Eastern throne. 'When Ranji passed out of cricket,' wrote Sir Neville Cardus, 'a wonder and a glory departed from the game forever.'

SIR CHARLES AUBREY SMITH

Captaining England on its inaugural visit to South Africa was just the first of a string of authority roles for the stately star of more than a hundred Hollywood films between 1915 and 1949, where he was usually cast when some stiff upper lip, augmented by moustache, was required: colonels, lords, generals, deans, and twice the

Duke of Wellington (in *The House of Rothschild* and *Sixty Glorious Years*). Other cricketers have looked like film stars; no one else got to co-star with Greta Garbo (in *Queen Christina*).

CHUCK FLEETWOOD-SMITH

Victorian who bowled slow and lived fast in the otherwise staid 1930s: a lady-killer with a dandified air, Clark Gable looks and a taste for cravats. He spun the ball prodigiously and could be as generous with runs as he was with favours. In his case, however, the glamour was perishable. When his cricket was over, alcohol and eventually poverty took its place.

DENIS COMPTON

Charming, cheerful, carefree, sometimes careless, hard to dismiss, even harder to dislike. 'Never was such a hero as Denis Compton in those first post-war years,' averred E.W. Swanton. 'Never has Lord's rung to such affective affectionate applause.' The compleat sportsman: seventy-eight Tests, fourteen football caps for England, and numberless friends across the world.

IMRAN KHAN

Made into a star, then a stud, by World Series Cricket, he became the figurehead of Pakistan cricket's only true personality cult, culminating in the 1992 World Cup, and then parlayed his profile into a political career. As likely to be seen on the social as the sporting pages, especially in 1995, when he married Jemima Goldsmith, daughter of the Anglo-French takeover baron Sir James.

TED DEXTER

Charismatic, copiously gifted, a natural patrician, popularly ennobled as 'Lord Ted'. His batting carried on amateur traditions in an era of professional austerities. His ambitions were more modern: he ran a public-relations company, owned racehorses, modelled clothes and flirted with politics. 'A T.E. Lawrence of the cricket field', reckons Christopher Martin-Jenkins; Dexter had a similar flair for speed, whether it was in the air, on the road, or on the flat. A generation has matured, alas, who can remember him only waxing astrological as England's chairman of selectors.

Bob Crisp

Many lives in one, all of them worth living. Medium-pacer, magazine editor, mink farmer and memoirist of improbably restless spirit: born in India, educated in Rhodesia, a cricketer for South Africa (nine Tests), a mountaineer in Tanzania (Kilimanjaro climbed twice in a fortnight), a decorated warrior in North Africa (five times wounded), explorer of Crete (as a pedestrian), resident of Greece (where he eventually settled). Stayed still long enough to write a history of Johannesburg's foundation, *The Outlanders* (1964).

C.B. Fry

Almost 31,000 first-class runs at more than 50 with ninety-four hundreds – and that was just the start. The last of a discontinued line of Englishman: an improbably handsome cricketer, footballer, rugby player, field athlete, scholar, journalist, naval officer, novelist, unflagging if unfulfilled politician, and candidate for the throne of Albania. 'Romantic at heart,' wrote J.B. Priestley, 'but classical in style'.

Wesley Hall

There have been taller, faster, and even better opening bowlers than Hall, but in the 1960s there was no more magnetic physical presence on the cricket field, with his superb run and bounding stride, signature crucifix dancing round his neck. 'There was never a dull moment when Wes was batting or bowling or fielding,' said Richie Benaud. 'He was just that sort of player.'

Aamir Khan

Apparently not much of a cricketer in real life, but the *beau ideal* of Bollywood batsmanship as Bhuvan in Ashutosh Gowariker's *Lagaan:*

Once Upon a Time in India (2001), of which he was also producer. One to watch, if only on DVD.

The Wisden Cricketer December 2004

ENIGMAS

The Enemies of Promise

Whom the gods wish to destroy, wrote Cyril Connolly, they first call promising. Cricket's gods are still more cruel: they will permit them to be designated champions. Almost every game, at whatever level, features noteworthy performances, yet we all know that outstanding individuals are rare. This means that for every legitimately great player, there will be a host of those who flatter only to deceive. The very mention of names such as Lawrence Rowe, Vinod Kambli, Greg Blewett, Narendra Hirwani, Bob Massie and Graeme Hick – players who, it was thought, would dominate cricket for decades to come – stimulates among cricket fans a wistful reflectiveness. Where did they go wrong that others, perhaps less vaunted at the equivalent stage in their careers, went right?

No one has scored more runs in their baptismal Test than the Jamaican Rowe, in February 1972: his 214 and unbeaten 100 for the West Indies against New Zealand followed 227 for his island against the same opponents. Thirty years ago he became the second the West Indian to achieve a Test triple-century, and after a dozen Tests averaged 73; thereafter, with occasional reminders of his talents, his career was an anticlimax.

In his first ten Tests, Kambli averaged 93.7, and was the fastest Indian to 1000 Test runs; from his last seven, he scavenged 147 at 14.7. Blewett dominated his first two Ashes contests, with centuries in each at home, and later added a double-century and century away; in forty-two other Tests, he averaged less than 27. Hirwani and Massie were heroes for five days, with 16 wickets in their debut Tests, but little longer; Hick was never a hero, though widely expected to become one, on the basis of his hundred first-class hundreds.

Once you begin thinking in this might-have-been vein, the names of those turned from headlines into footnotes come easily. How many saviours of English cricket have there been? How many graven idols and false dawns in India and Pakistan? And if you stop to ponder it, of course, the surprise would be were it otherwise. There've been about 2350 Test cricketers: a small proportion of those become established; a tiny subset of those last long enough even to audition for greatness. In order for distinction to matter, in fact, it is necessary that many must fail. Starting a career like a world-beater, moreover, means that disappointment, sooner or later, is almost predestined. That doesn't count simply in cricket, or even in sport: it is in nature.

In one of his enchanting books about numbers, mathematics professor John Allen Paulos turns his attention to the most famous hoodoo in American sport: the *Sports Illustrated* cover jinx. It is said that an appearance on the cover of America's best known sporting magazine invariably preludes disaster: indeed, a survey of half a century of covers, by the magazine itself two years ago, discovered that more than a third of honourees had suffered injuries, slumps or other misfortunes within two weeks of a cover appearance.

Well, yes, said Paulos. What was being witnessed was the mathematical phenomenon called regression to the mean: the tendency for an extreme value of an at least partially chance-dependent quantity to be followed by a value closer to the average. He suggested that the magazine 'consider featuring an established player who had had a particularly bad couple of months on its back cover': their form was sure to rebound.

Cricket is all about at-least-partially-chance-dependent quantities. What goes up must come down; or, in the case of a bowling average, what goes down must come up. The records of even great players fluctuate markedly before, if they are genuinely outstanding, achieving an equilibrium. Brian Lara's batting average has been as high as 62.61 (after his 375) and as low as 47.57, before stabilising in the 50s. After his first 90 overs in Tests, Shane Warne's bowling average was 335; it has since been as economical at 22.55 and as expensive as 26.72.

Cricketers with the world at their feet one minute and clay feet the next present us with extreme declines because their ascents are so precipitous. Laxman Sivaramakrishnan could scarcely have done other than disappoint after his 7–28 on his Ranji Trophy debut at the age of sixteen, for Tamil Nadu against Delhi at Madras in February 1982, and his 19 wickets in his first three Tests at an average of 21, after becoming India's youngest Test player. His seven wickets at 104 each thereafter were, in a sense, written in the stars before they were written in the stats.

The forces that drag a cricketer back to the mean – form, luck, injury, opposition, adaptability – are not far to seek. Batsmen do better against some attacks than others. In the 1970s and '80s, the West Indies made a habit of nipping promising careers in the bud. In his recent autobiography, Pakistani Javed Miandad describes the pressure he felt in the West Indies after a spectacular beginning to his career against New Zealand: 'Fresh from what was openly being regarded as a phenomenal debut series, I now had a reputation to keep ... I came under a great deal of pressure and didn't quite know how to handle it.' After 'too much too soon', he was dropped; forbearing selectors recalled him and he prospered.

Others weren't so lucky. Kambli and Blewett suffered their first form reversals against West Indian attacks. England's Tim Robinson was patient, played spin well and was strong off his pads. From his first ten Tests, against Indian and Australian attacks that bowled too straight at him, he wrung 931 runs at 66.5. But the pace attacks of the West Indies and Pakistan jammed him up and cut him off; excluding a century on a shirtfront pitch at Old Trafford, he averaged only 16.77 in his remaining nineteen Tests.

A spectacular launch to a bowling career, likewise, usually implies conditions strongly in one's favour; bowlers can struggle when those conditions aren't reproduced everywhere. A year after his arresting debut in England, Massie found himself in the West Indies, was so tamed by its hot weather and flat pitches that he did not play a Test, and never represented his country again. Like many an Indian slow bowler, too, Hirwani proved a lion at home (45 wickets at 16.6) and a lamb away (21 at 59).

Sometimes, a cricketer rises not because he has made an unassailable case for selection, but because he seems to fit a bill. The Indian hankering for speed since Kapil Dev's peak has exposed countless contenders: Salil Ankola, Subroto Bannerjee, Raj Ghai, Rashid Patel, Randhir Singh, Atul Wassan. Sometimes, figures flatter their takers. Sanjeev Sharma's 5–26 against the West Indies in the Champions Trophy at Sharjah in October 1988 was the best performance by an Indian against that opponent, but he never appeared remotely capable of improving on it. On other occasions, attention came too soon. Vivek Razdan was picked as a Test player twenty days after his first-class debut, and a year before his Ranji Trophy debut. His 5–79 in December 1989 warmed the cockles of his supporters' hearts, but he was ill-prepared to fight back from a subsequent loss of form.

Failure tests character; failure after early success tests it even more sternly. The temptation is to adhere to those methods that brought early success. Part of the reason for Blewett's eventual exile was his reluctance to listen to advice about his fallible front-foot technique. Allan Border mused aloud that Blewett's early results had been 'too good': 'Guys who make a great start to their Test careers often come back to the field within a few years.' Yet one can understand his stubbornness; in other circumstances, it might have been called perseverance and determination, or, in the vernacular of the current Australian team, 'backing yourself'. Luck is such a huge determinant in cricket that its influence can be detected everywhere, if one looks hard enough: that was a nice shot, except for the fielder standing where it fell; that was a good spell, had it not been for the half-volleys and full tosses. And impersonal forces there are, it is true; what varies is the extent to which they reveal personal susceptibilities.

Take the case of Lawrence Rowe. In the early 1970s, with Viv Richards still to come, Rowe was the West Indian glass of fashion. 'He became our hero,' said Desmond Haynes. 'He had such ... such style.' Michael Holding still believes Rowe 'the best batsman I ever saw', and that 'I could not imagine anyone ever batting better or being able to.' Then came the setbacks. Recruited by Derbyshire, he was routed by hay fever and headaches: of all things for a cricketer to be allergic to, he suffered a reaction to grass. When he then joined the West Indies on tour in India in October 1974, Rowe seemed to fall apart. He failed, tamely, thrice; even in the nets, he was stilted and fallible. Sent home for treatment of a stye on his eyelid, he was discovered by an ophthalmic surgeon to have eyesight better than 20/20: he could read the maker's name on the optical chart. But he was also suffering pterygium, a disease involving vision-blurring growths. A remedial operation damaged his eyesight; the prescribed contact lenses caused his eyes to water copiously.

For a batsman whose game had been built on an eagle eye, the deterioration in Rowe's sight must have been traumatic. West Indian cricket's most exhaustive chronicler, Michael Manley, described him as 'transfixed by misfortune'. But Rowe's afflictions also caused him to look more deeply into himself, and there he found hitherto-unacknowledged weaknesses. Holding's autobiography contains a fascinating vignette of the young Rowe, describing a country social game where he was the special guest. Folk came from near and far to watch but, amid acute disappointment, the great man refused to bat: 'There had been rain, the pitch was damp and he protested that, in the conditions, *he could not be the Lawrence Rowe the people were expecting*' (my italics).

Cases of unfulfilled promise, too, also involve some sort of reflection of the time-horizons of selectors. If the player chosen was good enough in the first place, it is reasonable to surmise that he has the ability and fortitude to fight back from adversity. Javed, cited earlier, is hardly on his own: every distinguished cricket career involves periods leaner than others. The Waughs, Langer and Ponting all spent time by the wayside. Not so long ago, Matthew Hayden and Andrew Symonds would have looked like cases of talent misspent. Scott Fitzgerald wrote famously that there were no second acts in American lives. But because talent is one thing and form another, cricketers can usually feel confident of a third, fourth and fifth if they stick it out long enough; the only question is whether they retain the indulgence of selectors for sufficient time to enjoy them.

Wisden Asia April 2004

FAST-BOWLER CAPTAINS
Too Hot to Handle

If you were to pick as decisive one of the many trends in cricket over the last century, it would probably be the rise and rise of fast bowling. A hundred years ago, the new ball was simply a piece of equipment necessary to the conduct of a match. Today it is a team's cutting edge, lavished with care, attention, sweat and spit for the three or four pace bowlers in every attack. Their emancipation, nonetheless, is incomplete. Fast bowlers might lead their attacks, but they seldom if ever lead their teams.

It was ever thus. Australia has given them especially short shrift. Ricky Ponting, Australia's forty-first captain, is the thirty-first batsman to hold the position. There have been four all-rounders (George Giffen, Monty Noble, Warwick Armstrong and Richie Benaud), three keepers (Jack Blackham, Barry Jarman and Adam Gilchrist), two finger spinners (Hugh Trumble and Ian Johnson), but only one fast bowler: Ray Lindwall, who was grudged a Test match when Johnson was ill, at Bombay in 1956. Never mind the ACB; such market dominance seems more like a case for the ACCC.

Australia isn't the only country to have this taboo. In England, Mike Brearley believes, the discrimination is a vestige of the game's old class distinctions that vested authority in gentlemen, and kept horny-handed sons of soil to do the hard physical toil. He recalls becoming aware of this in a school game against a Combined Services XI, which was composed of officers but for the opening bowlers, 'Stoker Healey and Private Stead'. But England (with Bob

Willis) and other countries have at least hazarded the experiment: the West Indies (Courtney Walsh), India (Kapil Dev), South Africa (Shaun Pollock) and Pakistan (Imran Khan, Wasim Akram and Waqar Younis). And if Australia is truly the country where Jack is as good as his master, why does it not seem to be so if Jack happens to have an aptitude for bowling quickly?

The traditional theory has been promulgated by, among others, Sir Donald Bradman: that bowlers in general are incapable of the detachment necessary in determining when and how much to bowl. 'The difficulty with a bowler,' he wrote, 'is the constant fear that he will bowl himself too much and thereby incur an undercurrent of dissatisfaction amongst his colleagues, or underbowl himself because of undue modesty.' Brearley added that this was especially so with fast bowlers because their art is so strenuous and consuming: 'It takes an exceptional character to know when to bowl, to keep bowling with all his energy screwed up into a ball of aggression, and to be sensitive to the needs of the team, both tactically and psychologically.'

There is some weight to these propositions. To bowl or not to bowl: that is certainly a question. And because fast bowling is physically enervating, the husbanding of energy it requires can breed a certain taciturnity. Even Ray Lindwall, wrote Ray Robinson, would grow tight-lipped while he thought through his bowling lures and traps: 'So intent was his watch that fellow players talking to him on the field got only monosyllabic answers, if that.'

The sort of scenario Bradman envisaged, nonetheless, would really apply only to a bowler about whom a team already nursed doubts, and there is no reason to think that batting captains are any less prone to selfishness or self-abnegation. One could argue the contrary, that a bowler-captain, accustomed to working batsmen out, and ideally placed to assess both his own physical state and the suitability of conditions to his methods, would be likelier to deploy himself at intervals most conducive to his probable success (nobody complains when batsmen captains do this, as when Steve Waugh continued to occupy his preferred slots at number five and six despite uncertainties higher in the order). And if a necessary attribute of leadership is the capacity to empathise with one's charges, who understands cricket's rigours more intimately than the individual whose job is the hardest yakka of all?

*

Essentially, it is an issue of image. 'The popular theory ... is that fast bowlers aren't all that bright,' complained Geoff Lawson. 'After all, how smart must you be to run in 30 metres, 120 times a day, in the searing Australian heat?' Fast bowling is understood to be visceral, intuitive, spontaneous. Its definitive explanation is Jeff Thomson's: 'I just shuffle up and go wang.' The ideal captain is, or at least is imagined to be, rational and reasoned, thinking ahead rather than living in the instant. Here the most famous line is Richie Benaud's: 'Captaincy is 90 per cent luck and 10 per cent skill ... but for heaven's sake don't try it without that little 10 per cent.'

Fair? Scarcely. And the cool clinician is really only one type of leader. Another prerequisite of captaincy, Benaud once contended, is 'tremendous confidence'. In *Benaud on Reflection* (1983), he wrote: 'I believe that the man in charge of a cricket team ... must have the conviction that he can, at the very least, do anything he sets out to do; on top of this, he needs to believe that occasionally he can achieve the impossible.' And no one embodied this more fully than a fast bowler, Keith Miller, whom Benaud classed 'the very best captain I ever played under'.

Miller was also a virile attacking batsman, of course, but his whole game was governed by the fast-bowling humours cited earlier: he was aggressive, dynamic, impulsive. And far from unsettling the New South Wales side that he led from 1952 to 1956, it galvanised them – and him. He made a century in his first match as skipper, took 34 wickets at 20 in his first season, then led them to three consecutive Sheffield Shields. His hunches kept his men guessing, and his opponents confounded.

Benaud describes how on the first morning of the game at the Gabba in November 1953, Miller summoned him to bowl his leggies in the sixth over. 'Nugget, the ball's still new,' Benaud remonstrated. 'Don't worry about that,' countered Miller. 'It'll soon be old. Just think about the field you want ...' Looking at the young slow-bowler's expression, Miller reassured him: 'It's all right, it'll spin like a top for an hour.' By lunch, Benaud had 5–17.

Like all distinguished captains, too, Miller was prepared to countenance defeat in the pursuit of victory. In February 1955, he set MCC an inviting 315 to win their tour match with more than a day to make them: a gauntlet that they were obliged to pick up and, at 3–145 with Hutton and May in command, looked set to slap his face with. Then, having breezed in to bowl May, Miller set his spinners loose, who secured a 45-run victory. And for all its casual air and risky undercurrent, Miller's was a formula that proved remarkably robust: he was defeated as captain only thrice in thirty-eight first-class matches.

*

As the economist Maynard Keynes once observed, however, unconventional success provokes more suspicion than orthodox failure. When the Australian Board of Control deliberated on Lindsay Hassett's successor in November 1954, Miller was passed over in favour of the conservative Victorian Ian Johnson. And while obscure, the reasons that Miller became what Benaud has called 'the best captain Australia never had' are not difficult to guess at. 'He's too wild,' the Tasmanian cricket potentate Harold Bushby once confided, and by prudish 1950s standards, when one could be controversial for crossing the road against the lights, he was too hot to handle. Then there was the attitude of the chairman of selectors at the time. It may have been with Miller in mind that Bradman, in the chapter concerning captaincy in *The Art of Cricket* (1958), made clear that 'sheer sporting prowess is not regarded as the sole qualification for a player' and that a captain's 'private life must be beyond reproach'.

Since Miller, most Australian states have dabbled in fast-bowling skippers, if only in emergencies, from Dennis Lillee (two wins, one draw, no defeats) and Jeff Thomson (three wins, five draws, five defeats) to Geoff Dymock (one win, seven draws, three defeats) and Carl Rackemann (one win, five draws, four defeats). Few have given the impression of natural gifts. Rodney Hogg observed drolly after his only game as captain, in November 1980, that it could be a lonely job: when he sought team-mates' advice as India were making 9–456 in their first innings, he noticed them edging away from him; when India folded for 78 in their second innings, everyone had a suggestion.

Miller's reputation, funnily enough, may have done as much harm as good to the advancement of fast-bowling skippers. They are still perceived as the bold alternative when a choice from among the batsmen is not obvious; and if they do not succeed, they are construed as a reflection on the concept rather than on either the individual or the team. In fact, with the exception of Imran Khan, none of the bowling captains to which other countries turned during the 1980s and '90s was notable for their leadership flair. But this no more invalidated the idea of the fast-bowling captain than Kim Hughes' record means that nobody from Western Australia should ever lead Australia again.

Miller's experience may be instructive in different ways. He was fortunate to be leading a supremely competent team: Benaud, Arthur Morris, Norm O'Neill, Bob Simpson et al. A more callow bunch might have been disarmed by his mercurial temperament and laconic cue for the field to disperse: 'Scatter.' His gift was pushing established talent beyond its existing limit by his innate aggression and inspirational example. His experiences found an interesting echo in those of Geoff Lawson, who led New South Wales into three Sheffield Shield finals between 1989 and 1992 with similar imagination and initiative. Lawson was strongly convinced that bowlers should make naturally competent captains, their analytical faculties honed by experience with the ball: 'I spent many hours down on the fine-leg fence over the years and I used that time to play the game of captaincy constantly. It may have been a shock to many observers that I made an excellent fist of the job when I got it ... but really I had been preparing a long time.' Being a fast bowler, moreover, made him aggressive: 'It is the nature of bowling, and fast bowling in particular, that you have to be aggressive to be good.'

Lawson noted in *Henry* (1993), though, that fast-bowling captains required of their colleagues a minimum level of cricket sense, because their supervision, at least while the captain was bowling, was inevitably not total. 'When you're running into bowl,' he wrote, 'your concentration should be focused on where you want the ball to go – and not whether your fine leg has swapped over for the left-hander.' Lawson depended, especially in tight one-day matches, with their arithmetic challenge to permutate allocations of overs, on 'the co-operation and concentration of all players all of the time'. With the likes of the Waughs, Mark Taylor, Mike Whitney and Greg Matthews in his team, he seldom had to do without it. 'They were fine allies, always forthright in their advice – and I appreciated it greatly.'

There are now new forces that militate against the rise of the fast-bowler cum captain. One-day matches, such an important form of cricket, are essentially a batsman's game: it is hard to impose yourself on a match in only 10 allotted overs. And, ironically, the rise and rise of fast bowling has had the effect of making its practitioners incomparably valuable. They are to be petted and cosseted, spared when possible, rested when necessary. Anything that smacks of an additional burden and might compromise their effectiveness is to be rigidly eschewed; even Lawson and, more recently, Paul Reiffel had to wait until their Test careers were over before they were entrusted with leadership roles. Having been thought too obtuse to do the job of captain, they might now be felt to be too important.

Inside Edge: The Fast Men – A Celebration of Speed (2004)

TEST SERIES
The Makings of a Classic

When Australia visits India in October, a degree of disappointment will be inevitable. No matter how dramatic the events or stellar the individual performances, their excellence will be unable to surprise us. After the series of 2001 and 2003–04, expectation is strung to such a concert pitch that almost anything short of extraterrestrial intervention will feel anticlimactic.

Nobody anticipated the grandeur of the 2001 series; at the halfway point, in fact, it looked like a walkover. The pinch-me-I'm-dreaming power of the Laxman–Dravid revival arose precisely because there was no foretelling it. When India then came to Australia last year, it startled by playing cricket of the utmost dedication. So what now, since we have come to expect the wild, the freakish, the brave and the bold from India – qualities that Australia, indeed, seems peculiarly capable of provoking? While it may be exhilarating if Tendulkar, Dravid and Laxman make a ton of runs, it will scarcely be unanticipated. As Oscar Wilde said when an American invited him to share in the wonder of Niagara Falls, 'The wonder would be if the water did not fall.'

It is true that the opportunity exists here for one of the greatest cricket contests of our time, pitting against one another two outstanding teams with excellent recent records, both as fit, fresh and close to full strength as can conceivably be expected. Yet it is also worth reminding ourselves how habitually such predictions go awry. After all, the last time a Test rubber was anticipated so keenly as this was when South Africa and Australia staged reciprocal visits in 2001–02. Having approached one another like runaway trains bound to collide, however, the teams turned out to be on a funicular railroad, with Australia ascending and South Africa descending.

So what does it take to produce a great cricket series, comparable, say, with the West Indies tour of Australia in 1960–61, Australia's tours of the West Indies in 1995 and 1999, the Ashes of 1882, 1902, 1930, 1961 and 1981, and any or all skirmishes of India and Pakistan? It might be easier, initially, to discuss what's inessential. It seems axiomatic, for instance, that great players are a precondition of the best cricket, but it's not. Great players can play terribly tedious cricket, too. Perhaps the classic example was the keenly anticipated 1962–63 Ashes series in which Richie Benaud's Australians, featuring Neil Harvey, Alan Davidson, Bob Simpson, Bill Lawry, Norm O'Neill and Wally Grout, met Ted Dexter's Englishmen, marshalling Fred Trueman, Brian Statham, Colin Cowdrey, Ken Barrington and David Sheppard, and played cricket colourless and soporific even by the standards of the era.

Sometimes, counterintuitively, it is the absence of great players that heightens a game's intensity, by either evening up the standards of the respective XIs, or begetting opportunities for the upwardly mobile. Would the 1981 Ashes series have been nearly so memorable had Greg Chappell been available? Would Australia's capture of the Frank Worrell Trophy in 1995 have felt so stirring had it not been engineered by the ersatz attack of Glenn McGrath, Paul Reiffel and Brendon Julian? It might be truer to say that the presence of great players needs to be leavened by that of great players in the making: the young, the ambitious, the fearless, keen to make their own reputations by knocking over a few existing ones. In this sense, Irfan Pathan and Michael Clarke might prove as important to the texture of the forthcoming Tests as Sachin Tendulkar and Matt Hayden.

It is tempting to imagine that the best cricket requires the suspension of all other variables, 'a fair field and no favour', to use the old English expression. And, to be sure, there has seldom if ever been a memorable cricket contest without impartial and competent umpiring. Nothing poisons cricket more quickly or critically than inept officiation; it has been toxic to more than a few encounters between Australia and India. Conditions, however, need not be similarly neutral – and they never are when Australia and India meet. Ponting's men will feel themselves playing not merely eleven cricketers from India, but India itself, in all its sweltering, stifling, sprawling hurly-burly. That is the very essence of international cricket.

It would also appear logical that the opponents in any historic series draw on some pre-existing narrative of the contests between them; which, in their last seven Tests for the Border–Gavaskar Trophy, India and Australia have assuredly built up. But again this doesn't seem a prerequisite for memorable cricket. When Frank Worrell's men toured Australia in 1960–61, for instance, there had not been a West Indies tour for nine years. The visitors' recent record, moreover, was mediocre, and they were soundly beaten by New South Wales on the eve of the First Test: that improbable, unimprovable tie. When India and Pakistan play, it doesn't seem to matter how long has elapsed since their last encounter; even the captains' handshake is pregnant with meaning.

By the same token, the forthcoming showdown in India has already demonstrated the advantages – offsetting the host of disadvantages about which we ritually complain – of a frantically busy international schedule. Bizarrely, after the prodigies of 1960–61, the West Indies did not tour Australia again for eight years, by which time only Garry Sobers and Wes Hall carried over from that earlier meeting, and attempts to rekindle its excitement largely failed. Where 200,000 watched the parade that farewelled Worrell's West Indians, only 200 watched the last day played by Sobers' men.

The 'back stories' in India, by contrast, will be composed of fresh memories. Who can have forgotten Dravid's poise and Tendulkar's self-denial in Australia? Likewise, Hayden's heroics and Gillespie's courage in India? Past failings add an edge to the performances of others. We need hardly be reminded, for example, that Adam Gilchrist, Ricky Ponting and Shane Warne have unfinished business in India. Discounting Gilchrist's solitary big day out at Mumbai, their collective returns in India have been 306 runs at 12 and 20 wickets at 52: paltry in their Test totality of nearly 12,000 runs and almost 950 wickets, catches and stumpings.

*

Getting to the heart of this question entails reconsidering another: why countries first began playing cricket against one another. No one has significantly improved on the historian Bill Mandle's argument that playing cricket allowed those at the imperial periphery to prove their prowess and pluck to those at the centre. Playing cricket against England – because that's what helped define cricket in the countries it colonised – challenged the imported culture and validated it at the same time. And far from frustrating us, cricket's ceremony and duration invested it with a certain majesty. It looked like – to use that polysemous word – a Test.

What was in it for the English? Imperial condescension? Social control? Apprehensions about their own decline? In his book *Ornamentalism: How the British Saw Their Empire* (2001), the British historian David Cannadine has delineated conservative anxieties that underlay imperial expansion, the perception that institutions at home were imperilled by vulgarising capitalism and democracy. It may be that the English took up the cricket gauntlet thrown down by their subject peoples to stifle suspicions of decadence that they harboured about themselves.

What does this have to do with great cricket series? This: international cricket has never simply been about two teams of eleven getting together for a swing and shout; it has acted often as a metaphor for other struggles and quests. Thus the consuming passion for beating England, especially for the first time, and especially in England: in the annals of cricket in the West Indies, Pakistan, India, New Zealand and Sri Lanka, the years, respectively, of 1950, 1954, 1971, 1986 and 1998 are heavily engraved.

A typical recollection is Clyde Walcott's of the West Indies' win at Lord's in 1950: 'It was the first time we had succeeded at cricket's headquarters and it was a symbolic moment in our lives and in the lives of millions of countrymen. Many of them were arriving in Britain to build new careers in difficult circumstances because colour prejudice still lingered on. At the time I hardly drank but I had plenty that day ... We had beaten England, the country that brought cricket to the Caribbean, at their headquarters!' Or Hanif Mohammed's after Pakistan's victory at the Oval in 1954: 'It was a glorious moment for all of us ... The win gave Pakistan a visible identity. Not many had known about Pakistan until then.'

After a while, of course, England wasn't the only yardstick, for one could never beat them for the first time again. Thus C.L.R. James' moving rumination, at the end of *Beyond a Boundary*, concerning the aforementioned farewell parade for Worrell's West Indians: 'Clearing their way with bat and ball, West Indians at that moment had made a public entry into the comity of nations.'

In a post-colonial world, these former meanings remain only vestigially. To be sure, there are ardent rivalries in world cricket, deriving from proximity and similarities in culture: India and Pakistan, Australia and New Zealand. There are, too, antipathies based on specific personalities and issues: Australia and Sri Lanka because of the umpiring gauntlet Murali has run, Pakistan and England due to bad ball-tampering blood. But we no longer play one another today as an expression of something bigger, older, grander or deeper. We play now chiefly because it's what we've always done, because a system exists to facilitate it, and because there's a buck in it – and especially so when playing against India.

And the reason that we play so much cricket now – let's be frank about it – is the economic consideration that sport only has value to television when it is live. Unlike other broadcast content, like movies or TV series, sport's inherent value depreciates fast. If television's infatuation with cricket ended, if it was decided there were better forms of content and advertising space, there would be no need to play as much, if at all.

Which is not to say that this system doesn't provide cricket of quality and excitement; it can and does. But because the games exist only on the one level, anything other than the most brilliant feats and extraordinary results tend to pass very quickly from memory. It was fascinating when, before England's recent tour of the Caribbean, Brian Lara tried deploying the old imperial card. 'It's important for us to beat the old colonial masters,' he stated to the *Wisden Cricketer*. It sounded quaint, archaic and hollow, a sentiment decoupled from meaning, like a half-remembered line from a national anthem. And its success as a motivating tool can be judged from the verve and conviction with which his team proceeded to play.

This is not necessarily a development to be mourned. Sport can be a destructive force when it becomes a proxy for other tensions and disagreements: El Salvador and Honduras famously fought their 'Soccer War' in 1969 after an unruly World Cup challenge. Yet the fading former meanings of international cricket do leave a vacuum, being filled at present – with greater and lesser degrees of success – by hype, personality, money, marketing, and a kind of manufactured nationalism as deep as the war paint on spectators' faces. Australia and India 2004 may well turn out to be one of the greatest series in cricket history. But quite what that latter phrase means is, at the moment, in an intriguing process of renegotiation.

Wisden Asia October 2004

CONTROVERSY

Is It Not Cricket?

Sports marketing is not a product of the age of television and the cross-trainer. In an argument about sport's most successful marketing campaigns, the expression 'it's not cricket' would have to rank highly, not least because of the capacity it has demonstrated down the decades to survive such ceaseless buffeting. Was there ever a game so acutely conscious of its immanent spirit? Was there ever a game so conditioned to condoning offences against it?

For authors especially, the sentiment has possessed an irresistible allure. Variations have proliferated. Sid Barnes was sure that *It's Not Cricket* and Henry Blofeld even surer that *It's Just Not Cricket*, while Michael Down wondered *Is It Cricket?* and Frank Browne ventured that *Some of It Was Cricket*. We may be weakening. The best that match-fixing whistleblower Pradeep Magazine could come up with two years ago for his Indo-Augean stable was *Not Quite Cricket*. And while Simon Rae reverts to the robust formulation *It's Not Cricket* for his new 'History of Skulduggery, Sharp Practice and Downright Cheating in the Noble Game', he concludes by proposing that 'perhaps it never was'.

As the author of a superfine biography of W.G. Grace, gamesman extraordinaire, Rae is amply qualified to issue such a pronouncement. Indeed, it is not untrue to say that Grace is the star of this book as well, fabulous scallywag and/or petulant reprobate that he was, of his time and way ahead of it. In a sense, champion and

---

Review of *It's Not Cricket* by Simon Rae (Faber & Faber)

cheat, he is at the heart of cricket's ambivalence towards aggression and competitiveness: it is exquisitely ironic that during the phase of its development in which it took on so much of its moral ballast, cricket's leading practitioner was one so skilled in jettisoning it.

Rae writes with such knowledge and appreciation of Grace – variously sledging, intimidating umpires, fooling his opponents and fattening his wallet – that *It's Not Cricket* flags somewhat when he's not there. Players thereafter seem like mere simulacra, their peccadilloes and hypocrisies ultimately rather petty. That may be because they are less interesting; it may be because Rae is less interested. There is an excellent chapter on the old chestnut of 'to walk or not to walk', but the material on chucking, match-fixing, bouncers and Bodyline seems a tad routine, compiled as it is from some fairly well-worn secondary sources.

Which is not to say that the book is unenjoyable. An accomplished poet, Rae is often delightfully deft in prose, at turns elegant ('People generally look back on the 1950s as a halcyon age, whose probity was sometimes guaranteed by [Peter] May's immaculate parting'), epigrammatic ('Sledging is like spying, deplored as widely as it is practised') and engaged (he observes of fast bowling in the 1970s that officials 'like negligent schoolmasters ignoring fights in the playground … let the players mete out their own rough justice'). He crafts arresting similes, like deciding that the war-painted Allan Donald 'would not have looked out of place in Peter Brook's film *Lord of the Flies*', and makes interesting conjectures, such as the idea that the English aristocracy patronised cricket partly because 'the game seems naturally to embody the idea of hierarchy' and 'those playing it remain physically aloof from those they play against' (although, strangely, he takes the opposite view a few pages later, contending that 'once at the wicket cricketers could largely forget the social and financial inequalities that reigned so rigorously off the field of play').

What *It's Not Cricket* is not, though, is a serious attempt to analyse cricket's moral universe, to interrogate why it contains both such a strong sense of the ethical and such a self-torturing history of ethical violation. Is it to do with cricket administration? Is it to do with nostalgia? Is it to do with young men having to play by old men's rules? In general, there is too little comparative analysis, and there is a tendency to see cricket as its own ecosystem, rather than in social, historical and cultural contexts. It surprised me that Rae did not pursue the fairly obvious point that today, as a global rather than an explicitly English game, the consensus about what is and is not cricket must inevitably be the subject of contestation. What is 'cricket' in Pakistan? What, for that matter, is 'cricket' in Australia?

Rae's general commentary on recent history that 'the post-Packer period has been notable for the central role money has assumed in the game' also seems a tad wishy-washy, especially when he has gone to great lengths earlier in *It's Not Cricket* to demonstrate that the game has an ancient and irreducible connection with greed and corruption. Lest this be thought carping, I should reiterate my view that Rae is a fine writer and a serious student of the game. The subject, moreover, is a worthy one: as I said, the expression 'it's not cricket' is a remarkable marketing success story. But the caveat about marketing is that the consumer must look extra hard to disentangle fact from fancy.

The Yorker Autumn 2002

ODD MEN IN

TOM HORAN

Felix on the Page

In the past few weeks, I have exchanged a number of emails with a young Indian eagerly immersing himself in a dissertation on Australian cricket writing, and full of questions. What did I think of Ray Robinson? Jack Fingleton? Peter Roebuck? (Peter will be gratified to know that he's now seen as one of us.) I answered these enquiries as best I was able, then made my own modest proposal: if he was a serious scholar in the field, he should probably acquaint himself with Tom Horan.

When answer came there none, I was not especially surprised. If Horan rings a bell at all today, it is as a player in the very first Test in 1877, and on the Australians' inaugural tour of England a year later, where he enjoyed the signal honour of the winning hit in their rout of the MCC. Born in County Cork on 8 March 1855 and brought to Melbourne as a boy, Horan became a steady top-order batsman, worth 4027 first-class runs at 23 and considered good enough to captain Australia at a pinch in 1884–85 when more uppity team-mates decided to hold out for a few extra shillings. By then, however, he had commenced a far greater contribution to cricket's common weal: the 'Cricket Chatter' columns in the *Australasian*, the weekly sister paper of Melbourne's *Argus*, which he would compose for an extraordinary thirty-seven years.

This transition was, in its time, highly unusual; in fact, distinguishing. Australian cricket was well supplied with competent scribes before World War I, notably J.C. Davis and A.H. Gregory in Sydney, and Donald McDonald and Harry Hedley in Melbourne.

Only Horan, however, had represented his country, at home and abroad. There was no television to apparently drop the fan into the middle of the game; on the writer fell the entire responsibility for bringing the game to the fan, and no one in their time was on such intimate terms with cricket at the top level. It wasn't merely out of Hibernian loyalty that Bill O'Reilly described Horan as 'the cricket writer par excellence'; it was, he explained, because Horan was 'a writer who really did know what he was writing about'.

'Felix', as he was pseudonymously known, was not an adventurous stylist: he wrote, instead, with his ears and eyes, with a sense of the telling remark and the evocative detail, such as in his recollection of his first encounter with Victor Trumper in 1897: 'While on the Melbourne Ground the veteran Harry Hilliard introduced me to him and I was struck by the frank, engaging facial expression of the young Sydneyite. After a few words he went away and old Harry said to me: "That lad will have to be reckoned with later on." My word! But do you know what particularly attracted my attention when I first saw Victor fielding? You wouldn't guess in three. It was the remarkably neat way in which his shirt-sleeves were folded. Not loose, dangling down, and folding back again after a run for the ball, but always trim and artistic.' I have never failed since to note this detail in Beldam's famous image of Trumper jumping out to drive.

My own acquaintance with Horan dates from the early 1990s, thanks to Australia's grand old man of cricket bibliophilia, Pat Mullins of Brisbane. Horan was Pat's great favourite, for his other great enthusiasm was all things Irish, and he had dedicated years of effort to compiling voluminous scrapbooks of Horaniana. When he foisted these on me at our first meeting, I accepted them with some reticence; seldom have I been so completely converted.

Horan knew everyone, and reported their deeds in a prose as breezy and inviting as his personality. When he is recounting the experiences of the English team of 1884–85 on tour, for instance, it is as though you have a seat at their table: 'Barnes says that at Narrabri the heat was simply awful, and immediately up in the ranges at Armidale he had to wear a top coat and sit by the fire to keep himself warm ... It would do one good to hear Ulyett, little Briggs or Attewell laugh as they detail some of their Australian experiences; how Flowers was frightened of the native bears on the banks of the Broken River at Benalla; how Ulyett jumped from the steamer on a hot afternoon on his way down from Clarence; and how little Briggs came to grief on a buckjumper at Armidale. Briggs to this day maintains that the horse had nothing to do with unseating him, it was simply the saddle. His comrades, however, will not believe him ... Briggs gives a graphic description of a murderous raid he made one night upon the mosquitos in Gympie, and how, when that proved futile, he quenched the light and pulled his bed into another corner of the room to dodge them.'

In January 1893, the *Australasian* commissioned from 'Felix' a regular supplementary column called 'Round the Ground'. Horan's preferred vantage point at the MCG was under an elm tree near the sightboard opposite the pavilion; from here he would embark on long peregrinations round the arena and through his memory, each personal encounter bringing forth a fund of reminiscences. It was during one of these ambles, in January 1902, that he committed to print perhaps his most famous passages, which concern the dying moments of the inaugural Ashes Test at the Oval in 1882, in which he had played. Subsequently cited by H.S. Altham in *A History of Cricket* (1938), these lines have been unconsciously paraphrased by scores of writers since: 'the strain even for the spectators was so severe, that one onlooker dropped down dead, and another with his teeth gnawed out pieces of his umbrella handle. That was the match in which for the final half-hour you could have heard a pin drop, while the celebrated batsmen, A.P. Lucas and Alfred Lyttelton, were together, and Spofforth and Boyle bowling at them as they never bowled before. That was the match in which the last English batsman had to screw his courage to the sticking place by the aid of champagne, when one man's lips were ashen grey and his throat so parched that he could hardly speak as he strode by me to the crease; when the scorer's hand shook so that he wrote Peate's name like "geese", and when in the wild tumult at the fall of the last wicket, the crowd in one tremendous roar cried "bravo Australia".'

That inaugural Ashes Test had, I suspect, another impact on Horan's writing. He was not the last Australian journalist to be struck by the vehemence of the local criticisms of his English opponents: 'The very papers which, in dealing with the first day's play, said, in effect, that the English cricketers were the noblest, the bravest and the best; that, like the old guard of Napoleon, they would never know they are beaten, now turn completely around, and, with very questionable taste, designate these same cricketers as a weak-kneed and pusillanimous lot, who shaped worse than eleven schoolboys.'

Even after his playing days were over, Horan remained at heart a player: 'Felix' rejoiced in successes, and sympathised with failures, understanding sensitivities and susceptibilities as only one who has been there can. If he felt a point of order worth making, he did so with utmost even-handedness, the lightest touch and a peculiarly Victorian circumlocution. 'All this should be enough, indeed, to make one long to be in possession of Cagliostro's famous secret, so that one might have everlasting youth to enjoy to the full and forever the glorious life of a first-class Australian cricketer,' he wrote of the frequency of cricket tours in the 1880s. 'Though, to be sure, one must not forget that the thing might pall upon the taste in the long run, for does not the sonnet tell us that "sweets grown common lose their dear delight".' No danger of that with Horan's writing today; its sweetness is still well worth savouring.

Cricinfo March 2006

ARCHIE MACLAREN
Pride and Prejudice

In his final year at Harrow, Archie MacLaren had as his fag a particularly 'snotty little bugger', uppity but damn near useless, with
no aptitude even for sport: the youth had actually once been pelted
by boys with cricket balls, and felt an everlasting shame from
having cowered behind trees. Embarrassing, really – for MacLaren,
even as a teenager, was marked out for great attainments. He
would that year compile an effortless maiden first-class century
for Lancashire; within four years he would set a record score in
England to withstand all rivals for nigh on a century. That dam-
nable, feeble fag. Never amount to anything, that Winston blessed
Churchill.

MacLaren lived long enough to see the schoolboy upstart
achieve fame throughout the world; one wonders if it ever occurred
to him that his own closest brush with international renown
beyond the cricket field was his walk-on part as a monocled veteran
of the Crimean War in Alexander Korda's *The Four Feathers*. Likewise, while Churchill's greatness endures, MacLaren is nowadays at
best a period curio, like an antimacassar or an aspidistra.

If ever a cricketer was the creation of a single writer, it is
MacLaren, the luminous majesty with which he is associated owed
in very large degree to his youthful acolyte Neville Cardus. In one
of the most famous passages in *Autobiography* (1947), Cardus parallels his first glimpse of MacLaren with his first experience of the
actor Henry Irving ('They wakened the incurable romantic in me
which saves a grown man from foolishness'); later, he elevates the

cricketer to the stature of creative genius ('MacLaren was not just a cricketer any more than Wagner was just a composer') and supreme English artist ('Among exponents of the recognised arts in England there is only Sir Thomas Beecham whom I have found fit to compare in character and gusto of life ... with A.C. MacLaren, on or off the field').

Like Jad Leland in *Citizen Kane*, unable to wash from his memory the idle adolescent glimpse of a woman in white, Cardus never forgot that initial sight of MacLaren, on 'the greenest grass in England', playing a drive 'far to the distant boundary, straight and powerfully'. The memory turned him back into a twelve-year-old in the sixpenny seats at Old Trafford. 'I cannot remember the bowler's name; he has passed with all other details of the match into the limbo, but I can still see the swing of MacLaren's bat, the great follow-through, finishing high and held there with the body poised as he himself contemplated the grandeur of the stroke and savoured it ... This brief sight of MacLaren thrilled my blood, for it gave shape and reality to things I had till then only vaguely felt and dreamed about of romance.'

Other observers verify the spacious flourishes of MacLaren's batting. 'He lifted his bat round his neck like a golfer at the top of his swing,' recalled a contemporary, C.B. Fry. 'He stood bolt upright and swept into every stroke, even a defensive backstroke, with dominating completeness.' But, for Cardus, it was the thought of MacLaren as much as the deeds that did the trick. The climactic moment of their relationship was MacLaren's invitation to Cardus to Eastbourne in August 1921, where his ramshackle English XI was taking on the might of Warwick Armstrong's unbeaten Australians. MacLaren made a first-ball duck. In the *Manchester Guardian*, Cardus nonetheless spent 150 words describing it: a passage, I might add, that is startlingly moving, drenched with disappointment yet incandescently admiring. The faith was repaid when MacLaren's team won two days later, not only handing Cardus the scoop of a lifetime, but also vindicating his romantic effusions.

Yet then, MacLaren was by most measures a failure. Clinging

tenaciously to his amateur status, he had hazarded a host of careers: from banker to teacher; from Ranji's secretary, warding off his army of creditors, to limousine salesman with 'a gaudy line in patter and a sunny indifference to his customers' real needs' (to quote a lovely essay on MacLaren by Jeremy Mailes). Eternally beyond his means, he had been invalided out of the army and run a failed magazine; he'd go on to start an unsuccessful stud farm and an inhospitable hotel; he would fail in attempts to manufacture cricket bats from Spanish willow, and inflatable pads.

Nor were these misfortunes: on the contrary, they were nothing but the failures of a frankly unpleasant personality. Cardus admired him from the perfect distance. Team-mates and business partners alike found MacLaren brusque, boorish, overbearing. Even admirers who grew close enough came away disabused. 'It is disillusioning to one of my youthful loyalties,' wrote the Etonian littérateur George Lyttelton to his former pupil Rupert Hart-Davis, 'to realise that the Majestic MacLaren was an extremely stupid, prejudiced and pig-headed man.' In *Batter's Castle* (1958), Ian Peebles recalls perhaps MacLaren's most notorious habit: 'I have heard old timers say he was liable to enter the dressing room clutching his head and saying, "Look what they've given me this time." Or "Gracious me! Don't tell me you're playing!" Which cannot have been very good for morale.'

No, indeed. Without Cardus, in fact, MacLaren might have faded altogether: *Autobiography*, today probably the most read of Cardus's works, still tends his monument, if in a slightly unusual way. MacLaren was a cricketer like many others, a lion on the field, a lamb everywhere else; Cardus's MacLaren is the archetypal object of youthful devotion to whose faults and failings we are impervious. There was only one MacLaren, but everyone has *a* MacLaren.

Cricinfo July 2006

CHARLIE BLYTHE

Painted Figures

Wednesday week marks a hundred years since a game of forgotten feats but immemorial imagery. Over three days from 9 August 1906, Kent overcame Lancashire at Canterbury's St Lawrence Ground by an innings and 195 runs, thanks largely to 176 from their elegant amateur Kenneth Hutchings and destructive fast bowling from Arthur Fielder, en route to securing their first county championship of the modern era. But it would have receded into antiquity like myriad others of the period had not it become the subject of an extraordinarily detailed likeness by the salon painter Albert Chevallier Tayler.

E.W. Swanton reckoned it 'one of the finest ever portrayals of distinguished identifiable cricketers in action'; it is by some way the most valuable, having fetched £600,000 at auction last year. The eye falls first, out of habit, on the striking batsman: the diminutive figure of Lancashire's Johnny Tyldesley, who had taken the Kent bowlers for 295 earlier in the season, and whose dismissal for 19 and 4 here was a leading indicator of Lancashire's eclipse. But the image is set in motion by the figure of Kent's slow-left-arm hero, Charlie Blythe, about to release from the pavilion end, where he was favoured by a slight slope, in the setting where his 281 wickets cost less than 15 runs each.

The opposition is an intriguing one. Although Hutchings and Fielder were the match's undoubted stars, ahead of greater feats the following year in Melbourne, where the former made a hundred in a session and the latter conjured the winning runs in a single-wicket victory, Lord Harris apparently insisted that Blythe be the bowler in the picture. By homing in on Blythe's duel with Tyldesley, Tayler makes the game's defining contest, in a period defined even in the writings of C.L.R. James as a belle époque of amateurism, that between two skilled professionals. What's more, they strike attitudes of exquisite poise. Tyldesley's trim figure, still but relaxed, is nearly upright, the high-gripped bat placed daintily in the block, the toe of his front foot poking toward cover. And Blythe hovers above the crease, face fixed, body tensed, front foot arched in space, concealed arm about to begin its upswing – Blythe's arm, in fact, came, with a studied nonchalance, from behind his back, hiding the ball until it left the hand.

Harry Altham's description of Blythe in action might well serve as the painting's caption: 'The very look on his face, the long, sensitive fingers, the elastic back sweep of the arm before delivery with the right hand thrown up in perfect balance against it, the short dancing approach, the long last stride, and the final flick of the arm as it came over, all these spoke of a highly sensitive and nervous instrument, beautifully co-ordinated, directed by a subtle mind, and inspired by a natural love for its art.'

Blythe came from unpromising material, the son of an engine-fitter at the Arsenal. 'Blythe lived at Deptford,' wrote his Kent mentor, Captain William McCanlis, 'a place one would hardly go in search of cricketers. The lads of this town have only the roughest parts of Blackheath on which to play their occasional cricket.' McCanlis first spied Blythe as 'one of the crowd' bowling idly at Walter Wright when Kent visited the town; impressed by what he saw, McCanlis invited the boy to trial at his Tonbridge 'nursery'.

Observing his slim build and high forehead, Neville Cardus, the junior romantic, nurtured an elaborate fantasy of Blythe's aristocratic past, until it was rudely disturbed by hearing him twit a team-mate: 'I'll 'it yer on top o' the nose in a minute!' Yet he began his portrait of Blythe in *Good Days* (1934) with an aesthete's appreciation: 'Blythe of Kent – what a name, how perfect for the prettiest slow left-handed bowler of his, or surely any other, period!' And he was right to sense delicate sensibilities behind the deceptive flight. Blythe played the violin with his supple spinner's fingers; likewise on big occasions, the tendency exacerbated by epilepsy, was he strung up to concert pitch.

A year after Blythe's canvas immortality, he achieved cricket indelibility, taking 17 Northants wickets in a day at Northampton, then, in the Test at Headingley the following month, 15 South African wickets for 99. C.B. Fry called the latter game 'the tautest cricket match in which I have ever played', and perceived the toll on its star: 'The strain of the match was severe, especially on Colin Blythe, who was completely knocked up. From start to finish he never bowled a single ball except of impeccable length. The situation was that three bad overs could have lost the match.' The strain was such, in fact, that in the next ten days, a wan Blythe could winkle out only 4 county batsmen for 313. He bowled well at the Oval, then on the Ashes tour that winter failed altogether: Philip Trevor could hardly believe it was 'the real Blythe', as 'he often found it difficult even to keep a good length.'

It was situations rather than opponents that troubled Blythe, for he removed batsmen in county cricket with almost surgical deftness: thoroughbred batsmen, too, including Gilbert Jessop nineteen times, and Tom Hayward and his protégé, Jack Hobbs, seventeen times each. Yet now a reputation for frailty would precede him, preventing improvement on his 100 Test wickets at 18.63, and his accumulating more than three Players caps against the Gentlemen. As well, there was the availability of the perhaps less artful but certainly more arch Wilf Rhodes. Unlike Rhodes, for example, Blythe was singularly uninterested in batting, and conveyed that indifference to spectators – so much so that correspondence broke out in the columns of *Cricketer* in 1978 about whether he was right or left-handed; it was answered finally on the authority of his team-mate Frank Woolley: 'He was a right-hand batsman who spent very little time at the crease, say at the most four balls.'

In his last season, Blythe was as potent as ever, striking with undisturbed regularity for 170 wickets at 15: he was thirty-five, and might have bowled on for a decade and more. But young men with his socio-economic background went mainly in one direction after September 1914. Enlisting in the Kent Fortress Engineers soon after the outbreak of war, and attached to the Yorkshire Light Infantry, he lost his life to a random shell-fall on the railway between Pimmern and Forest Hall two days *after* the capture of Passchendaele village, the news coming soon after another shell claimed the life of Hutchings. He was to be twice remembered at his happiest hunting ground: as a soldier, his two shrapnel-streaked wallets on display in the pavilion, and as an artist in Tayler's painting, his heel hovering an inch or two above the ground, forever.

Cricinfo August 2006

PADDY MCSHANE
Missing in Action

Next month the Melbourne Cricket Club will unveil a tapestry marking its sesquicentenary, designed by artist and member Robert Ingpen. Measuring almost 19 square metres, it teems with life and lives, some famous, some obscure – and none like Paddy McShane's. Everything came easily for McShane in sport. Classed 'the best all-round athlete in Victoria' 120 years ago, he represented his colony at football as a ruckman, his country at cricket as a left-handed opening bowler, ran fast and jumped long. Daily cares took greater toll. Few sportsmen have met more squalid ends.

For those fond of records, McShane's name has never lost currency. Only one Australian has returned an analysis superior to his 9–45 at the Sydney Cricket Ground in March 1881, for a Combined Victoria–New South Wales XI against Billy Murdoch's national team, then just returned from England garlanded with glory. And nobody has paralleled his feat at Adelaide Oval a month later: an all-run seven, without overthrows, from a straight drive.

McShane has an indelible place in history, too. After a successful career at Essendon Football Club, including its vice-captaincy, he helped found Fitzroy Football Club in September 1883. Club meetings were held at his hostelry, the Leicester Arms in Leicester Street, and McShane became their inaugural captain in April 1884. Broad-shouldered, massively moustachioed, arms akimbo, he looks impatient for action in Fitzroy's first team photograph.

His taste of big cricket against England almost a year later was then an unusual one, following a mutiny among players about their

242

rightful share of gate-monies which deprived Australia of its choicest talent. In the unruly summer, McShane filled several breaches. Named twelfth man for the Fourth Test in March 1885, he umpired when the original appointment withdrew. Managing not to offend anybody in this awkward role, he made his Test debut the following week. Scores of international cricketers have become umpires; McShane is one of only two to stand in a Test before playing.

McShane fulfilled all parts of his potential except those which might have guaranteed his future. He capriciously resigned Fitzroy's captaincy in August 1885 to further his track-and-field career, where he won golden opinions as a sprinter and recorded a 6.5-metre long jump. But his two further Test appearances were inconspicuous, and he ultimately obtained only a sole wicket, albeit a poignant one: English slow-bowler Johnny Briggs, who was destined to die in Cheadle Asylum in July 1902, prostrated by epilepsy. By that time, McShane was similarly confined.

McShane came from a working-class Roman Catholic family, and was never well off. When he wed twenty-two-year-old Jeannie Brown in February 1887, he was a travelling salesman – a regular recourse of the hard-up. St Kilda Cricket Club offered more commodious employment as a curator in November 1889, to the delight of Tom Horan, the *Australasian*'s avuncular cricket correspondent: 'During recent seasons he has been somewhat like the rolling stone which gathereth no moss, but now he has brought himself to an anchor … let us hope he will not slip cable for many a day.'

The anchor, however, steadily became a weight. Within six years, McShane was providing for six children on essentially a labourer's wage. Notes recording his committal to Kew Asylum in September 1901 detail the defeat of McShane's health and hygiene: the filth in his hair, the vermin in his beard, and a febrile restlessness curbed only by doses of chloral hydrate. Still more complete was the rout of his reason.

What we would probably call schizophrenia, doctors a century ago called 'mania'. They dutifully documented McShane's kaleidoscope of delusions. 'Thinks all the wealth in the British kingdom is his,' reads one entry. 'That a ventilator in his room was really the hangman's drop and he had seen a man hanged there.' Sporting prowess counted for nothing here: his confinement was grindingly typical. By comparison, indeed, not even his visions were especially noteworthy. One 'mania' victim admitted around the same time asserted that the ocean had no bottom; another claimed to be representing God on a mission to convert the Jews.

The environment was hardly one to inculcate reassurance and relief. By the time McShane arrived, Kew Asylum was thirty years old. Its architectural grandeur attested the wealth of colonial society at the time of its building, its abysmal conditions the eternal marginalising of the mentally ill. British Medical Association visitors described it in November 1879 as 'the worst-managed institution in the colony', being 'an imposing building on a magnificent site with an internal appearance and arrangement that would do little credit to a workhouse'. Good intentions weren't lacking. The so-called Lunacy Commission of 1884 had made various proposals for mitigating its overcrowding and disorganisation, including the separation of those suffering mental disorders from the criminally insane and alcoholics. Depression in the 1890s had thwarted them all. For a population exceeding 1000, the Asylum had only three medical officers.

McShane's case history reflects prevailing mental health precept, being dedicated largely to restraint. When he began sedulously shredding his own clothing, for instance, he was simply issued canvas attire and gloves. He lapsed briefly into lucidity in February 1902, after being permitted to watch a cricket match on the asylum's green, but the grip of hallucination tightened again. 'Talking of impossible schemes,' scrawled a doctor visiting six months later. 'That he is going to make millions out of a travelling group and wants half the patients in the asylum to become members of it.' The only treatment mentioned explicitly is an enema administered the day before his death, of influenza, on 11 December 1903.

While Paddy McShane is an inconspicuous presence in the MCC's tapestry, there largely to fill out the original Fitzroy strip and hose, it is nevertheless a happy event that Robert Ingpen should have woven in this loosest of historical threads. McShane's story reminds us that misfortune, like sport, is no respecter of reputations.

Age July 2004

BOB FOWLER

The Student Prince

July 1910 was a month of headlines a mile high: the ascension of a new king, George V; the chase for an infamous murderer, Dr Crippen; magnificent men in flying machines at Rheims; grey-beards grinding out the Triple Alliance, the Russo–Japanese Agreement, the Pan-American Conference and the Pan-Slav Congress, not to mention repunctuation of the Lord's Prayer. Yet for a moment, their import was equalled by a most unlikely athlete: no cricketer has known fame so great for a match so minor as Robert St Leger Fowler, captain of Eton, in the annual match against Harrow at Lord's.

'A more exciting match can hardly ever have been played,' decreed *The Times*, likening its 'electric rapidity' to that of the inaugural Ashes Test at the Oval twenty-eight years earlier, and Fowler's performance to that of Fred Spofforth, albeit that 'to boys the bowling of Fowler was probably more formidable than Spofforth's to England'. *Wisden*'s verdict was even more emphatic: 'In the whole history of cricket, there has been nothing more sensational … The struggle … will forever be known as Fowler's match. Never has a school cricketer risen to the occasion in more astonishing fashion.'

Eton v Harrow a century ago, after more than a century of exchanges, was at the zenith of its prestige as a fixture. Games drew as many as 20,000 to watch and promenade, transforming the playing field at intervals into a sea of top hats and parasols. As *Cricket* summed it up in previewing the 1910 match: 'Men who have become famous as statesmen, orators, scientists, authors or in some other manner, have done their best for their school at Lord's, and have probably without exception always referred with greatest pride to the fact that their cricketical skills gained them a place in the XI.'

These were the sons of the elite, and the nation's future leaders. In the 1910 match were a field marshal (Harold Alexander), an air vice-marshal (C.H.B. Blount), and an attorney-general (Walter Monckton) in the making, alongside sundry sons of dukes and earls. And it is certainly true in this case that none of the participants ever quite got over the experience. 'In the minds even of non-cricketers, the very mention of "Fowler's match" may arouse a faint movement, as of something rare and strange,' said Alexander's biographer, Nigel Nicholson, in *Alex* (1973). 'To those who took part in it, the memory turns old men into boys.'

Nineteen-year-old Bob Fowler was at home in this exalted company. Descended from a Protestant clergyman who had settled in Ireland in the 1760s, he was a son of a professional soldier in Enfield, County Meath. The Anglo-Irish aristocracy at the time would no sooner have schooled their offspring at home than belted out a chorus of 'Sean South of Garryowen'. When he brought the fundamentals of cricket home from his prep school, Mr Hawtrey's in Westgate-on-Sea, he practised by bowling interminably at a chalk mark – with a footman to do the retrieving.

At Eton, Fowler came under the influence of his housemaster, the Middlesex amateur Cyril Wells, who turned him into an off-break bowler of formidable accuracy: his 11 for 79 had almost won the annual fixture for Eton in July 1909. A year later, the challenge was steeper. Only one player other than Fowler carried over from the previous game; Harrow had seven veterans of the rivalry. Their splendoured fixture list had also yielded rather different fortunes: Eton had lost to Free Foresters, Authentics and Butterflies; Harrow was unbeaten, having disposed of Free Foresters, Harlequins, Quidnuncs and the Household Brigade, and was very pleased about it, in a muscular Christian kind of way. English public schools, of course, could be bleak places for the sport intolerant: the young Nehru found Harrow 'a small and restricted place' where boys talked of nothing but cricket. To be fair, though, they had a good deal to be excited about, two Old Harrovians, F.S. Jackson and Archie MacLaren, having led England in the preceding five years.

Harrow began the match on Friday, 8 July, full of purpose, compiling 232 under grey skies on a pitch turning appreciably but slowly. A callow keeper conceded 18 byes as Fowler and his leg-spinner partner, Allan Steel, son of the Test player A.G., shared 8 wickets. Nothing suggested that it would not be a match of patient application and minor advantages. But Eton crumbled at once in reply, finishing the day at 5 for 40: a situation *The Times* already thought 'almost desperate'. Fowler's 21 ended up being the only double-figure score in Eton's eventual 67 from 48 overs.

When Steel was caught in the second innings, Eton's score following on had dwindled to 5 for 65. Spectators began leaving. It was a Saturday. The Gentlemen and Players were playing a tight game at the Oval; perhaps there was more entertainment there. With 100 needed to make Harrow bat again and only the tail remaining, however, Eton rallied. Harrow's fast-bowler captain, Guy Earle, the only future Test player in the match, unaccountably spelled Alexander, who had already secured 5 wickets in the match with his leg-spin, and Fowler found an ally in Donald Wigan, with whom he added 42.

Fowler then teamed up with William Boswell to wipe away the rest of the arrears. In the face of Fowler's controlled hitting – his 64 contained eight fours, a three, ten twos and nine singles – the fielding grew ragged, and Eton's spectators became as boisterous as Harrow's were solemn. A.B. Stock fell quickly, but the last wicket was prolonged by the two junior aristocrats Hon. John Manners and Kenelm Lister-Kaye, who thrashed 50 in a hectic half-hour.

There should still have been no question of the result. With Harrow needing only 55 to win, Earle requested the heavy roller to subdue the pitch; Eton faced a challenge of almost exquisite hopelessness. F.S. Ashley-Cooper reported that confidence was still general: 'Harrovians, feeling at peace with all men, settled down with a languid air to watch the runs hit off for the loss of perhaps a couple of wickets in half an hour or so.'

So quickly did the face of the match change, in fact, that anxiety must have been lurking. Perhaps there was even the seductive sense that all were playing a part in an improbable romance. Any writing about public schools cricket before World War I demands reference to Sir Henry Newbolt's martial doggerel *Vitai Lampada*, in which the youthful cry of 'Play up! Play up! And play the game!' rallies first a counterattacking cricket team, then a beleaguered regiment in a colonial battlescape. It seems sadly apposite here: of the aforementioned boys, Steel, Stock, Manners and Boswell would all be killed on active service in the Great War, then barely four years away; likewise the three Harrovians, Geoffrey Hopley, Tom Wilson and Thomas Lancelot Gawain Turnbull, who succumbed in Fowler's first two overs. At the time, though, the elision would not have seemed so crude. Fowler was a soldier's son, destined for Sandhurst. Maybe he invoked Gordon at Khartoum, or Chard and Bromhead at Rorke's Drift; perhaps he enjoined his boys to fight on with the famous words of the expiring colonel at Albuera: 'Die hard, 57th, die hard!' Whatever the case, they did fight, fielding tigerishly, catching brilliantly, keeping composedly, preserving that 55 like their vital spark.

Fowler, meanwhile, bowled as he can seldom have bowled. Charles Eyre, an Old Harrovian, felt a grim foreboding at the sight of his first ball: 'It looked to break a yard and come off the pitch like a rattlesnake.' But conditions were not the determinant. Under such circumstances, slow bowlers can panic, either trying too hard, or expecting the pitch to do all the work. Fowler did neither, simply adjusting his line a little and continuing to vary his pace so that driving became treacherous, and runs nearly unobtainable. Opener Tom Jameson spent forty minutes on 0. Middle order batsman Walter Monckton, equal to the strain of the abdication of Edward VIII twenty-six years later, didn't last that long.

'Walter took guard and played his first ball safely,' recalled his biographer Lord Birkenhead in *The Life of Viscount Monckton of Brenchley* (1969). 'Then Fowler, by an inspiration of genius, tried him with a slow full-toss, and to the dismay of all his friends and to every Harrow supporter, Walter was clean bowled, and had to make the silent and terrible return to the pavilion.'

The most delightful description of Harrow's second innings, however, is an almost unimprovable passage in Lt Col C.P. Foley's *Autumn Foliage* (1935), which merits quoting at length: 'I was going to spend that Saturday to Monday at Coombe with General Arthur Paget, and, not being in the least anxious to see an overwhelming Harrow victory, I left the ground and called in at White's Club to pick up my bag. Providentially, as it turned out, my hair wanted cutting. Half way through the operation Lord Brackley looked in and said "Harrow have lost four wickets for 21 runs," and a few minutes later, "Harrow have lost six wickets for 21 runs."

'That was enough. I sprang from my chair with my hair half cut and standing on end, and we rushed together into the street, jumped into a taxi, and said "Lord's! Double fare if you do it in fifteen minutes". We got there in 14 minutes 21 5/8 seconds (I carry a stop-watch), paid the man, and advanced on the pavilion at a pace which is called in the French army *le pas gymnastique*.

'The shallow steps leading to the pavilion at Lord's form a right-angle. Round this angle I sprang three steps at a time, carrying my umbrella at the trail. A dejected Harrovian, wearing a dark blue rosette, and evidently unable to bear the agony of the match any longer, was leaving the pavilion with bowed head. I was swinging my umbrella to give me impetus, and its point caught the unfortunate man in the lower part of his waistcoat, and rebounded from one of its buttons out of my hand and over the side rails of the pavilion.

'The impact was terrific, and the unlucky individual, doubling up, sank like a wounded buffalo on to his knees, without, as far as I recollect, uttering a sound. I sprang over the body without apology, and, shouting out instructions to George Bean, the Sussex pro, who was the gate attendant, to look after my umbrella, dashed into the pavilion and up the many steps to its very summit, where I hoped to find a vacant seat.'

No sooner had Foley taken his seat than Fowler bowled Straker to reduce Harrow to 8 for 29. Jameson, usually a free scorer and later an amateur squash champion, was also bowled by Fowler after finally scavenging a couple to get off the mark, leaving Harrow 23 from victory with a wicket left.

Joining his friend Ogilvie Graham at the wicket was Alexander. He was another *beau ideal* schoolboy. He had been three years in the first XI, played in the rugger XV, excelled in the Rifle Corps, had won the year's cross-country run by 200 metres, and come narrowly second in the mile-and-a-half. According to one account, he had stuffed himself with bun in expectation of a restful afternoon, but now went indomitably about the deficit, cheered to the echo with every run. 'If he had succeeded,' noted Nicholson, 'it would have been known as Alexander's match instead of Fowler's.' He fell 10 short, nicking Steel to slip, leaving Fowler with 21, 64, 4–90 and 8–23; Alexander had to be content with later defeating Rommel's Afrika Corps.

What *The Times* described as 'most pardonable pandemonium' ensued, continuing into the following week, for Eton's VIII also won the Ladies' Challenge Plate at Henley. In celebration, there was a ritual 'hoisting', where Fowler, Manners, Boswell and two rowers were carried quickly, if somewhat uncomfortably, through the college, to the cheers of a throng of past and present Etonians: an event, rather remarkably, considered worthy of a detailed report in the *Daily Telegraph*: 'The members of Pop assembled on Barnes Pool Bridge at 7.30 p.m., some attired in flannels and ducks and other wearing top hats.'

Fowler's crowded hour, however, was over. A few weeks later he emulated his father by enrolling at Sandhurst, where he won the Sword of Honour the following year and became a cavalryman. With the 17th Lancers, 'the death or glory boys' famously bloodied at Balaclava who sported the skull and crossbones on their regimental colours, Captain Fowler lived out the Newboltian vision by winning the Military Cross during the defence of Amiens from Ludendorff's *Kaiserschlacht* of March 1918. Fowler's cricket henceforward was confined to games for Army and Free Foresters, apart from a couple of games for Hampshire in 1924, soon after which he was diagnosed with the leukaemia that killed him the following year, aged thirty-four: a melancholy case of promise unfulfilled.

It is doubtful that Fowler mourned missed sporting opportunities. Testimonies to him suggest a young man consumed by martial and filial responsibilities: 'His simplicity, straightforwardness, courage and pertinacity were as noticeable in afterlife as they had been at school,' wrote his obituarist in the *Chronicle* at Eton. What survives of him is not, however, a career of brave soldiering: his enduring fame lay not in the corner of a foreign field, but in the middle of a local one, where he became the schoolboy cricketer *in excelsis*. What good came of it at last? As Old Kaspar answered Peterkin: '"That I cannot tell," said he, / "But 'twas a famous victory."'

Cricinfo May 2006

FRED ROOT

Gentleman Player

One day at Worcester eighty years ago, when the home team was playing Glamorgan, the visitors' openers, Arnold Dyson and Eddie Bates, were involved in a mid-pitch collision that left both prostrated on the pitch as the ball was returned to the bowler, Fred Root. Root paused, then generously chose not to break the non-striker's stumps: the batsmen seemed quite badly injured. 'Break the wicket, Fred, break the wicket!' shouted a keen amateur teammate. Root was annoyed: 'If you want to run him out, here's the ball; *you* come and do it.' The amateur explained hastily, 'Oh, I'm an amateur. *I* can't do such a thing.'

Root, as he recalled it, was irked – as, in a twenty-three-year career bowling inswing for Leicestershire, Derbyshire and Worcestershire, he often was by just such hypocrisies. English cricket between the wars is generally regarded as a period of prelapsarian innocence, one in which cricket was simply a game and everyone knew their place. Jack Williams writes in *Cricket and England* (1999): 'Assumptions about cricket being an expression of English morality were not restricted to the inter-war period, but they were probably no stronger at any other time.' Root, with his earthy name, burly physique and open mien, looks like one of those cheerful toilers that were the backbone of the county-cricket economy. Except that, as his fascinating autobiography *A Cricket Pro's Lot* (1937) reveals, he wasn't.

Root, the son of Leicestershire's groundsman, was not to be deflected from his boyhood ambition to become a cricket pro. As a fifteen-year-old, he visited his vicar in search of a testimonial. The vicar asked whom it was for. 'Please sir, to Mr Robson, the secretary of Leicestershire Cricket Club,' explained Root. 'And I am going to be a cricketer.' The clergyman harrumphed: 'I couldn't possibly allow it to be used for the purpose you propose.' No matter: there were other vicars. When Root was shot in the chest as a dispatch rider in 1916, an army doctor told him he was to be discharged but could not realistically expect to play cricket again; Root arranged a contract in the Bradford League from his hospital bed.

Root's book is unwaveringly loyal to those of his vocation. Of the best dozen batsmen and bowlers he chooses from his career, eleven are professionals. His hero was selfless Dick Pearson, who always went without wages if money was short and 'thought it an honour to wait'; he delighted in 'Nudger' Needham, who wore his street clothes beneath his flannels so he could hasten to catch the same train every night from the station. He also admired those amateurs who played like professionals, such as Johnny Douglas, whom he once heard coaching a young left-arm spinner: 'Joe, if you bowl that sort of tripe again I'll punch your head.'

There are no statistics in *A Cricket Pro's Lot*: Root deprecated them as a measure of merit. Instead there is a calculus of his productivity per pound of wages. Root explains that he budgeted 1500 overs a season for 150 wickets, and 47 innings for between 800 and 1000 runs. For this, he complained, he could expect just £300, less hotels for away games, and taxis, insurance and incidentals; he had even to pay for his own rubdowns. 'It is popularly supposed that there is quite a lot of money in first-class cricket,' wrote Root. 'If there is I have not found it. It is the worst paid of all the professional games.'

The advice section of *A Cricket Pro's Lot* is occupational not inspirational, aimed not at producing champions but at assisting the jobbing cricketer with a lifetime of tradesman's tricks: one learns to use talcum powder for chafing, methylated spirits for skinned fingers, and not to forget an extra pair of socks for support. Find your limits, is the message; don't let them find you. Don't try bowling fast: 'Not one in a hundred youths can bowl really fast.' Don't try moving it too much: 'The most dangerous ball is the one that "moves" a little.' Don't waste energy as you get older: 'A cricketer is as old as he fields.' And don't forget to contemplate your mortality: 'The professional cricketer's boom years are few … When age takes its toll, it needs a man with a very strong will to adapt himself to the humdrum of ordinary life … and days are long and prosaically uneventful. Many of the cricket heroes of the past are getting what consolation they can out of their memories – and an unskilled job of work at a mere pittance of a wage.'

Early in his career, Root complained to 'a well-known official holding high office at Lord's' about being required to do so much hackwork in the nets before games. The official upbraided him: 'I am surprised at you, Root. You are lucky to be playing in the match at all. Please realise that professional bowlers are nothing more or less than the hired labourers of the game.' Nothing in *A Cricket Pro's Lot* is described with such relish as him getting the better of such stuffed shirts. Root describes, for instance, how he persuaded the poor-mouthing Worcestershire committee to guarantee him a benefit of £500. The club secretary pleaded, 'If we had any money, Fred, we would make it a thousand pounds, but, knowing as we do, how you so richly deserve all we can possibly afford, shall we agree on £250?' Root simply fished out the offer of a Lancashire League contract worth £600 that he had just received; the request was granted.

Root's particular grievance, however, was not austerity itself; it was the inequality of the burden of sacrifice. The lucky amateur, he complained in a passage with a familiar ring, did well from the game: 'Manufacturers of well-known goods from fountain pens and energy restoratives to easy chairs and hair-oil shower their samples with lavish generosity in much the same manner as they accommodate film stars. "Stars", too, often sign on the dotted line beneath a newspaper article which bears their name but which sometimes they do not even read, and afterwards they sign the endorsement on the back of the cheque in payment … And so

the game goes on, full of make-believe; and yet everybody intimately connected with cricket knows all about it.'

The cricket pro of Root's period was meant to be unimaginative
and deferential, even obsequious. Root's prognostications about
cricket, however, prove to be remarkably farsighted, and expressed
with the nerve of a man who once had the temerity to tell Lord
Hawke to stop talking in the slips. Root urged officials to 'adapt
themselves to the type of cricket which pleases the patrons and is
demanded by them', and even traced the outline of a limited-over
knockout tournament among the counties: 'Make the matches
sharp and snappy. So many overs to be bowled by each side if you
like, but aim at a definite result in a specified time ... The public
do not want extensions, they cry out for contractions.' Root lived
just long enough to see one of his wishes granted: the appointment
of a professional captain of England, for which 'these democratic
times' cried out, because 'a title and lots of money doesn't assure
the scoring of centuries'. Others, like a transfer market, he did not;
a few, like penalties for scoring at less than a run a minute, have
remained fancies.

Root didn't want to be seen as a 'red revolutionary'. Various
grandees – such as Lady Warwick, whose son he coached, and Lord
Coventry, who would take the Worcestershire side to shoot game
with him – feature in *A Cricket Pro's Lot*, in admiring cameos. Ultimately, his narrative is a reinforcing one: 'This cricket is a great
and glorious game. It is played by grand fellows. In spite of my
grouses I shall try to play it until the "reaper" bowls me out.' But
the Gilbertian air of the title is surely not coincidental: a cricket
pro's lot is not a happy one.

Cricinfo January 2006

HARRY OWEN ROCK
The Immovable Dr Rock

In the statistics of Australian cricket, Dr Harry Owen Rock is a jut-
ting outcrop, with a first-class average of 94.75 – just a chip shy of
Bradman's 95.14. Indeed, his Sheffield Shield average of 112 gives
him a slight edge on the Don: something John Howard would
probably regard as un-Australian. The record is, of course, a trick
of the mathematical light, for Rock's 758 runs were gathered in
half a dozen games. The 1920s, too, saw runs being made in industrial quantities around the world, ahead of their full-scale mass
production in the 1930s. But the arithmetic progression of Rock's
scores has an undeniable authority: 127, 27 not out, 235, 51, 151,
12, 35, 81, 39. Even *Wisden* thought he 'must surely have ranked
among the great' had his career not been truncated by the call of
medicine and thirty years as a general practitioner in Newcastle.

Rock, a son of a Cambridge cricket Blue, was a prodigious
junior athlete at King's School, where he was coached by Mick
Waddy and Gerry Hazlitt. He was from the first a fine driver with
a long reach, whose slight build belied his power, and one of only
three King's players to pass 1000 runs in a season. War service with
the 3rd Brigade Artillery not only cost him run-bearing years, but
also altered his style. After damaging ligaments in his knees while
trying to shift horse-drawn artillery pieces bogged in the mud, he
refashioned his stance on upright lines, holding the bat raised. It
made him a quaint sight at the crease: opponents were often
unsure if he was quite ready to take strike. The impression did not
last. When he began playing cricket for Sydney University, while

undertaking medical studies, stiff legs became more of a problem for bowlers.

To infiltrate the powerful New South Wales team of the '20s required luck and patience. Rock had to wait until November 1924, when Collins, Macartney, Bardsley, Taylor and Scott were all unavailable; as it was, the team still featured past and future internationals Kippax, Oldfield, Andrews and Mailey. In any event, Rock lost nothing by comparison with any of this exalted company, his debut hundred requiring just two hours and twenty minutes. The *Referee*'s venerable J.C. Davis deemed his fourteen fours 'as classic as anything seen this summer from any of the international batsmen' – a sample, incidentally, that included Ponsford, Ryder, Hobbs, Sutcliffe and Woolley.

Davis, then the game's most respected newspaper critic, was even more appreciative of Rock's six-and-a-half-hour sequel at the SCG against Victoria in January 1925: 'H.O. Rock is a veritable stoic at the wickets. He takes his stand with ease, and has no semblance of movement or mannerism until he moves the bat to meet the ball. Everything is done with mechanical accuracy that makes batting look an easy or effortless thing.' This was the highest possible praise, an anticipation of the kind of Fordist production logic that would be admired in 'run machines' like Ponsford and Bradman.

Rock's career, however, was not a linear progression. The availability of the state's Test stars, and his own medical examinations, precluded further matches that season: he satisfied himself by topping the Sydney grade averages with 655 runs at 55. There seemed much to look forward to when he began the 1925–26 season with 151 in a helter-skelter session against Western Australia at the SCG, but he was dynamited out by Jack Gregory and stranded by Arthur Mailey when representing the Rest in a pre-Ashes-tour trial game against Australia a fortnight later. There were no further opportunities. Rock went all the way to Adelaide to be twelfth man for New South Wales soon after; his remaining two first-class innings were at number seven, beginning at 5 for 291 and 5 for 465, and Australia sailed for England without him.

There may have been some pique involved in Rock's decision to renounce the game when he graduated as a doctor in 1926. Australian cricket had already featured its share of doctors: Tup Scott, John Barrett, Roy Minnett, Percy Charlton, Roley Pope, Claude Tozer. And in the mid-1920s, doctors – and also dentists – were surprisingly thick on the ground in Sheffield Shield cricket: New South Wales had Eric Barbour; Queensland had Otto Nothling and Percy Hornibrook; Victoria, Roy Park and Albert Hartkopf; South Australia, Harry Fisher and Norman Williams.

Examples known to Rock also suggested that a professional career need not have cramped his cricket style. One of his King's School contemporaries, Dr Reg Bettington, was at that stage a star leg-break bowler for Oxford and Middlesex; one of his Sydney University comrades, Dr Jim Bogle, also scored a century on debut for New South Wales before moving on to medical practice in Port Douglas. And Rock's New South Wales contemporary Johnny Taylor was still a Test player, despite the demands of his dentistry exams.

Perhaps Rock had diagnosed in himself an irreversible medical condition: age. He turned thirty in October. This need not have been a handicap, except that Australia was coming to the end of the cricket Kondratieff that had begun with the AIF team of 1919, and was heavy with famous, decorated but declining players: Collins (thirty-seven), Macartney (forty), Bardsley (forty-three), Mailey (forty) and even, by that stage, Gregory (thirty-one). Rock apparently queried captain Herbie Collins about his lack of opportunities and was informed that his knees had been held against him: there were concerns about his fielding. This was a little unkind – Rock had more than stood in for injured keepers in games – but was probably influenced by the decreasing mobility of the Australian Test team of the day.

Rock's example, then, reminds us that the establishment of a career needs more than just one's own excellence; the time must also be ripe. Donald Bradman's first nine first-class innings, not two years later, yielded only 282 runs – barely a third as many as

Rock's – but his state place was never in jeopardy: by that stage, Australia had lost the Ashes, taking that senior playing generation with them. Rock had to be content with leaving an outcrop submerged by the tide of events, which re-emerged to engage the browsing eye only with that tide's withdrawal.

Cricinfo February 2006

BERT IRONMONGER
Australian Son

The statistics by which we mostly know Bert Ironmonger are those of a long, hard, patient haul. He made his Sheffield Shield debut, in December 1914, in his thirty-third year; he waited another fourteen years for his first Test cap; his first-class career, packing in 464 first-class wickets at 21.5 and 74 Test wickets at 18, extended more than a quarter of a century. Yet Ironmonger not only played cricket in a different era, he might almost have played it in a different country. His was the Australia of rural hardship: he was the youngest of ten children in a farming family that had to abandon working an uneconomic block north-west of Ipswich, whereupon at twenty-five he became a labourer on the railways. His was also the Australia of long-term labour: after arriving in Melbourne in December 1913 and working as a barman and a tobacconist, he took a job as a gardener with the St Kilda City Council, tending parklands with a hand-mower until the age of seventy, even though his wages were suspended when he was away from work playing cricket.

Ironmonger is the member of a genus of Australians almost vanished from today's land of plenty, a man of what used to be called 'steady habits': he was frugal, conservative, neither smoked nor drank, and lived with his wife and children in the same unprepossessing house, with flower beds and vegetable patch, for forty years; they did not have a telephone until 1939, and never owned a car. His life spanned the decline of his type. The majority of Australia's population would not be urbanised until after World

War II, but the change was underway, embodied in Donald Bradman, the country boy who came to the big smoke to pursue his dreams, swapping farmer's togs for the smart suits and shiny shoes of retail, real estate and sharebroking. Ironmonger, his very name evoking a vanishing vocation, carried on, continuing to mow lawns for the elderly in his area even after retiring from work, his burly frame, broad shoulders and forearms a testament to the outdoor life. The Melbourne General Cemetery in Carlton, where he is interred, is thickly sewn with men of great deeds: prime ministers, governors-general, eminent jurists, distinguished writers. Ironmonger lies in a secluded corner near where the grounds-keepers store their maintenance gear.

Part of Ironmonger's life, it is worth recalling, was entirely extraordinary. As a boy, he lost half his left forefinger in a chaff-cutter on the family farm; his sister probably saved his life by plunging the copiously bleeding hand into a bag of flour. No fuss, however, attended Ironmonger's career; where today he might have become a poster child for the disadvantaged or disfigured, he instead turned the extraordinary into something utterly ordinary, spinning the ball off the stump of his finger as though it was as nature intended. And in a society in which stoicism was still admired, labour remained predominantly manual and a generation of men had been mutilated by World War I, this was the custom.

On 12 November 1932, the Melbourne-based weekly the *Australasian* published a lavish photographic spread headed 'Bowlers' Grips': colourised images demonstrating the metacarpal configurations preferred by ten famous bowlers, from Clarrie Grimmett and Bill O'Reilly to Harold Larwood and Hedley Verity. Of course, the reader has only the paper's word for the ownership of these disembodied appendages, but one there is no mistaking. 'H. Ironmonger: Left-hand spin from leg' shows a hand protruding from the sleeve of an Australian sweater, gnarled, wizened, coarsened by physical labour; the ball is clasped between a strong-looking thumb, an arching middle finger and a forefinger shortened to a stub, like the butt of a big cigar. The caption, though, makes no further comment; the impressionable might even assume that surgical sacrifice is integral to left-arm slow bowling.

Ironmonger is today an obscure figure, largely overshadowed by his contemporaries, Grimmett and O'Reilly. He might be considered ripe for rediscovery. No Australian bowler has been so economical, grudging runs at 1.7 an over. No Australian has been so deadly on a damp wicket, or is likely to improve on his match figures of 11–24 against South Africa at the MCG in February 1932. No Australian has been so excellent so old, bowling more than 400 deliveries in fifteen of the sixty-five first-class matches he played after the age of forty-five.

Unsurprisingly, almost everything else about Ironmonger now seems exceedingly quaint. He could not bat to save himself, a quarter of his first-class innings ending in ducks. He shambled in the field, and no more resembled an elite athlete than he did an eminent artist. But that is because, in Ironmonger's Australia, the athletes still resembled their countrymen, walked the same streets, inhabited the same sort of houses, might have served us in a shop or a bank, might even have mowed our lawn. Ironmonger's birthplace of Ipswich produced another fine Test-match bowler, Craig McDermott, and Ironmonger's native Queensland is represented in the current Australian team by Matthew Hayden or Andrew Symonds. But they are famous, wealthy young men, with big houses and expensive cars, who play a game for their living. And do you know anyone who looks like them?

Cricinfo January 2006

R.L. HUNTE

The (Bats)Man Who Never Was

R.L. Hunte very nearly had it all. He appeared in two Test match scorecards; his records appeared in *Wisden* for eighteen years; he had a contemporary corporeal counterpart. But when he vanished, it was as though he'd never been there. And, in fact, he hadn't. This is the story of a cricketer who did extremely well, considering that he didn't exist.

Errol Ashton Clairmonte Hunte was born in Port-of-Spain on 3 October 1905, and grew into a nimble keeper and a batsman good enough to open for Trinidad, although when chosen to represent the West Indies against the MCC team led by Hon. F.S.G. Calthorpe in January 1930 he was for some reason consigned to number eleven, making 10 not out and 1. Yet that was not the only confusing aspect of Hunte's Test baptism. Though *Wisden* 1931 recognised him in his debut appearance as 'E. Hunte', when he appeared in the Second Test in his hometown, scoring 58 and 30 at first wicket down, it was as 'R.L. Hunte'. This suggests a simple mishearing of Errol as 'R.L.', although there was also a real R.L. Hunte around at the time, 46-year-old Ronald Lionel, who opened the bowling, probably at sub-light speed, for British Guiana when the MCC played the island at their next port of call, Georgetown.

Also in Georgetown, Errol Hunte, now back to being 'E.', made his greatest Test contribution, helping Clifford Roach add 144 for the first wicket. At one stage, after the first of twin hundreds from Headley, the West Indies were 1 for 340, and beat a useful touring XI that included Patsy Hendren, Bob Wyatt, Wilf Rhodes and Andy

Sandham by 289 runs. Of Hunte's 53, *Wisden* reported that he was 'missed four times', the MCC's fielding being 'badly at fault'. But *Wisden* was not best positioned to be commenting on the deficiencies of others. For, in the average tabulations on page 689, Hunte's split personality had been further divided. 'E. Hunte' had been stripped of one of his Test caps, being left with only his debut match; 'R.L. Hunte' had been awarded two Tests, his average for 155 runs having been plumped to 38.75. The real R.L. Hunte, meanwhile, had played his last game for Trinidad, but his namesake would exert a subtle gravitational pull on cricket's records for almost forty years.

Errol Hunte's cricket was to be laden with disappointment. He went to Australia with Jackie Grant's team of 1930–31, but lost his role as first-choice keeper to Ivan Barrow, and lingered in first-class cricket only three more years. Perhaps he was not a *Wisden* reader. Almanacks probably didn't have a wide circulation in Trinidad; even C.L.R. James, who as a 'British intellectual long before ten' was devouring *Review of Reviews*, *Tit-Bits* and *Comic Cuts*, among other journals, doesn't mention *Wisden* coming into his purview. But if Hunte opened *Wisden* 1948 to consult its inaugural compilation of Test cricketers, what disappointment awaited him: 'R.L. Hunte' *still* had one of his Tests, and would keep it almost the rest of Errol's life.

Quandoque bonus dormitat Homerus, of course. And just as it's sometimes said that it's harder to get out of the Australian team than get into it, books of record can be the same: so intent on assimilating the present that, as Omar Khayyam warned, piety, wit and tears are no remedy – especially in an era when news travelled so slowly and in such confined circulations. In fact, while 'E. Hunte' lived his diminished life, 'R.L. Hunte' went from strength to strength, with each year's repetition embedding himself more deeply in cricket's past. You can hear the Charters and Caldicott conversations, can't you?

'Y'know, Charters, I can't fathom why they picked that E. Hunte for those two Tests, can you?'

'No, Caldicott, but they got it right when they picked that R.L. Hunte: he was up to the mark, eh?'

'My word, yes. Look, he not only kept wickets but opened the bowling for Guiana, too!'

'Wonder why he never played again. Inter-island jealousies, no doubt.'

'Ah yes – the ooold inter-island jealousies: the curse of Caribbean cricket!'

An immaterial alter ego, of course, is not without its uses: 'Another rum and coke, please, Harry. And put it on R.L.'s slate.' Yet, the torment of losing the credit for such a large part of one's career! Imagine, if you will, an encounter between Hunte and the anti-Hunte:

'So, we meet at last. I believe you have something of mine: one Test cap.'

'Hey, I didn't take it, pal. I was going along, minding my own business; next thing I know, I'm a Test player. I figure, hey, just go with it. And lemme tell you, the babes love it. They're always asking me to tell them about my half-centuries, being dropped four times, facing Rhodes, joking with Patsy Hendren, what Learie Constantine's really like. Did I tell I'm releasing my own tour diary?'

'You fiend! That should be *my* tour diary!'

'Tell someone who cares, buster. I'm in *Wisden,* and I ain't budgin'.'

It was almost too late before anything was done. To coincide with the arrival of Garry Sobers' team of 1966, *Wisden* assembled a sizeable supplement of West Indian records; one imagines it was then that editor Norman Preston realised he had a rogue cricketer on his hands, for in the 1967 edition the almanack restored to Hunte his lost cap, and 'R.L. Hunte' dematerialised with a last spectral chuckle.

All the same, the correction went unacknowledged in the errata, reserved instead for such instances of slightly preening pedantry as: 'Page 820. Add 100 for Australians: S. Trimble 164* v Barbados Colts at Bridgetown (not first-class).' And it is unlikely

Hunte derived much satisfaction from his rehabilitation, for he died on 26 June of that year. Of course, it's always possible that the book, being published as usual in April, was sped to his bedside as belated corroboration of that third Test; one can imagine his wife reading it aloud, eyes a-gleaming:

'Errol, look! "Hunte, E. 3: v E 1929 (3)." There it is, Errol ... Errol. Errol! Oh God ...'

'He's gone, Mrs Hunte. I'm sorry.'

Even then, the almanack didn't cover itself in glory. In 'Births and Deaths of Cricketers' in *Wisden* 1968, his entry was curtly amended to 'd 1967', and the obituarist guessed he was '62': in fact, he was 61 and 266 days. Those were the days, of course, when *Wisden* was a corner store compared to the hypermarket of today. It was a labour-intensive business, dependent on the diligence of contributors and the squinting eyes of a single hard-pressed proof-reader from Sporting Handbooks. Such inexactitude is nowadays almost inconceivable, with statistics updated by the second, and so many cricket-loving souls poring over them daily with access to email and chat: *Wisden* today discretely honours Hunte with his full name, and correct birth and death dates.

Mind you, check out the player page for E.A.C. Hunte on the Cricinfo website, if you will. We have, at last, corrected Hunte's mortal span at the top. But, because the obituary has been lifted direct from the *Almanack*, down below he is still sixty-two. Seventy-seven years after not playing a Test, 'R.L. Hunte' is still plaguing hapless Errol.

Cricinfo June 2006

KEN FARNES

Fast Action Hero

With our narrowing sense of what constitutes a properly athletic physique, cricketers of the past can seem increasingly remote. How did a figure so diminutive as Harold Larwood terrorise Australia, or a man as mountainous as Warwick Armstrong intimidate England? As for W.G. Grace, today he'd be nicknamed 'Dis'.

Ken Farnes represents a type far more recognisable, standing 200 centimetres, displacing 73 kilograms and bowling what would now be called a 'heavy ball', usually fast and often short. When he became one of only six Englishmen to secure 10 wickets on Test debut, he opened the bowling with the amiable forty-year-old pro George Geary; in his next Test he was partnered by the bespectacled and ungainly Bill Bowes. Yet nobody would fail to pick Farnes as a fast bowler in a cricket identikit parade today.

R.C. Robertson-Glasgow thought him a bowler 'who can suggest even by his run-up that the batsman would do well to stay firm', and batsmen stayed hit when he hit them. Jim Swanton offered his biographer, David Thurlow, a vivid aural vignette of Farnes in the 1932 Varsity match: 'I can still hear the ball thudding around Pieter van der Bijl's ribs and Pieter giving great groans. You could hear him in the Tavern.' And Player Bill Edrich left a memento of Farnes's 8 for 43 for the Gentlemen at Lord's six years later which has a distinctly modern ring: 'I tried to play back, a defensive back stroke while turning my head and lifting my hands. The next thing I knew was that someone was saying smoothly, "Have some water, there's no hurry."'

Long before cricketers began subscribing to the body cult, too, Farnes was an addict of physical culture, who undertook a Mr Universe course, and who was often pestered in dressing rooms to show off his stomach muscles (his party piece was to contract first one half, then the other). In every team photo where you find him, he exudes a very contemporary strength and youth. He could have changed in the next cubicle to Michael Bevan without coyness. However, in most other senses Farnes was a distinctly unusual cricketer, even in his time. Pace in 1930s England was a professional vocation: Larwood, Tate, Voce, Bowes, Clark, Nichols, Copson. Farnes, a housemaster at Worksop College, was the most serene of amateurs, and the last of a line to pursue such hard labour. And Farnes's attraction to fast bowling was not so much temperamental, for he was a gentle and charming man hard to rouse to aggression, as a combination of the aesthetic and the athletic.

Twelve-year-old Farnes watched Arthur Gilligan knocking a stump from the ground in a Test at Lord's, thought it 'a wonderful, unforgettable, inspiring sight', and never lost the love of doing it himself: 'The sight of a stump seen hurtling out of the ground has always struck me as one of the finest in cricket. It sends a shock through the spectators and from the middle you can hear a gasp all round.' To not then have bowled fast, with his physique and physicality, would have seemed like a denial of destiny. In anointing him a 'Cricketer of the Year' in 1939, *Wisden* called him 'essentially a natural cricketer', and this was perhaps about more than talent; he revelled in what Frank Tyson would describe so memorably as 'the glad animal action' and the 'thrill in physical power' of fast bowling. Some passages in Farnes's autobiography, *Tours and Tests* (1940), even have a kind of muted mysticism to them, like a recollection of fielding in the deep one day at Leyton against Kent: 'It was there too that a day's fielding in the late summer heat brought about in me an amazing evening's contentment. I cannot explain the reason – just positive physical well-being really. I had not done well myself, for Kent had thumped our bowling, but it was just the

end of the season and I still remember the glow of pure contentment that I felt that evening.'

Team-mates thought Farnes a little too susceptible to such rev-
eries. He was a mystery to Len Hutton, who thought the absence of
histrionics from his bowling suggested limited ambition. In fact,
Farnes's ambitions were broader and vaster than Hutton's professional imaginings. The salient exhibit in Thurlow's economical but
evocative biography is Farnes's diary of the MCC's 1938–39 tour of
South Africa, which gives surprising glimpses of his sensitive, restless, questing mind. Before the trip, Farnes set himself five objectives, none of them having anything to do with cricket; he would
try instead, for instance, to 'remain conscious of my inner, natural,
more realised self instead of being overcome by successive and
accumulative environments experienced on tour'. He wrote of
having seen some children in the East End, 'monstrous in their
lack of realisation', whose appearance 'seemed a horrible reflection on the state of civilisation or education'. Yet he also confessed
to feeling 'detached' and 'somewhat disgruntled with myself', and
pledged himself a 'subjugation of self' that he felt might induce
'the required metaphysical state'.

Farnes had long had a literary bent: he was an aficionado of the
orientalist poet James Elroy Flecker and the Irish novelist George
Moore. The diary reveals a fascination with the work of J.W. Dunne,
an engineer turned philosopher who had developed an abstruse
theory of sleep's effect on time after becoming obsessed with his
dreams. Dunne was an eccentric and obscurantist; even his friend
H.G. Wells thought his theories 'an entertaining paradox expanded
into a humourless obsession'. But Farnes was 'absorbed and
thrilled' by Dunne's *The New Immortality* (1939), and imagined himself 'glimpsing a new world' – which suggests that he was looking
for one. Farnes was also introduced in South Africa to the metaphysical lyrics of Rabindranath Tagore, which probably also resonated with him: 'The song that I came to sing remains unsung to
this day ... The time has not come true, the words have not been
rightly set; only there is the agony of wishing in my heart.'

As well as an expression of patriotism, then, Farnes's enlistment in the Royal Air Force at the outbreak of war smacks of a continuation of a search for fulfilment, for a transcendent cause or duty. In *Gitanjali*, Tagore asks: 'On the day when death will knock at thy door what wilt thou offer him?' Farnes, perhaps, wished it to be more than wickets. The day turned out to be 20 October 1941, when the thirty-year-old Farnes crashed during a night-flying exercise. There were no more amateur fast bowlers of note; within two decades of the war's end, there were no more amateurs. The love of speed remained, and the game now teems with towering athletes bowling fast. Yet to fast bowling's traditions, Farnes both belongs and does not: a big man in all senses.

Cricinfo March 2006

ROGER KIMPTON
Company Man

If a man can be measured by the company he keeps, Roger Kimpton has an enviable cachet. In a team photograph of the 1937 Gentlemen, the tight-lipped twenty-one-year-old Kimpton looks like a schoolboy minding his Ps and Qs, as well he might alongside seven internationals, including three Test captains. In a board-room image taken just over three decades later, included in a history of his family's flour milling and stockfeed dynasty, W.S. Kimpton & Sons, he is again unsmiling and intent amid exalted company. Next to him is the venerable Sir Ian McLennan, behind him stands a burly young John Elliott: the most influential Australian businessmen of their respective generations.

'Of all the cricketers known to me who from one cause or another achieved less than their desserts,' wrote E.W. Swanton, 'Roger Kimpton would top the list.' Which is quite a tribute, given the group constituted by 'all the cricketers known to' his Jimship; mind you, the 'one cause or another' in Kimpton's case were the consequences of a rich, full life. A grandson of W.S. Kimpton's eponymous founder and a son of its then proprietor, Roger was born on 21 June 1916, and bred in leisure and privilege, attending the elite Melbourne Grammar, and in May 1934 following the foot-steps of brother Stephen by leaving Australia for Oxford University. His enrolment at Brasenose College and in Modern Greats was probably for social rather than intellectual reasons. Family lore is that the principal told him, 'You won't pass, but I can guarantee you a good time'. He was right on both counts.

Kimpton seemed a pocket version of his boyhood hero, Stan McCabe: compact, fearless, fleet-footed, fast-scoring. 'My father believed in one principle of batting,' says his son Geoff. 'You never let the bowler get on top of you.' Kimpton's 160 in his second game – against Gloucestershire, boasting Tom Goddard, Charlie Parker, Reg Sinfield and Wally Hammond – included twenty-six boundaries in two and a half hours. Drafted also as keeper, he secured his Blue after only four matches, with 84 against Yorkshire in 105 minutes. He quickly gained a cult following; students, recalled Gerald Brodribb, 'would forgo many a lecture in the hope of seeing Kimpton bat'. For good measure, he won the Freshmen's Singles Title at tennis, and taught himself golf, whittling his handicap down to three within twelve months and winning another Blue.

Kimpton opened season 1936 with a brace of centuries against Gloucestershire, followed by a seventy-minute hundred against Lancashire, despite the handicap of a runner; with Sandy Singleton, an old Salopian, Kimpton added 105 in less than an hour. For the next few months, in fact, he led the chase for the two-year-old Lawrence Trophy. But in a Folkestone Festival game at summer's end, sportsmanlike Indian fielders hurrying between overs helped Les Ames to a sixty-eight-minute hundred. Impecunious undergraduate Kimpton, chagrined to see £100 slip away, consoled himself by finishing twelfth in the first-class averages.

Kimpton top-scored for the Gentlemen at Lord's in July 1937, and by the simple expedient of leaving a bag behind between visits to the Singleton family had qualified for Worcestershire. But his 1568 runs at 35 that year represented his career's pinnacle. He played district cricket for Prahran in 1938–39 on returning to Australia, but mostly dedicated himself to flying, taking early-morning lessons at Essendon Airport, then joining the Air Cadet Corps.

After such a carefree youth, Roger Kimpton grew up quickly. He married Moira Creswick, his sister-in-law, on 1 July 1940, the day that France fell. She was only eighteen and suffering measles; but, as Kimpton's son James says, 'In those days, you didn't wait.' Kimpton's best man, schoolmate Bill Newton, already in the Royal

Australian Air Force, would be awarded a posthumous Victoria Cross. After six months as an instructor, Flight Commander Kimpton joined 77 Squadron, serving in Perth, Darwin and New Guinea's infamous Milne Bay. One of his pilots, John Gorton, who became a good friend, would be the last Australian prime minister to see active service. Commanding 75 Squadron, Kimpton undertook eighty bombing and strafing missions in Kittyhawks; the citation for his Distinguished Flying Cross mentions 'outstanding courage on numerous operational sorties'. Yet his proudest moment, he thought, was when his father invited him, after the war, to become a partner in W.S. Kimpton & Sons.

Kimpton & Sons was then a somewhat antiquated company. Most of its haulage was still by horse-drawn lorry. As number two to brother Stephen, Roger helped modernise it, rebuilding the firm's exports to Indonesia, Thailand, Malaya, Singapore, Borneo, the Philippines, Hong Kong and Ceylon. Export flour, sold in calico bags with elaborate and eye-catching trademarks like 'Frog', 'Wild Boar' and 'Double Axes', boomed after the war, although rival Asian producers, plus tariffs and subsidies in Europe and the United States, steadily eroded the company's competitive advantages. Kimpton himself wrote ruefully of discovering that 'when dealing with officialdom of another country, how apt they are to protect their own nationals even if they are scoundrels.'

When profit pressures compelled industry consolidation, the Kimpton brothers agreed to a three-way merger in 1969 with rivals McLennan & Co and James Minifie & Co. The driving force was Sir Ian McLennan, tending to his family's old business in time off from chairing the board of Australia's biggest company, BHP; the plan was dreamed up by youthful John Elliott, then at the tony management consultants McKinsey. Stephen became executive chairman and Roger ran the flour division in the merged KMM Ltd, but Roger had retired by the time it was absorbed by Barrett Burston in April 1978. Within three years, Barrett Burston had become part of Elders IXL which, under Elliott, would be one of Australia's most rapacious corporate raiders of the 1980s.

Roger Kimpton reappeared just once for Worcestershire, against Nottinghamshire at Stourbridge in July 1949, where his unbeaten 93 in eighty minutes, wearing borrowed sandshoes, impressed John Arlott, who noted in *The Echoing Green* (1952) that Kimpton's name was 'always quoted when conversation turns to the "lost men" of cricket who might have been among the great had they remained in the game'. Yet Kimpton would hardly have thought himself 'lost'; on the contrary, life had been one discovery after another.

Wisden Cricketer October 2004

BRUCE MITCHELL
The Quiet South African

Bruce Mitchell was one of the shyest cricketers ever to represent his country at cricket. It wasn't simply that he was a quiet, formal and religious man who avoided the limelight; he sometimes gave the impression he would have preferred it had Test matches been played in private before empty stands and without the necessity for force or competition. For Mitchell, cricket was a pleasure preferably consumed in silence and deep contemplation. He stood apart in the weak South African teams of his time by seldom seeming to commune with his team-mates, being known for his obliviousness to whom he was batting with. He stood tall at the crease, tapping the ground with his bat gently – 'almost apologetically' said his contemporary Dudley Nourse. To each ball, he moved only minimally; his backlift was perfunctory, his running between wickets dainty, as though in dancing pumps. After each delivery, he would stand perfectly still over the blockhole and stare impassively back down the pitch, apparently husbanding energy for a later that never came, his only concession to animation an unconscious left-hand tug at his collar on the right. 'By nature, tense', decided John Arlott, and 'not an easy man to know', but one 'in whose brain there is careful labour'.

For twenty years, nonetheless, Mitchell was the personification of South African cricket, his 3471 Test runs at 48.8 the more impressive for the pristine orthodoxy with which they were acquired, and the desperate match situations that he often faced. He never mastered the limelight, becoming stiff and self-conscious when praised, and blushing when crowds clapped his fifties and hundreds; Nourse recalls him flushing with embarrassment after a score of 72 against England in which he had fallen short of his usual standards of solidity. 'You don't need to tell me it was a bad innings,' he confessed. 'I know it only too well ... I don't suppose I will ever live this down.' But, of course, he did: in the twenty years from 1929 to 1949, Mitchell's wicket was almost as integral to South Africa as Bradman's to Australia and Headley's to the West Indies.

Louis Duffus once likened Mitchell to a boy standing up in front of classmates to recite 'The Charge of the Light Brigade', and his earnestness seems to have been an abiding one. His cricket upbringing was unusual in that it was not, until later, with other boys. His first mentor was a devoted older sister, who bowled to him tirelessly, and gifted him with a prize Jack Hobbs bat that she had won in a girls' match. Mitchell treated it like a piece of the true cross, carrying it in his bag for the rest of his career, and explaining: 'I was always Jack Hobbs when I went in to bat.' Mitchell was then 'discovered' by E.A. Halliwell, South Africa's captain against Lord Hawke's Englishmen and a family friend. He took Mitchell as a pupil, bowling at him day after day on a dust-caked road to a mine in Witwatersrand, and prophesied that Mitchell would play Test match cricket in his teens. He was only five months out.

Mitchell's debut was more of a challenge than most. In common with almost all the young Springboks, Mitchell played his first big games on matting, and as a result mostly off the back foot. When he went to hook Larwood early in his first innings at Edgbaston in June 1929, the ball was on him far more quickly than he'd bargained for and dislocated his thumb, deadening his right arm and depriving him of all power. For such a retiring young man, however, Mitchell was almost preternaturally tough. He batted on in pain, his 88 compiled in seven and a half hours, with only his top hand, coming through like a pendulum – something he had cultivated by hours in front of a long mirror at home. He enjoyed a laugh – a private one – when a spectator asked whether he thought he was a war memorial.

Mitchell's greatest Test innings took him back to that matting *fons et origo*. In June 1935, the Lord's pitch was plagued by leather jackets – not the kind once coveted by Mitchell's countryman Cronje, but a grub that consumes grass at its roots. The dried mud surface, almost bare of grass, turned prodigiously but reminded Mitchell of home: he hit seventeen fours in a match-winning unbeaten 164, and looked nothing like the bookish student he usually resembled. Rather, said C.B. Fry, he 'batted like the schoolmaster of all the bowlers ever born'.

For the most part, Mitchell was a passive resister, and could look completely immured under pressure. During the wet Australian summer of 1931–32 that regularly reduced batsmen to helplessness, Mitchell almost had observer status. He topped South Africa's averages by quiet accretion, but at one stage went runless for seventy minutes against Grimmett and Ironmonger. Mitchell even, it is said, let that impassive visage slip, at least momentarily. At Brisbane, Cyril Vincent dropped Bradman, then only on 10, at second slip, and commenced a suitable chorus of effing and blinding. 'You should not say things like that, Cyril,' Mitchell said mildly from first slip. 'Not even when you have dropped Don Bradman.' Bradman was on 16 when he snicked another outswinger, this time straight to Mitchell, who also put him down. Mitchell looked at the ball on the ground, shut his eyes and said, almost inaudibly: 'Jesus Christ.' (Bradman eventually made 226.)

Mitchell was also a poor captain, too taciturn to engage others, too sunk in concentration to seize initiative. He may be the origin of a story deeply embedded in the game's apocrypha. In his autobiography, John Waite swears by a report of a game at Linksfield in which Mitchell was playing in an Old Johannians XI with the similarly lugubrious Russell Endean. The two stood beside each other behind the wicket for the duration of a 150-run partnership without exchanging a word, until Mitchell broke the silence. 'Don't you think it's about time our captain tried a change in the bowling?' he asked. '*You* are our captain,' Endean replied.

To shift him, however, was work fit for gelignite. He played late and straight, always with the swing or spin, from a grooved side-on position taught him by Herby Taylor; he looked, above all, like a man with a plan. He was once joined at the wicket by the ebullient Eric Rowan, who struck some rousing fours and tried to ginger up his partner. 'Come on, Emma,' said Rowan. 'Give it a bang.' Mitchell looked perplexed: 'What's the hurry? We've got two days.' Arlott found him a source of endless fascination: 'Mitchell is, by nature, a man who solves problems, who solves them for himself, by himself. There are few less obvious or more interesting men in cricket today.'

Mitchell was on the field for the Fifth Test at the Oval in August 1947 for all but fifteen minutes, moving like a tide toward 120 and 189 not out, which saved the game and almost won it. He batted through the final hours as if in a trance, guiding South Africa from 6 for 266 to 7 for 423, first with Tufty Mann, then with Lindsay Tuckett. After they had been together half an hour, Mitchell met Tuckett in the middle of the pitch, wearing a puzzled frown. 'When did Tufty get out, Lindsay?' he asked. If he could not find those private places and empty stands, it seems, Mitchell was capable of fortifying his own mind.

Cricinfo February 2006

ROY MARSHALL
Fear Is the Key

Roy Marshall felt that cricket contained two kinds of madman: the fast bowler, because he expended his energies so wildly and thriftlessly; but also the opening batsman, for it required another species of lunacy to deal with madmen of one's own volition. As an opening batsman, and one of the most spectacular of his generation, Marshall knew whereof he spoke. In his own case, he confessed, he did not like opening, was worried by extreme pace and often exceptionally nervous. But the alternative was worse: 'I am not ashamed to say that there have been many occasions in my life when I have been frightened as I went out to face a fast bowler for the first time in a match,' he confessed. 'The plain truth is that I just cannot bear hanging round.'

Few cricketers have been so honest. Maurice Leyland allowed that 'no one liked fast bowling, but some show it more than others.' But, generally, fear is not something batsmen own to. Marshall, too, was a visible worrier before batting. If bowling of truly speedy repute was in the offing – and his years as the hope of Hampshire took in Tyson, Trueman, Statham, Loader, Snow and Ward – Marshall would fall quiet in the dressing room. He would tense up. He would dislike being spoken to. He would fiddle with his thick glasses, without which he stumbled round blindly. He was disturbed by Trueman's propensity for visiting the opposition dressing room before games. 'Why doesn't he get the hell out of here?' Marshall would think. 'What right has he got to come in here cracking jokes at this moment when in a few minutes' time he'll be trying to knock my head off?'

All of which makes his cricket the more remarkable. For, in the middle, Marshall hurled himself at the bowling with an almost vindictive fury. No county cricketer of the 1950s and '60s drove more lavishly, or cut more fiercely: standing in the gully to Marshall was not for the faint of heart, and most learned to stand some yards deeper than usual. His eye was as good as his nerve. 'All right,' Frank Tyson announced in the middle of an over one day. 'Let's have all the fielders out and we'll play baseball.'

Marshall would have been remarkable anyway. A scion of the Barbados plantocracy, he toured England and Australia with West Indian teams of the early 1950s without immediately looking the part. About this, again, he was acutely honest: 'Being a white West Indian myself, the son of a planter and living a fairly sheltered life, I suppose I did grow up with slight racialist feelings. It was never anything that was said or done but just that I was brought up in a white man's world and white men, at the time, probably ruled the day-to-day life in Barbados.'

Ironically, Frank Worrell became his idol and also one of his staunchest admirers, while Marshall made an enemy of white Jeff Stollmeyer, whose Trinidadian faction with Gerry Gomez dispossessed captain John Goddard on the 1951–52 tour of Australia. It was in youthful disillusionment with inter-island jealousies that, having already represented Lowerhouse in the Lancashire League, he took the county shilling, thereby forsaking international cricket: a choice and a sacrifice that today seems altogether bizarre, but was made by scores of players at the time, mainly Australians like Somerset's Bill Alley and Nottinghamshire's Bruce Dooland, but also South Africans such as Sid O'Linn and Stuart Leary at Kent, and West Indians, including Ron Headley at Worcestershire and Shirley Griffiths at Warwickshire.

Marshall's success was more or less instantaneous. In his first game, against the 1953 Australians, he belted 71 in eighty-five minutes, including five sixes. His first full season contained 2115 runs; at his peak, he surged past 2000 in five consecutive years. Worrell twice implored him to return to Test cricket to partner Conrad Hunte. There was nothing doing: 'I had a duty to Hampshire who had shown faith in me in the first place.' For if his batting sometimes smacked of carelessness, Marshall was anything but casual; he could even be a bit of a prig. For example, he heartily disapproved of sledging, of which he found a startling amount to complain, even in what is usually regarded as a period of gentler mores. 'I think the thing that shocked me more than anything else was the amount of swearing I heard on the field,' he recalled of his first season. 'I've learned to ignore the language hurled about but don't let anyone fool you that cricket is always a gentlemanly pursuit.' He once rounded on the famously salty Wilf Wooller, who had been cursing him from short leg: 'For a Test selector, I think your behaviour is absolutely disgraceful.' Even Wooller was momentarily lost for words.

Coming from West Indian cricket, Marshall found that county cricket had its own form of exclusion: the distinction between amateurs and professionals, which Marshall thought 'totally wrong'. Unapologetically, outspokenly professional, Marshall declared, 'If someone is ill, he does not call for an amateur physician to attend him. If someone needs legal advice, he doesn't seek out the barrack-room lawyers.' He was especially irked at Hampshire by 'amateur players coming along in the summer holidays and wanting a game', who were 'often found a place in the side, although they did not possess half the talent of the professional player they displaced'. Marshall was such a pro, in fact, that one season when he found himself in line for the £100 Lawrence Trophy, presented to the compiler of the season's fastest hundred, he paid £25 to buy an insurance policy against a faster century: no gay blade, this.

Then there was that batting. If fear was in the mix when he faced pace bowling, it never showed; 'indeed,' noted John Arlott, 'at times he seemed positively to enjoy it.' At Canterbury in August 1957, Marshall top-edged Kent's hard-working swing-bowler Fred Ridgway into his own face, shattering his glasses and opening a wound under his eye requiring six stitches. Hampshire's next fixture was on their fast Portsmouth wicket, against Surrey's extremely rapid Peter Loader, whose action was of dubious purity. Marshall's captain, Desmond Eagar, offered him the game off; Marshall would not hear of it. Loader bounced him to hell and back, at one stage striking him a glancing blow on the temple just inches from his stitches. Nonetheless, Marshall made 56 out of 120, then 111 out of 230, in a masterful display. 'No finer display of batting,' wrote Eagar, 'has been seen in Hampshire since the war.'

When Eagar's successor, Colin Ingleby-Mackenzie, staked money on his Hampshire team to win the 1961 championship, he was influenced by one man alone. It was Marshall's benefit year: that would surely imbue him with that 'extra little killer instinct'. His 2607 runs were crucial; his opening partnerships with Jimmy Gray as decisive as they were often imbalanced. Of the 155 they added against Somerset, for instance, Gray contributed 38. Marshall was finally dismissed for 212, with the score at 317.

Marshall bowed out of the game with little evidence of decline. If anything, his attacking style was more refreshing than ever. On day one at Derby, in August 1972, he made 203, with twenty-nine fours and two sixes; on day three, the hosts batted for 136 overs, 65 of them maidens. He left a residue of rare candour. Batting against fast bowling, he reminded us, is a physical challenge and a mental test. To feel fear and overcome it is no small thing; bravery without fear is simply insensate, automatic, a form of miscalculation *in extremis*. Marshall may have been right to view a taste for opening the batting as a kind of madness, but it is surely the very finest kind.

Cricinfo September 2006

DUNCAN SHARPE

The Big-hearted Boy

'Hurry up Griz,' hissed Richie Benaud to his wicketkeeper, Wally Grout. 'Give us the ball.' He'd beaten Test newcomer Duncan Sharpe first ball, and was intent on a clinical coup de grace. It didn't happen. Though a contemporary local account of the First Test between Pakistan and Australia, at Lahore in December 1959, seems to have been blessed with unusual long-sight, Sharpe assuredly did not panic. 'Instead he looked up and had a grin on his face,' it reads. 'Duncan smiled as Benaud raced back to his mark for his second delivery. This one the big-hearted boy punched toward the mid-off boundary with the style and grace of a seasoned batsman.'

And there he is, Duncan Sharpe, bent over scrapbooks in the living room of the Cranbourne home where he and his wife have raised six children. He's a nimble fifty-eight, hair still brylcreemed like his idol, Denis Compton, and speaking in a delighted singsong of Benaud's Australians: 'Magnificent, the greatest cricketers we had ever seen. And the language! Australians were the worst. This fellow O'Neill, it was, "Fuck this! Fuck that! If I'd had so many chances I'd've made a fucking double-hundred." All this while you were playing.' There are still vestiges in his speech of the Pakistani cricket vernacular, like 'the cancel-break': an off-spinner's arm ball bowled to drift away.

Not only is he proud to have repelled Benaud and Davidson and Lindwall, and played with five Mohammed brothers, but Sharpe laughingly offers his handclasp as one that shook the hands of two presidents. As it did. One was Pakistan's post-partition strongman, Mohammed Ayub Khan, the other Dwight D. Eisenhower – still the only US head of state to watch a Test, on a numbing December day in 1959 that still ranks as Test cricket's second slowest. Wearing a Pakistan blazer given to him as a gift, Ike asked captain Fazal Mahmood, 'Is this the young man who's done so well?'

Sharpe appears in cricket history as a mysterious interruption to the alphabetical progression in Pakistan's Test honour roll from Shakeel to Shoaib. He was, it transpires, the son of second-generation Anglo-Indians of Yorkshire extraction, born in Rawalpindi in 1937; his father worked as an assistant engineer on the Indian Railways and his mother as a nursing sister. The latter's appointment to Jinnah Central Hospital in Karachi after Partition pushed the family over the border when Sharpe was ten. The boy's cricket, self-taught from a copy of Len Hutton's *Cricket is My Life*, was first seen to advantage on the mats of the Multan Cricket Club.

Though he excelled at once, Sharpe was mortified, at sixteen, to be invited to Lahore for a trial before the national captain and cricket grand vizier, Abdul Hafeez Kardar. 'My heart sank when they said it: "Come down to the nets, the captain of Pakistan wants to see you,"' Sharpe recalls. 'And I had to face this off-spinner, Zulfiqar Ahmed, a Test player and very heady. He bowled the cancel-break, which I'd never seen before, but I managed to get some good strokes away and I heard that Kardar was impressed: I was a "bit rough" but I was "a good lad".' It was enough to gain Sharpe a place in the unofficial systems of patronage that still provides for Pakistani cricketers: in his case he was offered a 'job' with Pakistan Railways. When he cautioned that he had no qualification, the arrangement was explained: 'Don't worry about that. We will have you on the books but you won't work. You will come in once a month, collect your pay, and then we do not want to see you except when you play for Railways.' Nominally, Sharpe was posted to Gujranwala; but he laughs, 'I've never been there in my life!'

Sharpe's introduction to international cricket was playing for Railways at the end of 1955 against an MCC 'A' side weighted with talent, from the Surrey stars Ken Barrington and Tony Lock to Donald Carr and Peter Richardson. Lock, his left-arm crooked as though cocked for a game of 501, made Sharpe the middle victim of a hellish hat-trick. 'His arm came over so fast that he was unplayable on the mats, and I was caught at slip by Fred Titmus,' Sharpe recalls. 'But Mohammed Aslam, who was next, said he simply didn't see the ball that knocked his middle-stump out of the ground.'

Sharpe nonetheless continued to advance for Quetta and Lahore, and first brushed international cricket when he was nominated twelfth man for two Tests against Gerry Alexander's West Indians in March 1959. His pale face stands out clearly in a combined-teams souvenir photo behind the young Garry Sobers. Programs introducing Saeed Ahmed's apprentice squad of Pakistan Eaglets on their 1959 England tour dwelt on the twenty-two-year-old tyro: 'It is by dint of merit alone that this fair-complexioned, unassuming young batsman owes his place in the side ... he pushes the ball off his feet without any backlift of the bat – a quality found in a few. He also pushes the ball on the off-side, which gives aesthetic pleasure.'

A visit to Trent Bridge to play Notts Club & Ground afforded Sharpe an opportunity to emulate his hero, Compton. 'He was my golden boy, the batsman I most wanted to play like,' says Sharpe. 'And Nottingham, that was Compton's ground of hundreds. I thought, Denis Compton seemed to score a century every time he batted here. I must score one, too.' The local captain forewarned him that Notts' 6-foot, 6-inch Jamaican, Vincent Lindo, could be dangerous. But he revised his opinion when Sharpe made 58 and 176 not out, including 135 before lunch. 'I must apologise,' he said to Sharpe. 'He was quick, but you were quicker.' Sharpe learned much about English conditions as he broke Hanif Mohammed's Eaglet tour record with 1608 runs, and a little more about Pakistan cricketpolitik when Saeed installed him as vice-captain midway through the trip, at the expense of Ahmed Mustafa. 'I was from Lahore, Saeed was from Lahore, Ahmed was from Karachi,' explains Sharpe. 'That was Pakistan cricket.'

Fazal Mahmood shifted Sharpe into a final sixteen before the First Test against Australia at Dacca Stadium. Showing zeal befitting of a member of the Pakistan police, Fazal drilled his team with constabulary discipline by punishing errors at fielding practice with laps. At one stage before play on the first day, the skipper stood deserted while his entire team was circling. 'Fazal, he was a lion-heart; his leg and off-cutters, in and outswingers, all with the same action,' Sharpe enthuses, then sighs. 'But the fielding practices: we were worn out before we got on the field.' Those enervating preparations, and five drinks breaks compelled by the heat, may account for Pakistan's paltry first-day return: 3–146 from 77 overs. But Sharpe was unbeaten on 35 at the close, and climaxed his debut next morning by hooking Davidson for an emphatic four to reach his half-century.

The surge of pride returns as Sharpe recalls the pleasure of that blow: 'I just knew he was going to bowl that bouncer. I was back quick, and smash, one bounce into the pickets. I thought, That's it! And Davidson, he came down the wicket and shook my hand. Lovely, lovely man.' It was Norm O'Neill, of fearsome bat and banter, who finally ended Sharpe's stay, at 56. The debutant answered the call of partner Israr Ali, but the stumps exploded ahead of his run as O'Neill's throw picked them out from cover.

O'Neill then towered over the Second Test at Lahore with his bat: a brutal 134, his maiden Test century. Sharpe watched from gully as O'Neill set about them, wincing as the Australian pulled Mohammed Munaf through the hands of the square leg, Haseeb Ahsan, before he could blink. 'One bounce, four,' Sharpe chuckles. 'Poor Haseeb. He was just standing there wringing his fingers.' Ike paused over Sharpe at the players' parade in the Third Test, and also over Australian Wally Grout. President Ayub had explained the provenance of bat and ball, but wicketkeeping clobber was baffling.

There wasn't much else, although Sharpe finally realised a cherished ambition of facing Ray Lindwall – and became a victim of his bouncer: caught for 26 off a mis-hook on the long-leg boundary by

Ken Mackay. And it was at the end of that match that Sharpe first thought about Australia as a destination. Having become friendly with South Australia's Barry Jarman during the tour, he met Australian ambassador Sir Roden Cutler at a post-match reception. Indignant at omission from Pakistan's touring party for India a year later, Sharpe hatched a plan to emigrate, with Jarman as his sponsor. He recalls: 'I was first standby for the tour but I said, "That's not good enough. Pick someone else." In Pakistan they always have their friends. I was only the third Christian to represent the country, and the message I got was that it was felt I wouldn't fit in.'

Cutler warned Sharpe that he might find Australia difficult to fit into as well: there would be no domestics there to cook and clean for him. But Sharpe insisted that he and his young wife, Gillian, would adjust, and fretted for six months while Canberra scrutinised their emigration papers and X-rays. They boarded a Qantas Boeing 707 in Lahore in May 1961 with a total of £30, but without – Sharpe admits, with a little regret – any further thought.

Though Les Favell's South Australians were congenial and almost overwhelmingly friendly to the newcomer, Sharpe was too homesick and headstrong to enjoy his 1961–62 summer. Taking part-time jobs to supplement a stipend from carting covers and mowing outfields at Adelaide Oval for forty hours a week, he struggled to combine work and play. There were all manner of local customs to absorb, like the distribution of the standard stumps-ration of two-dozen bottles of beer. Watching Neil Hawke in the shower funnelling restorative fluid down his throat, the previously teetotal Sharpe took a mouthful that he promptly spat out. 'I have made up for it since,' he smiles.

In addition to the fabulous Sobers and the young Ian Chappell, Sharpe's comrades included the freakish left-arm unorthodox spinner David Sincock. As Sincock's wrist went to work, Sharpe would join the general rousing: 'C'mon, Evildick.' But few impressed Sharpe so much as a tall, fair-headed prodigy who struck three seismic centuries that season: Ian McLachlan, destined for a straight drive into politics as a minister in the first Howard administration.

Sharpe was the non-striker in December 1961 throughout McLachlan's rampant 120 at the MCG, watching his partner's dander rise as Ian Meckiff took a second new ball. Laughter fills Sharpe's voice as he recalls: 'Oh, Ian McLachlan, he picked up the first ball off the back foot and smashed it past Meck's left ear as he followed through. Meck, he just stopped, laughed, looked at me and said, "Jeez, Duncan, can't this bastard hit?"' A pair against Queensland a fortnight later terminated Sharpe's season, Wally Grout apologetically stumping him for a second duck off Tom Veivers' 'cancel-break'. At stumps the solicitous keeper counselled Sharpe to fasten on to the first woman he saw: he was due to score.

Ian Chappell had become a twenty-one-year-old Test player when Sharpe was recalled to the SA side in 1964–65, and was emerging as a rather irascible character as well. Sharpe remembers, 'Ian Chappell'd say, "Well, who'd you play for?" And I'd say, "I played for Pakistan, a country of seventy-five million compared to your fourteen million, and I made 56 and 34 against the strongest attack in the world. How about you?"' Chappell had played against Pakistan at the MCG and made 11. 'Ian just gave me this look and said, "Sharpie, I'll catch you a bit later." And if Ian had been in Pakistan you probably would never have heard of him. He was a very stodgy player in those days and the selectors here stuck with him for eleven Tests before he made his first century. In Pakistan they'd have looked at him once and said, "He'll never make it. Out he goes."'

Despite its brevity, Sharpe's Test career had left a forceful impression on Australian manager Sam Loxton. Encountering Sharpe in a Melbourne street after the 1965–66 Shield season, Loxton enticed him east to begin a prosperous career with his district club, Prahran. Now, as Sharpe points out, he's lived in Australia longer than he did in Pakistan. The hand that greeted presidents later rolled pitches at Wesley College, and he now walks his dog round Cranbourne as a part-time greenkeeper with Waverley City Council. All that remains are the scrapbooks – which his Australian-bred children find difficult to believe – and the accent. It's unmistakable. Or, at least, unmistakably foreign. 'I was lucky to come here when I did,' Sharpe says. 'Because Australia was booming. After two years I'd never have gone back. But it's always been clear, as soon as I open my mouth that I'm from somewhere else. People have called me German, Irish, French, Italian. I've really been everywhere. Once I said I was from Mars.' Not quite so exotic, but almost.

Australian September 1994

AJIT WADEKAR

Gentle Persuader

The formidable Indian team of the early 1970s is one whose stature has been significantly enriched by hindsight. Looking at the side now, the names have a magic aura. But even with Jaisimha, Vishwanath, Bedi, Prasanna, Chandrasekhar, Venkataraghavan, Abid Ali, they had almost succumbed to New Zealand, then been soundly defeated by Australia at home in the second half of 1969.

The touring party that left for the West Indies on 1 February 1971, moreover, was noteworthy mainly for its exclusions: the captain, 'Tiger' Pataudi, his deputy, Chandu Borde, and keeper Farokh Engineer, the last in gratuitous retaliation for putting county before zonal cricket. History tells that the failure of Bengal's Datta Ray to attend the critical meeting was crucial, leaving the chairman of selectors, Vijay Merchant, to choose with a free hand: choices vindicated when the rehabilitated Dilip Sardesai and the ripening Sunil Gavaskar dominated India's unexpected victory, with 1416 runs between them.

Perhaps, though, Merchant's most perceptive pick, using his casting vote, was the captain. It was not, Merchant explained later, because he had seen any particular genius about Ajit Wadekar's prior leadership of Bombay; nor was it because Wadekar showed an avidity for honours, even in batting. The great man noted disapprovingly, 'Unfortunately he is not very ambitious – ambitious for runs.' The quality Merchant detected instead was serenity. Wadekar was never flustered or fretful; his bearing was unaltered by success or failure; he described himself as 'pretty cold-blooded'. After the humours of the mercurial Pataudi, with his royal blood and the looks of a Fellini male lead, Wadekar was a gentle persuader and conciliator.

The circumstances of his appointment set the tone for his tenure. On the day the party was chosen, Wadekar was out with his wife shopping for curtains, returning to find his modest State Bank of India home surrounded by reporters and well-wishers. His first gesture was to solicit the involvement of his predecessor. Pataudi thought on it, and declined; some of his anger, further inflamed by the Congress Party's recent abolition of princely entitlements, leaked out in published criticisms of Wadekar. Wadekar said nothing, dismissing the remarks as understandable disappointment, and would studiously avoid the regional feuds and petty jealousies to which every Indian captain seems heir. He took Pataudi's great friend Jaisimha as his vice-captain; he championed the debonair Durrani and the poor but pawky Solkar alike. Only under his captaincy was it possible to fantasise, Chandra would observe, that 'there was no politics in Indian cricket'.

The detached and philosophical air was bred in the bone. Though Wadekar grew up amid the maidans of Bombay's Shivaji Park – the *locus classicus* of Indian cricket from which have sprung Gavaskar, Tendulkar, Kambli, Agarkar, Patil, Amre and others – he played no cricket at school. His father, intent that he should hone innate talents as a mathematician in order to become an engineer, expressly forbade it.

Even after Wadekar's father relented slightly, rewarding his son with a Stuart Surridge bat for securing a perfect grade in an important algebra examination, Wadekar fitted cricket into his life rather than his life into cricket. At college, science pracs overlapped with net practice. Though it meant he hardly ever had the opportunity do more than field, he never failed to finish his experiments. The training, he reasoned, could do no harm – and rightly so: Wadekar became a sure-handed slip, and it was his direct hit from cover to catch John Jameson napping that began England's subsidence at the Oval in August 1971.

Indian selectors also forced him to wait. Tall, lean, feet wide apart in an open stance, gripping the bat high and swinging it freely, Wadekar looked as he was, a homespun stylist. He was twenty-five and in his sixth first-class season when finally trusted with his first Test cap, failing at his first three attempts. But here were first seen the lineaments of that unflappable temperament, coming in on a pair for his fourth innings, at Chepauk, against an attack of Hall, Griffith, Sobers and Gibbs, with India 1 for 0. He drove Hall for four, then hooked him for six, and proceeded to top-score in a near-victory.

Wadekar joined India's line-up in the exposed promontory of number three, filled by six different batsmen in the six preceding Tests and rendered almost uninhabitable by India's constant churning of openers. And while there was a good deal of pace bowling about – including the likes of Snow, McKenzie and Pollock, as well as the aforementioned Hall and Griffith – India had none of it. At Edgbaston in July 1967, they notoriously delegated the new ball to their deputy keeper, Budhi Kunderan – who, when asked what he bowled, replied gravely, 'I'll have to bowl one to find out.'

Wadekar thought that the impunity with which other teams could rotate their pace bowling was a damaging disadvantage to India: 'In big cricket it is a real test to go out and face genuine fast bowlers who have tasted blood in the early overs. Without a fast bowler we have never been able to give visiting teams a taste of their own medicine.' He often bore the brunt of it. When India toured Australia in 1967–68, they were scheduled to begin their tour at the WACA, world famous for its pace and carry, and as remote from their home conditions as mud from lava. Wadekar had a tooth knocked out by a bouncer and was yorked next ball in an overwhelming defeat.

The lesson was not lost. As captain, Wadekar made it a point not to flinch. In his first match, at Sabina Park against Jamaica, he was hit on the hand by the West Indian tearaway Uton Dowe, and bled into his glove from a burst blood vessel in the finger rather than show discomfort, grinding out 70 in four hours. At Lord's in July

1971, India came face to face with Snow, who had recently humbled Australia. 'I decided to get at him in my first encounter,' Wadekar recalled. Coming in at 1 for 1, Wadekar received a bouncer first ball and hooked it for four; three times the dose was repeated with the same result. He made 40 of the first 50 runs, and a priceless 85 out of 125.

One of the most telling tour incidents had actually occurred a day or two before the Test, when Wadekar's team had arrived in London from Bournemouth to find themselves booked into a charmless, shabby hotel of the type it was hard to imagine Australians being prepared or expected to tolerate. On their previous tour, the Indians had been humble, deferential; the manager, Kunderan complained, was 'always crawling to the English'. Now Wadekar and his upstanding, martial manager, Lt Col Hemu Adhikari, demanded successfully that the accommodations be upgraded.

Their cricket upheld this assertion that Indians would no longer be treated as second-class citizens: having held out for draws at Lord's and Old Trafford, India was able to secure a fabled rubber at the Oval, where Wadekar's 48 and 45 in a low-scoring game helped guarantee that Chandra's prodigies were not wasted. Most famously, when Wadekar was run out first thing on the last morning, leaving India 100 short of victory with 7 wickets remaining, he conveyed his calm by creeping off for a snooze in the dressing room. 'Like Montgomery before Alamein,' wrote the *Daily Mail*'s Alex Bannister, 'he had laid his plans in advance and retired to confident sleep.'

Hemingway defined courage as grace under pressure, and Wadekar needed courage in plenty in the years ahead. In short order in 1973–74, he lost the Irani, Ranji and Duleep Trophies. Expectations further raised by victory at home against England were dashed in the 1974 rematch, when India were routed at Old Trafford, Lord's and Edgbaston; recriminations included Wadekar's sacking from the West Zone team, which forced him, huggermugger, into retirement.

But his reign should not be recalled for its end. In December 1976, for example, he was also the first Indian cricketer to visit Pakistan in twenty years, a role to which his natural tact was well suited. And he provided a lasting example for Indian captains, not always followed, by burnishing the reputations around him rather than tending chiefly to his personal advancement.

Cricinfo August 2006

COL HOY

The Hoy Boy

It was cricket's great good fortune that the unflappable Col Hoy should be officiating at square leg shortly after 6 p.m. on 14 December 1960, as Australia's Ian Meckiff lunged for the crease to complete what would have been the winning run of an already unforgettable Test match against the West Indies. When the striker's stumps reeled from the impact of Joe Solomon's return, Hoy made what might have been a difficult decision – after a day of exacting, heart-in-the-mouth cricket – appear deceptively simple.

The Queenslander, who died in Brisbane on 24 March 1999, was inclined to downplay his contribution to the lore and legend of what became known as the Tied Test. 'God, it was easy,' he insisted of the final decision. 'He was miles out. There was no-one there.' But umpires have faltered under less pressure, and one suspected on meeting him a certain pleasure in the reflected renown. Years later, when his name was called at a luncheon of the Motion Picture Industry Club, guest of honour John Cleese's ears pricked. 'Not the cricket umpire?' asked the British comic. Hoy liked that.

Born in Windsor on 9 May 1922, Hoy was a keen schoolboy sportsman, having been introduced to cricket and Australian Rules football at the local state school, but came to his umpiring vocation almost by accident. He had not troubled the scorers for four innings as a reserve-grade opener for Valley when, in November 1951, state player Mick Harvey wondered aloud if he'd considered umpiring. As it happened, the Queensland Cricket

Association was then in dispute with its umpires. So when Hoy rang the association's secretary, Ted Williams, and introduced himself as 'Col Hoy, the umpire', the only question he was asked was, 'Are you available?' After one and a half grade games, Hoy was appointed to stand in a Queensland–Western Australia match at the Gabba.

Umpiring in the 1950s was far from glamorous. Hoy had to fork out for his own kit: a pair of black trousers bought at McDonnell & East, cricket boots and a white barber's coat. The pay was also menial: in his first Test match, at the Gabba in November 1954, Hoy stood five days in enervating heat for a princely £35. When Hoy came to Melbourne for his first Test interstate a month later, he and colleague Mel McInnes lodged in the Commercial Travellers' Club in Flinders Street and commuted to and from the MCG by tram.

Umpires' efforts, moreover, often went unappreciated. One anecdote Hoy often retold involved the aftermath of that Melbourne match, which finished at the stroke of lunch on the fifth day. The umpires were slipping into their civvies when a stranger burst in and began haranguing McInnes about his final judgment. Eventually he identified himself: 'I'm the caterer and that decision of yours has cost me 10,000 bloody pies.' Nonetheless, Hoy's personal qualities came to the fore as an official. Considerably younger than most officials then standing, he won the trust of players with both his coolness under pressure and his relaxed affability. 'In his era,' says Queensland cricket historian Warwick Torrens, 'he was probably the best umpire in Australia.'

As a raconteur, Hoy also had more stories than the Bible. He enjoyed Sir Robert Menzies' greeting when they met at the opening of a paper mill at Petrie in the 1950s. 'Still cheating 'em?' enquired the prime minister, with a wink. Hoy also spun a tremendous yarn out of offering a cigar to his father, then explaining that it had been a gift from Menzies: 'Dad was a rabid Labor man, used to attend all the branch meetings and hated Menzies with a passion. I can still see his eyes crossing as he looked down at the cigar in his mouth, working out whether his love of the Labor Party should be allowed to interfere with his love of cigars. There was a pause I can only describe as pregnant. Then he kept puffing.'

Hoy and South Australian Col Egar stood in all five Tests in the intoxicating 1960–61 Australia–West Indies series, after which the Worrell Trophy was inaugurated: only the fifth time in the century that one pair of umpires had stood for the duration of a rubber. There were several taxing umpiring moments, yet the visiting captain, Frank Worrell, commented, 'I would be happy to have the same umpires again.' But Hoy retired after nine Tests and twenty-six first-class matches, returning to club cricket with Valleys, though he made a brief comeback twenty years ago with the World Series Cricket tour.

Hoy's working life otherwise was varied. There were spells with an engineering firm, and with the retailer D.W. Murray. He joined Ansett in 1963 as a group-travel representative, and covered Australian Rules football for the *Brisbane Courier-Mail* in the years when the game was far from fashionable. One of his chief joys was film, of which his knowledge was encyclopaedic – the legacy of many years working as a doorman at the Elite Theatre in Toowong while his wife Bev ran the candy bar. His life as a retiree was also busy: he took a job in 1984 as a driver for the US Consulate and, having served at Milne Bay with the 61st Cameron Highlanders, was a wholehearted organiser and participant in the 'Australia Remembers' campaign four years ago. Hoy is survived by Bev, to whom he was married fifty-three years, his brother Keith, son Ken and daughter Desley.

Australian March 1999

DENNIS AMISS
Search Party

Thirty years ago, Dennis Amiss published an autobiography entitled *In Search of Runs*. Australian readers would have queried the use of the plural: 'In Search of Run' might have seemed a fairer reflection of his form. The book had clearly been commissioned on the basis of Amiss's 1974, when his 1379 runs at 69 had just failed to break Bob Simpson's decade-old Test-run record for a calendar year. It had reckoned without Amiss's 1975, including 19 runs from his last seven Ashes innings, during which he had personified the crumbling of the English bulwark in the face of Australian pace. At my primary school in country Victoria, he was known, rather cruelly, as 'Dennis A. Miss'.

Seldom can a batsman of international quality have been reduced to such helplessness. 'Many a time I walked out to the middle in a Test match knowing it was virtually a waste of time carrying a bat,' Amiss said of facing Dennis Lillee and Jeff Thomson. 'I knew it would not so much be used to make strokes as to fend the ball off my body.' In hindsight, he reflected, it might have been wiser to stand down before the selectors did the standing. In the end, though, failing was the simpler option. 'It takes a certain moral courage for a man to stand up and admit that he is not mentally and physically equipped to play for his country at Test cricket,' he recalls. 'Looking back, I can see that I was not brave enough to ask to be omitted from the England team. Conscience does indeed make cowards of us all.'

The last line is a remembered snatch of Hamlet's 'To be or not to be': the Dane's soliloquy on suicide, whose attractions are weighed against the dread of 'the undiscovered country from whose bourn no traveller returns'. Unusually for a sports book, it is perfectly chosen, for Amiss's choice was also Hamlet's: 'Thus conscience doth make cowards of us all / And thus the native hue of resolution / Is sicklied o'er with the pale cast of thought.' And the line actually fits quite tightly with the totality of his story.

Amiss was a slow-ripening cricketer, who took five years to win his county cap for Warwickshire, then five years to make his first Test half-century, being 'completely overawed' and 'horribly nervous' at the top level. His choleric county coach, 'Tiger' Smith, 'more than once ... reduced me to tears'; he was left 'near to tears' by a pair against Australia at Old Trafford in 1968 and a hostile reception from the crowd.

Amiss did not play his cricket in a tight-lipped fury or with a triumphal hauteur. He was a 'walker' throughout his career, even once in a Test against India where he thought he merely *might* have hit the ball, and left because it was 'such a loud, confident appeal'; his batting partner, Alan Knott, told Amiss afterwards that he'd been nowhere near it. It is of a piece with a suggestible personality: on one occasion, he was hypnotised over the phone while padded up, waiting to go in during a Test match against Pakistan.

There is even something slightly apologetic in the title of his book. 'Searching' for runs? The impression was of someone peering round the corner, hoping to find a few that someone else had discarded: not altogether inappropriate given his recent travails, as observed, but on the meek side even by the standard of the times. That summer, Fred Trueman published *Ball of Fire*; Derek Underwood, *Beating the Bat*; John Snow, *Cricket Rebel*; and Mike Procter, *Cricket Buccaneer* – but here was polite, popular, pipe-smoking Amiss foraging furtively for a run or two, if nobody minded, and it wasn't too much of a bother.

Yet Amiss was not too nice a guy to succeed. Against opposition other than Australia, Amiss's simple technique and cast-iron concentration made him for several years England's most formidable batsman. His record *ex* his Ashes Tests is 3307 runs at 57, and he was the last English-born batsman to reach a hundred first-class hundreds until Graham Gooch's equivalent landmark. Something clearly clicked in Amiss's career that made him capable of double hundreds against strong West Indian sides at home and away, and marathon innings against the best slow-bowlers in the world in India. And that, I suspect, might have been Geoff Boycott.

The penultimate chapter of *In Search of Runs*, 'A Man Called Boycott', reminds the reader what an enigma the Yorkshireman was to the public, and even his team-mates, at the height of his career. Amiss opens with a vivid memoir of their first partnership, in a Prudential Trophy match at Old Trafford in August 1972. 'Good luck,' said Amiss, as they walked out. No reply: he learned later that Boycott did not approve of such a comment in a game of skill. Boycott burst through the gate first, forcing his junior partner to jog after him, which was also a habit: a picture shows the great man brandishing his bat and surveying the field well ahead of a shyly smiling Amiss. In the middle, Boycott said nothing, and it would be some time before he did. Calling? Watch and learn.

'At first if I called for a run which he rejected, he would give me a filthy look. And if I refused one of his calls he would look at me as if to say, "Don't you know who's in charge out here?" Eventually he said he would do all the calling in that first partnership and I accepted because I think we both felt that I was only a temporary partner and we would not be seeing too much of each other.'

When next they opened together at Trent Bridge in June 1973, however, Amiss had the nerve to call – and, even worse, the nerve to countermand a call. Reconsidering a second, Amiss sent Boycott back. Boycott kept coming. Amiss buried him: 'I turned my back on him and, as you can imagine, he said a few well-chosen words as he walked past.' He then compounded the offence by making a fluent hundred, his first at home. The story goes that, head swathed in a towel, Boycott saw not a ball of Amiss's unbeaten 138, and wailed self-pityingly when the landmark was reached: 'Stop it! Stop it! They're my roons yer clappin'!' The one-way feud continued afterwards: Boycott refused to speak to Amiss, claimed that his partner had run him out on purpose, and threatened to turn the tables when next they batted. It took captain Ray Illingworth to broker a settlement, pulling Boycott aside at the dinner before the next Test and telling him, 'Dennis has apologised. Now you stay here and sort this out, otherwise you'll never play for England again while I'm captain.' And there it *did* end. Amiss, by his own account, came to relish opening with Boycott: so sure, so correct, so tough.

These days the story of that Trent Bridge run-out is part of the bulging official Boycott-as-Selfish-Bastard File: it's aired again in Leo McKinstry's excellent *Boycott* (2000). Yet the implications for Amiss were also profound: perhaps even the making of him at Test level. This most retiring of cricketers had asserted himself in the presence of the most forthright; he had demonstrated he was not a pushover, in his own eyes and those of others; he had proved that conscience need not make one a coward *all the time*.

Everyone deplores the cricketing egotist, but the challenges such personalities pose to other egos can be the making of them. Phil Edmonds, for instance, relished Boycott's prickly personality, how in the nets he would seize on loose deliveries and leer, 'Anoother fower!' It put Edmonds, to use Mike Brearley's phrase, 'in touch with his combative powers'. The statistical evidence suggests that the same was true of Amiss. When he first batted with Boycott, his Test average was less than 20. In the dozen Tests they played together, his average was 66. In the two Ashes series from which Boycott then abdicated, Amiss's average dwindled to less than 15.

It is not the *whole* story of Amiss's career, for when he published his autobiography he was also on the brink of an astonishing come-back at the Oval, with next to no assistance. But it is, I think, a *part* of the story, because cricket is not simply the search for runs and wickets, but also for the environments, the conditions and the comrades that best suit our getting them.

Cricinfo May 2006

ROY FREDERICKS

The Fastest Gun in the West

In November 1977, when World Series Cricket came to my home-town of Geelong, my grandmother's flat overlooked the forecourt of the Travelodge Motel, the town's swankiest hostelry. From her balcony I watched the West Indian players milling about their min-ibus preparatory to embarking for Kardinia Park, giants in repose, but still exuding a predatory air: the towering presence of Lloyd and Garner; the lounging power of Richards and Greenidge; the limber athleticism of King and Julien. The one to watch, though, was Roy Fredericks, 163 centimetres, not even 65 kilograms, neat down to his closely trimmed beard, bearing himself a little sol-emnly, perhaps even lugubriously. Heavens, he was so small, so unprepossessing; a bantamweight at best. He had played his first big cricket while still a clerk at the Blairmont sugar estate on the Berbice River, and would still have looked at home in collar and tie, behind a desk or a counter.

Yet it wasn't two years since, in a whirl of left-handed strokes, I had watched him lay waste one of Australia's greatest attacks on the world's fastest pitch. This cricket was quite a game, it crossed my young mind, if a good little 'un could take down so many mighty big 'uns. I'd soon experience the same sensation while admiring the balance and poise of Sunil Gavaskar and Gundappa Vishwanath against Jeff Thomson. But Fredericks remained unique: with the power-to-weight ratio of a sports car, driving himself with foot to the floor. That 169 in the teeth of Lillee, Thomson, Gilmour, Walker and Mallett at Perth took just three and a half hours and 145 balls. It was the day that Jeff Thomson let go what remained for years cricket's fastest recorded delivery, at 99.68 miles per hour – to Fredericks, as it happens. No one records the treatment meted out to the delivery, but if it did not vanish from a blazing bat at twice the speed, it got off lightly: Thomson's first 3 overs cost 33; Fredericks' first 50 took 33 balls.

The shot that stands out in memory is the hook from Lillee's second delivery. In the World Cup final six months earlier, Fredericks had swung Lillee for six so violently as to lose the traction of his ripple soles and swivel into the stumps. Now he went even harder, as willingly as a cowboy throwing a punch in a Dodge City saloon. Carried by the strong south-westerly at Lillee's back, the ball flew fine, entering the crowd just to the leg side of the sight-screen. That makes it sound a little ungainly. In fact, a photo I've seen since of the shot shows him comfortably inside the line, upright and balanced. What he'd done, simply, was make the unconventional look entirely natural: something seen with only the best batsmen. He'd also made a great bowler look distinctly ordinary. This was Lillee's happy home hunting-ground, where he'd slain the World XI four years earlier; now, his first 5 overs cost 35, and the West Indies were 91 when Fredericks' ersatz partner, Bernard Julien, was out after an hour.

It was a contest of two natures. The Australians knew no other way to bowl, and Fredericks favoured no other sort of batting. At Glamorgan, where he spent three seasons, he was known for his succinct expressions of intent: 'I tink I'm agoin' to pelt some lash at de ball, man.' He had a substantial backlift, but with reflexes honed by table tennis, at which he had also represented Guyana, was seldom late on his stroke; his follow-through was similarly expansive, feet often leaving the ground as he cut and pulled. The WACA that afternoon was wreathed in smoke, the new City Centre skyscraper having caught fire. As Fredericks also smouldered, his bat threw off sympathetic sparks: for one spell of Gilmour's, the analysis read 1–0–22–0. In his book on the series, Frank Tyson recalls that his old captain, Sir Leonard Hutton, was a guest of the

WACA during the match, and watched proceedings 'with the amazement of the purist opening bat written all over his features'. Hutton's erstwhile rival Lindsay Hassett, then commentating for the ABC, was less circumspect, pronouncing it simply the best innings he'd ever seen in Australia.

Fredericks had not always played this way. On his debut in Australia, seven years earlier, he had been rather more obdurate, making up for in guts what he lacked in flair. He was hit on the head by Graham McKenzie in Perth, coming back after a brief retirement, and by Alan Connolly in Sydney, not retiring at all; admiring Aussies nicknamed him 'Cement Head'. That did not change. He eschewed helmets, and once during World Series Cricket responded to being hit on the head by Len Pascoe with a contemptuous V-sign. He scorned chest protection; his sleeves, always buttoned to the wrist, were bare of guards. But it steadily became a kind of proclamation, from a batsman intent on dishing punishment out rather than taking it, usually in the company of his like-minded protégé, Gordon Greenidge.

Eight months after his plunder at Perth, he and Greenidge belted 192 in the first two and a half hours of a Headingley Test, then an unbeaten 182 in two hours, twenty minutes at the Oval; Snow, Willis, Underwood and Greig came undone alike. In what proved his farewell Test, he and Greenidge turned a low-scoring game on its head with 182 for the first wicket of the West Indies' second innings; Imran Khan and Sarfraz Nawaz were among the tamed.

Fredericks had officially 'retired' from Tests by the day, almost thirty years ago, that I glimpsed him across that street, wondering at the power he packed. But Jeff Thomson was among those for whom he couldn't finish quickly enough, finding him a redoubtable opponent even when WSC visited the West Indies in 1979, by which time Fredericks was in his thirty-seventh year: 'He was a thorn in our side, and we were always glad to see him go.' Thomson remembered; and, from my balcony of memory today, so do I.

Cricinfo January 2006

WASIM RAJA

Bearded Wonder

Raja: the very name has a hint of the toff. And when Wasim Raja represented Pakistan in the 1970s and '80s, he always gave you the feeling that cricket was there for his pleasure, not he for its, with all the thrills he could pack into it. Kevin Pietersen at the Oval equalled his record for sixes in a Test series: fourteen. But Raja set his mark in the Caribbean at the zenith of Roberts, Garner and Croft, unprotected by headgear, and apparently unencumbered by care: a brand from the burning, if ever there was.

Footage of cricket from those days now seems from slightly longer ago than it actually is. Players not encrusted with helmets, not upholstered with protective equipment, with stances and techniques not pressed from a coach's template: as a game it almost more closely resembles club cricket than the pasteurised, homogenised, globalised game played today.

Raja had methods so homespun that they might almost have been designed to engage the eye. He bent low from the waist in his left-hander's stance, peering eagerly down the pitch, pounding his looping preliminary pick-ups into the earth like a woodsman bisecting a log. He was all eye and wrist, hands at the top of the handle, feet tending to follow his strokes rather than lead them, with a bravura backlift that no coach would condone now and selectors distrusted then, excluding him from twenty-eight Tests amid the fifty-seven he played. And you can't entirely blame them either. While Javed Miandad called Raja a 'breathtaking stroke-player', that was doubtless partly from sighs of exasperation.

Yet it looked great, and so did Raja, assuredly one of the hand-somest men to grace a cricket field, with a natural ease of move-ment, a willowy physique, and a helmet of black hair that he later complemented with a suave beard. So when Raja failed, it was like a cavalryman's fall: not war, to reverse Marshal Bosquet's formula-tion, but magnificent. A glimpse of him can be found amid footage of Botham's Test-best 8 for 34 at Lord's in 1978: while his comrades poke and prod at the swinging ball, Raja hurls himself at an inswinger, eyes ablaze with defiance, then throws his head back as the bowler accepts a return catch from his leading edge.

I particularly recall Raja taking guard at Perth in November 1981, with Pakistan 4 for 17. Lillee greeted him with a bouncer, which was hooked thrillingly, fecklessly, for four. Lillee followed with another bouncer, faster, fiercer, straight from his salad days, straight at the outside of Raja's right eyebrow. It was a trap, but Raja couldn't help himself. The voluminous backlift uncoiled, the body pivoted, the centrifugal force almost swung him off his feet: the result was the latest of top-edged hooks to the finest of deep fine-legs, having travelled little more than head-height all the way. It was a ridiculous, reprehensible, culpable waste of a wicket in a total of 62 that barely lasted 20 overs, yet somehow ennobling.

For when Raja came off, it was in essentially the same proud and prodigal way. He did everything with style. He bowled speculative leg-breaks with a whippy action, his arms blurring like those of a juggler, once bowling Pakistan to an 8-run one-day victory at Adelaide by winkling out four West Indians in half an hour. He prowled the covers with a sinuous walk, and chased the ball with an improbably elastic stride that ate up distance. It was a Pakistan team full of grandees in those days – Imran, Majid, Asif Iqbal, Zaheer Abbas – but Raja lost in comparison with none of them.

And in that Caribbean summer almost thirty years ago, he topped the batting and bowling averages: 517 runs at 57.4 and 7 wickets at 18.7. A few players successfully thwarted the West Indian teams of Clive Lloyd and Viv Richards, but perhaps none so extrav-agantly as Raja, displaying a kind of fighter ace's disdain for danger, feet off the ground as he slashed over point, skedaddling down the pitch to take advantage of any slow bowling he saw, enjoying the slight freedom of movement available to the left-hander, and perhaps also a scenario in which his mercurial ways were best. Majid said that Raja seemed during those five Tests to 'hit a six when he liked'; and liking was the essence of the effort.

Raja's average of 57.43 from eleven Tests against the West Indies in the Lloyd–Richards years, in fact, surpasses even those of Sunil Gavaskar (53), Graham Gooch (45), Allan Border (39), Mohinder Amarnath (38) and Allan Lamb (34): an astounding statistic, not least from a batsman who never gave the appearance of contemplating them, let alone coveting them. A toff, perhaps, but one to lift one's lid to.

Cricinfo December 2005

EWEN CHATFIELD

Man and Machine

At its cricket zenith in the 1980s, New Zealand had the better of Australia, was a match for the West Indies, and could even get away with taking the field in beige polyester body-shirts. They had larger-than-life luminaries such as Richard Hadlee and Martin Crowe; yet they were somehow personified by the lesser-than-life figure of Ewen Chatfield.

Hadlee and Crowe: these were stars by any definition. But 'Chats', with that deadpan demeanour, pudding-bowl haircut, side-burns and moustache? He could have come from no other country: a singular and resourceful land that specialised in harnessing its abilities to the last atom. He trundled in at a uniform pace and ran through the crease in a continuous movement, as though his bowling life was just one endless delivery. But the basics were so right and so robust: the upright delivery, the high arm, the big striding follow-through, and the nagging, nagging, nagging accuracy that grudged only 2.3 runs an over.

Team-mates called Chatfield 'Mer' – short for 'farmer', as if anyone needed reminding of his origins. His farming family lived in the hollow of a hill at Waione, on New Zealand's North Island, near Palmerston North. Actually, 'near' is correct only in the sense that nowhere in New Zealand is geographically far from anywhere. Waione is a speck on the map, often cold, eternally cloudy, known, if at all, for wool … and, in later days, Ewen Chatfield.

Such cricket tutelage as he had was from his father Neville, a fair player before being swept up in the fall of Crete and spending

309

most of the war as a prisoner in Germany. Otherwise, Chatfield's initiation in the game was listening to it on a radio out in the family orchard, for potential playmates were few: he travelled 20 kilometres by car and bus to sit in a class of one at a school at Akitio.

Hutt Valley and Wellington team-mate Graham Newdick recalled his first sight of the junior Chatfield, looking like he had walked straight 'out of the bush', with hair down to his shoulders, a baggy old sweater in his Nanae Cricket Club's colours and size-14 boots. A haircut followed, and a change of deportment: every night on tour, Chatfield would proudly hang his Wellington blazer and lovingly fold his tie. But the self-containment never changed: he spoke when spoken to, and would have bowled all night as well as all day if permitted. For, like a good farmer's boy, Chatfield was formidably fit, and remained so. Well into his thirties he was outrunning young team-mates, and leaving peers far behind. 'Chats could outrun me holding a suitcase,' said his captain, Jeremy Coney.

When he wasn't 'Mer', Chatfield was 'The Machine', team-mates joking that he had less need of a physiotherapist's ministrations than a mechanic's. For Chatfield's cricket was rational, functional, pared back. Born to bowl, he did not trouble with the game's other faculties. Unlike many negligible batsman, he did not even swing wildly, instead playing boringly and predictably down the line … well, *a* line, because it was generally the wrong one. With the ball, he was only slightly more elaborate. No one polished a ball quite so devotedly, like a collector caring for a precious antique. But there were no histrionics, no sledges or stares; Chatfield didn't even particularly like appealing. 'It's just one of those little idiosyncrasies I've always had,' he explained.

In fact, for all the regularity of his habits and reliability of his performances, Chatfield was a remarkably idiosyncratic cricketer, his lack of mannerism becoming itself a kind of mannerism. His book *Chats* (1988), deftly put together from some unpromising material by Lynn McConnell, is self-effacing to the point of personal erasure. Over the course of its 200 pages, what accumulates most are Chatfield's aversions. He doesn't like team meetings. He doesn't enjoy chatting on the field. He isn't one for talking about the day's play afterwards. He's reluctant to watch cricket on television. He can't explain his motivations: 'When asked about what really stirs me up, I cannot really answer.' Not even his wife seemed to know: 'There have been times when he has been hurt by his disappointments, but he deals with these by himself.'

The most redolent story is related by keeper Ian Smith, who describes rushing up to share his joy with Chatfield after catching Viv Richards down the leg side at Lancaster Park in March 1987. Amid the laughs and backslaps, Chatfield merely commented, 'It should have gone for four.' The most telling images are two photographs of Chatfield's hundredth Test wicket, which show him first with arms raised, although more in relief than exultation, then the first to peel away from still-celebrating team-mates and head back to his mark.

The tendency today, an age where every cricketer has a hundred-dollar haircut, an earring and a tattoo, is to find Chatfield a little comical. But, without defiance or demonstration, he was undeniably his own man, and unmistakably of his own land.

Cricinfo June 2006

VINTCENT VAN DER BIJL

Lost in Translation

There was some dubious head-shaking when *The Times* published John Woodcock's list of eternity's hundred greatest cricketers, in 1997. Nine Englishmen in the top dozen smacked, to non-English-men anyway, of nationalism; Woodcock's preference for W.G. at the top over the Don seemed, at least to Australians, like lese-majeste. The burly rosbif Alfred Mynn looked suspiciously over-promoted at number four; Steve Waugh's Bradman-like batting certainty at the time made it difficult to credit that he barely scraped in.

One pick, however, passed with remarkably little objection, despite being the only twentieth-century player not to have repre-sented his country. At number seventy-eight, Vintcent van der Bijl was deemed by the Sage of Longparish to have been a fast bowler superior to Harold Larwood, Curtly Ambrose, Bob Willis, Jack Gregory and Allan Donald, among others. Wooders was surely onto something, big Vince's 767 first-class wickets at 16.54 being hard to overlook: all the same, no better career can have passed in deeper obscurity.

Van der Bijl's autobiography is entitled *Cricket in the Shadows* (1984); that shadow has subsequently lengthened and darkened. In the 1970s and '80s, at least, it was common to mourn 'the lost generation' of Springboks, from Test cricket untimely ripped. Mind you, they never seemed altogether lost: the names Pollock, Procter and Richards came trippingly off the tongue. And, well, unless you lived under the sport-and-politics-must-not-mix rock, it was hard to disagree they were lost for good reason.

312

Strangely, it is since South Africa re-entered Test cricket on a wave of post-apartheid goodwill that they have really sunk from view. The heroes of the 1970s and '80s are now those who kept the guttering flame of multiracial cricket alight, even though their efforts would have been set at nought had not political change extended the franchise and expedited black-majority rule. Perceived as dupes of the regime, the white cricketers of that period have become a source of quiet embarrassment; the rebel tours that provided their international opposition now give off a seedy reek of opportunism and hypocrisy.

There's nothing tragic about van der Bijl not playing Test cricket; as Richie Benaud observes, tragedy is when the *Titanic* sinks. But there is something melancholy to it, especially in an era when Test caps are so cheap and profuse. There's no doubt that van der Bijl deserved the honour and would have valued it, his Rhodes Scholar father, Pieter, having been a patient Test opening batsman and an Oxford boxing Blue before war wounds ended his active sporting life. The only picture in *Cricket in the Shadows* of van der Bijl *père et fils* shows Pieter congratulating Vince on his selection to tour Australia in 1971–72. Not even the formulaic nature of the newspaper cliché can disguise the warmth between them; not even the warmth can obscure the futility. The caption notes: 'Both of us knew when this photograph was taken that the tour would not take place.'

Pieter van der Bijl apparently stayed right out of his son's cricket upbringing; that, he felt, was rightly the domain of his son's school cricket-master. It wasn't until the eve of his first big cricket, during South African Universities Week in Cape Town, that Vince received a letter signed by 'Your loving Dad', with simple advice: 'Whether you make runs or take wickets, or do neither, always think of the other fellow ... It is so easy to win, and so easy to make excuses when things go astray. Mum and I will never be disappointed when you are not successful in the matter of making runs or taking wickets. We like you to do well only for your own sake. May you enjoy yourself.' During that week, with the aid of a coaching manual and a co-operative team-mate, the lanky youth developed a priceless outswinger; the attribute of visibly enjoying himself in all his cricket likewise lasted his whole career.

Van der Bijl benefited early in his career from the counsel of Peter Pollock and Trevor Goddard, and his methods were disarmingly smooth for one displacing 115 kilograms and with bald head topping out more than 2 metres above his size-14 boots. His run-up always seemed on the brink of being ungainly without ever becoming so, like some huge steam contraption with exquisitely oiled ball-bearings. His fingers rolled over a ball that always seemed half reluctant to leave his caress; his contemporary Jimmy Cook noted how he invariably seemed to hit the top half of the bat, even when the ball looked overpitched. When van der Bijl followed through, he seemed to eat the pitch up with his stride, descending on the batsman as though to chill him with the length of his shadow. Yet geniality kept bursting through his aggression. Once, when his captain Barry Richards asked him to bowl a bouncer at a tailender who had outstayed his welcome, he replied, full of concern, 'But I might kill him, Boer.'

By the late 1970s, big Vince was legendary in South African domestic cricket. But thanks to that country's outcast status, this meant he enjoyed fame only a notch above that of the best shuffleboard player in Estonia. Mike Brearley was peeved when, on England duty in Australia, news reached him that Middlesex had signed van der Bijl for the 1980 season. 'Who the hell is this van der Bijl guy?' asked his team-mate John Emburey. Brearley said he had no idea, but he'd be registering his displeasure when they returned to Lord's. In fact, van der Bijl had lots of demerits: he was thirty-two, had played only a handful of first-class games abroad, and then did nothing in the pre-season fortnight to suggest he was county material. He travelled up to Trent Bridge for the opening of the county season full of foreboding.

Van der Bijl's first ball pitched leg, jagged away, and beat the groping bat outside off stump; he was even more delighted to observe Brearley turning to keeper Ian Gould and chatting excitedly.

At the close of play, after taking 4 cheap wickets, he then grabbed a beer and walked into the Nottinghamshire dressing room. From the looks of greeting, he realised this was not the done thing at all ... but, well, it *was* where Vince came from, and he did not leave until the Notts players had been thoroughly acculturated.

Van der Bijl took 85 wickets at 14.7 that summer, and made 331 rumbustious runs at 25.5; it was in the manner of his cricket as much as the matter that he appealed to observers. Among spectators, he was naturally outgoing; among comrades, he was seldom downhearted long, and ensured against collective brooding. On one occasion, the Middlesex dressing room was silenced by the loss of a close one-day game. 'It's my fault,' Vince announced finally. 'I bowled a half-volley in my third over.'

At a peak of fast bowling, van der Bijl was the equal of Roberts, Holding, Garner, Croft, Marshall, Lillee, Thomson, Kapil Dev, Hadlee, Imran: for at least a couple of years he was probably the most penetrative new-ball bowler in the world, and certainly the most reliable, being apparently impervious to injury and a glutton for overs. Returning to Natal, he took a further 54 wickets at an outrageous 9.5. When the SAB England XI broke the sanction to visit South Africa the following season, he mowed down 75 wickets at 14.9. In his valedictory season in 1982–83, moreover, he read the portents right. He had no truck with the idea that the rebel tours were, as the South African Cricket Union insisted, fully-fledged internationals: 'If someone asks me how many Test wickets I have taken, my reply is none.' Having been disbarred from Tests for eleven years, he foresaw an exile as long again for a South African game 'further than ever from international acceptance'. He warned, 'Politics and sport have become one and a new era is upon us.' And, John Woodcock aside, that new era had no place for him.

Cricinfo July 2006

DILIP DOSHI
Left-arm Heterodox

Anyone who grew into their cricket in the 1970s will remember how crisply the world then divided. From Australia came moustachioed bandidos in baggy greens. In the West Indies originated towering, raw-boned fast bowlers. England provided the dour professionals and resourceful defenders. And India? India was the home of spin: apparently, in fact, its last bastion, in an era besotted with pace supported by a crescent of slips.

Everyone knew the chief quartet: Prasanna, Bedi, Chandra and Venkat, so original and so different from one another. Then there were others, who had to make the best of limited opportunities: left-arm slow-bowlers as good as Rajinder Goel, Rajinder Hans and Padmakar Shivalkar, and the excellent off-spinner Shivlal Yadav. *Primus inter pares* in that group, though, was Dilip Doshi.

Doshi was thirty-two by the time he found a niche in Tests, and already steeped in the traditions of which he was part. He was a negligible batsman, and with his unathletic physique, baggy creams and thick, square spectacles reminded Alan Ross of a French semiotician, a Barthes or a Levi-Strauss. It was a subtle analogy, for Doshi's bowling was full of double meanings and hidden depths, both inviting and aggressive, patient and probing.

In Australia in 1980–81, Doshi was a revelation. It's often said that Australians favour visiting players who seem to reflect, and thus endorse, their own mores: Botham and Flintoff have, in their days, been typed 'almost Australian'. Yet touring cricketers have also become popular here for the opposite reason, that they savour of distant places and different ways of life. Patsy Hendren, Maurice Tate, Freddie Brown and Ken Barrington were quintessential Englishmen; Garry Sobers and Wes Hall were archetypally West Indian; Imran Khan was no version of Australia Lite.

Doshi cut an unlikely figure, but his love of cricket was abundant and obvious, and he was incurably game; though he might be slow across the outfield, he never gave up a chase; even in adversity, his smile was never far away. He was brave, too, bowling 74 overs in the Melbourne Test with a fractured toe.

With a ball in his hand, he was never other than poised, setting the field like a finicky host setting the table. He had one of those approaches you could watch all day: a dainty run that turned him exquisitely side-on, followed by a delivery stride where his bespectacled eyes would be just visible over his high right arm. His body would pivot into a follow through that brought his left hand below knee-level.

Although Doshi could turn the ball an appreciable distance in responsive conditions, what left the strongest impression was how long he could make it hang in the air, as though suspended in a cobweb. Greg Chappell collared him in Sydney, but Doshi came back by dismissing him twice in Adelaide, sweeping at a ball that bounced too much in the first innings, then beaten in the air coming down the wicket in the second. Chappell turned on his heel without trying to remake his ground, bowed his head penitently, and stripped off his gloves in his few strides for the pavilion. 'Too good,' he seemed to say, 'too good.'

Australian spin bowling was then in a parlous state, and Doshi was a tonic to palates jaded by the monotonies of medium pace. 'Doshi taught us by example,' wrote Bill O'Reilly. 'Refined, thoughtful and brilliantly executed spin can offer the game an exciting future.' O'Reilly would live just long enough to see Shane Warne fulfil the prophecy he'd made while watching this improbable visitor.

Yet while Doshi took 114 Test wickets at averages and strike-rates in Bedi's class, he came and went quickly, not so much for reasons of form as because he was out of tune with the mores. The early days of the proliferation of limited-overs cricket was characterised by formulaic thinking, including the idea that spin was de trop. Doshi gave up fewer than 4 runs an over in his fifteen one-day internationals but could not keep his place; he took a fabled 8–7–1–1 in a Sunday League match for Notts against Northants and was left out of the county's next game. Even his pedantic way with field placings was held against him. Didn't he realise that spin bowlers were there to speed up the over-rate and kill a few hours while the fast men got their breath back?

Doshi's autobiography also makes it clear that he harboured his own objections to the game's trajectory. Most players are broadly in favour of commercialisation; certainly, they would no sooner object to it than fluoride in the water supply. In *Spin Punch* (1991), Doshi is almost entirely antagonistic to 'professionalism and money-mindedness'.

The Indian team, he says, had a 'one-track obsession' with money that he found 'quite disgusting'. The BCCI, meanwhile, was 'a government within a government, almost totally not accountable to anyone'. Doshi was, in his own account, a man apart. He reports that he declined the opportunity to write a newspaper column because it would 'bring out into the open what were essentially confidences'; he recalls being dismayed that 'players thought nothing of charging a fee to attend an event in the evening'; he thought throughout his career that advertising and endorsements were 'totally out of hand'. He even recalls a team meeting before the first one-day international in India where the conversation was entirely devoted to sponsorship, prize money, logo royalties and match fees: 'Cricket was discussed only as an afterthought.'

Hovering over the book is the figure of Sunil Gavaskar, now so gushing about the honour of representing India, but who Doshi depicts darkly as a petty tyrant 'bogged down in personal likes and dislikes', and 'either evasive or flippant' when challenged – as, for instance, when he instructed Doshi to take more time to complete his overs against England in 1981–82, then left the bowler to bear the brunt of criticism for India's abysmal over-rate.

Such selfishness, in Doshi's view, was contagious. In one vivid anecdote, Doshi recalls apprentice paceman Randhir Singh taking the ball on a green-top in a tour match at Canterbury. In a trice three catches were dropped by the 'stalwarts who stood in the slips apparently for no more than a pleasant chat amongst themselves'. Not only was apology tendered, but no one took any notice. This, said Doshi, was the 'crudest and ugliest face of Indian cricket'. If his own face did not ultimately fit, perhaps it is a testament to him.

Cricinfo April 2006

THE YARRAS

Octoberfest

'A funny month, October,' mused the writer Denis Norden. 'For the keen cricketer, it's when you realise that your wife left you in May.'

Norden, an Englishman, was describing how the end of the northern summer could be a harbinger of domestic surprises. For the keen Australian cricketer, by contrast, October ushers in a period when wives, sweethearts, children and pets are drowned out by the siren song of practice, selection nights and long hot Saturdays. Our problem month is March. But March, at this stage, can take care of itself.

On Saturday, tens of thousands of Victorian men and women will take the field in thousands of games of club cricket. Or at least, they fully intend to: practice at my club, the Yarras, this week has consisted of indoor cricket games with a broom and tennis ball, followed by pool and pizzas. But rain is ingrained in the ritual, too. Round one is like our sacrifice in propitiation of the weather gods, as integral to the season as the first dropped catch and the first strained groin.

Park cricket, in fact, is quite an enterprise. None of us is obliged to do what we do. We're not being paid. Nobody is coming to watch. We aren't made to feel particularly welcome by the councils whose grounds we rent; our outfield this season looks like it's been attacked by the gopher in *Caddyshack*. These days, even residents are apt to complain. One club in our association this season has had to placate locals by deeming that a straight six will count for no runs; a second straight six will be considered 'out'. The one-hand–one-bounce rule cannot be far away.

Yet it still happens. Governments today spend millions of dollars trying to encourage people to perform simple actions in their own interests, such as picking up their litter. But our game restarts unbidden every year, when we flock to our grounds like migratory birds recognising the change of seasons or salmon surging upstream to spawn.

Or so it seems. Truth be told, the actions are more conscious. Most park cricketers will have been practising for a month or two already, under cover of football. I've been enjoying a regular hit over winter with a group of diehards, with the result that I've already peaked half a dozen times and am now hopelessly out of form. Some even use the winter months to get fit. Our coach, Macca, surprised us a few weeks ago with the disclosure that he'd been going to the gym, and had been there as recently as the previous week. 'Were you buying your lunch?' he was asked sceptically. 'Getting a massage,' he replied.

A smaller but still significant core of participants will have sat through a number of meetings of their clubs' committees. The Yarras' year commenced in June with the arrival of a $3500 utilities bill, which did rather more than offset the $50 we had in the bank; perhaps, said our president, Doc, we could consider running the club without electricity.

Our treasurer, Sven, then presented a very impressive spreadsheet demonstrating what had long been suspected, that the most profitable option for the club would be to play no cricket at all and simply hold barbecues. Obviating the need to pay umpires, curators, associations or insurers, this would result in a tidy surplus. Existing debt could be extinguished by offering free tickets to our trivia night in lieu.

This organisational effort could all be lightly dismissed. We are, of course, doing this for ourselves, so we have our precious games to play, and ready excuses where renovations and scary family gatherings are concerned. But it's not so simple. I should perhaps let you in to a big, poorly kept but often-unacknowledged secret of park cricket: a lot of us are no bloody good.

There are some lines concerning Sir Donald Bradman by the wonderful English broadcaster John Arlott that I have always appreciated: 'I do not think cricket is under Bradman's skin but I believe it is under his skull – in close control. Therefore he has missed something of cricket that less gifted and less memorable men have gained.' This means a lot to me. I am one of those infinitely less gifted and less memorable men. My thirty years as a club cricketer have offered so little to write home about that I almost count as a missing person. Fortunately, ability walks, but availability talks.

Don't get me wrong. I don't revel in being bad. On the contrary: I relish it when, just occasionally, I get a glimpse of what it would be like to be better. But I think it applies to most park cricketers that it is not solely their own pleasure and satisfaction they're seeking; they could never live by their skills alone. They find instead the fun of sharing, and the sense of contributing to the common weal. This is an arena where what you do matters, but the spirit in which you do it counts as much, if not more.

Cricket clubs erect legends on wickets, runs, catches and flags. But they also build legends around guys who pick teams, roll pitches, erect nets, take minutes, keep accounts, stock bars, sweep and scrub clubrooms, drag out covers when it's wet, stand there watering practice areas when it's dry. For that is how clubs survive: on myriad independent, uninstructed, unsupervised, unrewarded actions by people who could be doing other things but choose not to.

One evening last season, while enjoying a post-match beverage, I watched a spellbinding display of self-mastery by young Lazza, the Yarras' very talented and somewhat wayward all-rounder. Lazza is a boy with a big heart, a short fuse and some eye-catching tattoos. He seems to live on his motorbike. His career plans are to be either a DJ or a commando. He usually arrives at games with a minute or two to spare, hot-foot from some bizarre escapade, generally sleepless, occasionally a little disoriented, sometimes off with the pixies. He is, nonetheless, a smoulderingly intense cricketer, up to most opponents in standard, his only weakness being a tendency to dismay when he doesn't do himself justice.

This night, through the encroaching darkness, I watched him amble over to our practice wickets, which are staked out by four poles strung with a rope – a token effort at reminding dog walkers that we'd prefer their mutts didn't take a dump just short of a length. This rope has a tendency to grow severely tangled. By this stage of the season, it looked like a laboratory model of the human double-helix. I imagined that Lazza would simply do the standard half-arsed job and hurry in for his beer, but no.

Over the next half hour, every time I peered through the gloaming, there was Lazza, patiently unravelling knots; unself-conscious, unbidden, unrecognised, just because he thought he should. I don't think anybody else observed this act, yet it was strangely moving. There'd have been few occasions in Lazza's life when he'd had to apply such yogic patience, even for his own ends; here he was doing so, essentially, for others. That makes me as proud of my club as any premiership.

The pretext for this community writ small, of course, is cricket. It's not everyone's favourite game, nor even most people's. It's slow, archaic, complicated and makes no sort of sense – which is, of course, what we love about it.

Last summer, for instance, the Yarras played a semi-final at Cheltenham, and defended a typically ragged 100; in reply, our opponents inched to 4–87. By all objective measures, the game was lost. Faced with the equivalent situation at work or in a relation-ship, you'd have been forgiven for chucking it in and walking away. Yet when I looked around the field at this juncture – reading the grim set of the faces, checking the resilience of the body language – I was surprised. 'Crikey,' I thought. 'You guys actually reckon we can still win this.' I thought further: 'Bugger it if I don't, too.'

It was a heady moment, almost euphoric: I was one of eleven men who, in the face of overwhelming evidence to the contrary, had independently arrived at the same nonsensical conclusion.

And, it turned out, this was one for the true believers. Easty, the skipper, threw the ball to Tavo, whose remaining brain cell was still swimming against the previous evening's tide of scotch. He let loose a low-flying full toss. Backward point levitated and took the catch in his outstretched hand. It was the first of 6 wickets winkled out for 11. We won by 2 runs.

In a sense, though, the instant we won that game was the one where to all intents we were beaten yet held fast to our common purpose. There'll be little dramas like that played all over Victoria this weekend. October's a funny month all right. The funnier the better.

Age October 2004